# Unions in the 21<sup>st</sup> Century

# Unions in the 21<sup>st</sup> Century

## An International Perspective

Edited by

Anil Verma and Thomas A. Kochan

First published 2004 by
PALGRAVE MACMILLAN
Houndmills, Basingstoke, Hampshire RG21 6XS and
175 Fifth Avenue, New York, N. Y. 10010
Companies and representatives throughout the world

PALGRAVE MACMILLAN is the global academic imprint of the
Palgrave Macmillan division of St. Martin's Press, LLC and of
Palgrave Macmillan Ltd. Macmillan® is a registered trademark in
the United States, United Kingdom and other countries. Palgrave is
a registered trademark in the European Union and other countries.

ISBN 1–4039–3505–X hardback

This book is printed on paper suitable for recycling and made
from fully managed and sustained forest sources.

A catalogue record for this book is available from the British Library.

Library of Congress Cataloging-in-Publication Data
Unions in the 21st century : an international perspective / edited
   by Anil Verma and Thomas A. Kochan. – Unions in the
   twenty-first century
      p. cm.
   Includes bibliographical references and index.
   ISBN 1–4039–3505–X (hdbk.)
      1. Labour unions. 2. International division of labour.
   3. International labour activities. I. Verma, Anil, 1949–
   II. Kochan, Thomas A.

HD6476.U55 2004
331.88–dc22                                              2004042732


10    9    8    7    6    5    4    3    2    1
13   12   11   10   09   08   07   06   05   04

Printed and bound in Great Britain by
Antony Rowe Ltd, Chippenham and Eastbourne

*This book is dedicated to the memory of:*
*Noah M. Meltz*
*1935–2002*

Professor Noah M. Meltz earned a Bachelor of Commerce from University of Toronto and his Master's and PhD from Princeton University. He then returned to the University of Toronto in 1964 and by 1971 became a full professor. A remarkable scholar, Meltz was also a gifted administrator. He was appointed Director of the Centre for Industrial Relations in 1975, a position he held for ten years. After serving as Assistant Dean of the School of Graduate Studies from 1985 to 1987, Meltz served as Principal of Woodsworth College at the University of Toronto from 1991 to 1998. He also served as the President of Canadian Industrial Relations Association. His primary interests were unionisation in Canada and the United States, industrial relations theory, labour market analysis and human resource management. He published some 18 books in the field of industrial relations, contributed chapters in 40 others and was the author of numerous papers and articles. Meltz also served as adviser and consultant to many government and labour-management agencies. A frequent contributor to *Relations Industrielles*, he also chaired its Editorial Board for three years.

# Contents

# List of Tables

# List of Figures

# Foreword

This book comes out of a series of discussions we had with our friend and colleague, Professor Noah Meltz, after he had retired from a long career at the University of Toronto. Noah had worked in a number of areas of industrial relations over his long career but no topic made him as animated as did the question of the future of trade unions. He believed that liberal democratic societies were intricately linked with free trade unions. Yet, he realised, given his training as an institutional economist, that conditions that made trade unions a growing movement during the last century had changed unalterably. He wanted researchers and policymakers to think anew the possibilities for trade unions or other possible forms of worker representation. We acknowledge our debt to Noah by dedicating this volume of research essays to him.

These papers were written towards this end, i.e., to explore the possibilities for unions, both pessimistic as well as optimistic, across a wide-range of endeavour. The result, contained in the chapters to follow, reflects this range. The pessimistic view is not only well represented but also well researched and documented in this book. On the optimistic side, the contributors examine a range of options for unions from exploiting the internet for better organising to seeking growth in segments of the workforce where unions have not been strong in the past, e.g., women, youth, immigrants, white collar workers, etc. Better networking at home and abroad with other labour or 'progressive' groups, is also examined from various perspectives.

This book raises important issues and examines potentially useful directions for the future of unions. Even if some ideas in the book appear to be partial solutions, the analysis offers insights on ways to re-think the goals, structures and methods of trade unions. We hope readers can and will use the chapters of this book in creative ways to discuss and debate different approaches unions can take to fulfill their fundamental role of protecting workers within capitalist democracies.

This collection of papers would not have been made possible without the encouragement of Noah Meltz. We are also indebted to our colleagues (too numerous to name individually) within the Canadian Industrial Relations Association, the Industrial Relations Research Association and the International Industrial Relations Research Association, who made it possible to plan and bring to fruition such a diverse set of essays focused around a single theme. Financial support for inviting the papers to a conference is gratefully acknowledged from a variety of sources including: the Labour-Management Partnership Program of Human Resources Development Canada, the Toronto

Area Industrial Relations Association, the European Trade Union Institute, the Canadian Labour Congress, the Rotman School of Management and the Connaught Fund at the University of Toronto, and the Institute for Work and Employment, M.I.T., among others. Lastly, the editorial team at Palgrave led by Jacky Kippenberger provided exceptional support at all stages of the manuscript preparation, copy editing, and printing.

Anil Verma, *Toronto*
Thomas A. Kochan, *Cambridge, MA*

# List of Contributors

**John Burgess,** *University of Newcastle*
John Burgess is Associate Professor, Department of Economics, University of Newcastle. His research interests include employment restructuring, gender and work, and labour market policy. John is on the editorial board of the Australian Journal of Labour Economics and on the board of the Employment Studies Centre, University of Newcastle.

**Isla Carmichael,** *OISE/University of Toronto*
Dr. Isla Carmichael is a post-doctoral fellow at the Ontario Institute for Studies in Education, University of Toronto and the project manager of Capital Works: an international project on the social investment of union pension funds. She has held various senior positions at the Ontario Public Service Employees' Union (OPSEU). Her doctoral dissertation on workers' control of pension funds and social investment in Canada received the Canadian Policy Research Award from the Government of Canada. She is the author, with Jack Quarter, of *Money on the line: Workers' capital in Canada.*

**Rafael Gomez,** *London School of Economics*
Rafael is a Lecturer in Management, and Research Fellow, Centre for Economic Performance, London School of Economics. He is also a Research Fellow at the Centre for International Studies and the Centre for Industrial Relations, both at the University of Toronto.

**Rebecca Gumbrell-McCormick,** *University of London, UK*
Rebecca Gumbrell-McCormick (BA Yale, MA Princeton, PhD Warwick) is a Lecturer at the School of Management and Organisational Psychology at Birkbeck College, University of London, specialising in international and comparative industrial relations. She is a former Information Officer of the International Union of Food and Allied Workers' Associations (IUF) and Coordinating Editor of the Social and Labour Bulletin at the International Labour Organisation (ILO), both in Geneva. She has been a research officer on equal opportunities for the British union MSF, and is currently co-ordinating an EU-funded research project on trade unions, racism and xenophobia.

**Morley Gunderson,** *University of Toronto*
Morley Gunderson holds the Canadian Imperial Bank of Commerce Chair in Youth Employment at the University of Toronto where he has served as

the Director of the Centre for Industrial Relations. He received a PhD in Economics from the University of Wisconsin-Madison. Among other places, he has been a Visiting Scholar at the International Institute for Labour Studies in Geneva; the National Bureau of Economic Research and the Hoover Institution, both at Stanford University. He is also a Research Associate of the Institute of Policy Analysis and the Centre for International Studies, both at the University of Toronto.

**Raymond Harbridge,** *La Trobe University*
Raymond Harbridge is Professor of Management and Head of the School at the Graduate School of Management at La Trobe University, Melbourne, Australia. He holds a LLD from Victoria University of Wellington and a MA (Honours) from Auckland University. With Professor Pat Walsh he is a joint leader of the Employment Institutions Project, which for the last decade has been analysing the structure and operation of employment institutions in New Zealand.

**Richard Hyman,** *London School of Economics*
Richard Hyman is a Professor in the Industrial Relations Department at the London School of Economics. After receiving a DPhil from Oxford University, he was successively, Research Fellow, Lecturer and Professor at the University of Warwick. He has published numerous scholarly articles, chapters in books, and nine books. He has also edited numerous publications including the European Journal of Industrial Relations where he serves as the Founding Editor.

**Bruce E. Kaufman,** *Georgia State University*
Bruce is Professor of Economics in the Andrew Young School of Policy Studies and Senior Associate, W. T. Beebe Institute of Personnel and Employment Relations, Georgia State University. He received his PhD in Economics from the University of Wisconsin-Madison and currently does research and teaching in the areas of labour economics, industrial relations, and human resource management. He has published numerous scholarly articles and has edited or written 11 books, including *The Origins and Evolution of the Field of Industrial Relations in the United States*, winner of the 1992 Richard A. Lester award; and, *Government Regulation of the Employment Relationship*. Professor Kaufman is co-editor of *Advances in Industrial and Labor Relations*.

**Thomas A. Kochan,** *MIT*
Thomas Kochan is George M. Bunker Professor of Management at the Sloan School of Management, MIT. He has written or co-authored many books including: *Working in America, After Lean Production,* and *The Mutual Gains Enterprise.* His 1986 book *The Transformation of American Industrial Relations*

received the best scholarly book award from the Academy of Management. Prof. Kochan is a Past President of the International Industrial Relations Association and the Industrial Relations Research Association (IRRA). He was also named the Centennial Visiting Professor at The London School of Economics. During 1993–1995, he served as a member of the Clinton Administration's Commission on the Future of Worker-Management Relations.

**David W. Livingstone**, *OISE/University of Toronto*
David Livingstone is head of the Centre for the Study of Education and Work at OISE/UT and director of the research network on New Approaches to Lifelong Learning (NALL). He is also principal investigator of the OISE/UT Biennial Survey of Educational Issues. His recent publications include: *The Education-Jobs Gap: Underemployment or Economic Democracy*; *Down-to-Earth People: Beyond Class Reductionism and Postmodernism* (with Wally Seccombe); *Working and Learning in the Information Age: A Profile of Canadians; and Public Attitudes towards Education in Ontario 2000: The Millennial OISE/UT Survey* (with Doug Hart and Lynn Davie).

**Richard Locke**, *IWER, Sloan School of Management, MIT*
Richard M. Locke is the Alvin J. Siteman Professor of Entrepreneurship and Political Science at MIT. Locke has also taught at the Universita Degli Studi Ca' Foscari in Venice, Italy, the Georg-August Universitat in Gotttingen, Germany, and the Federal University of Rio de Janeiro. Locke received his PhD from MIT. His publications include *Remaking the Italian Economy*; with Thomas Kochan and Michael Piore, *Employment Relations in a Changing World Economy*; and with Kathleen Thelen, *The Shifting Boundaries of Labor Politics*.

**Graeme Lockwood**, *Kings College, London*
Graeme Lockwood is a lecturer in Industrial Law at the Management Centre, Kings College London. His main research interests are in the area of collective labour law and in particular, the information and consultation rights of trade unions.

**David Marsden**, *London School of Economics*
David Marsden is Professor of Industrial Relations at the London School of Economics and Political Science (LSE), and a member of the Centre for Economic Performance. Current research comprises a study of performance management and performance pay in the public services and its effects on motivation and performance, and an international study of pay inequalities and economic performance in Europe, Japan and the United States.

**Miguel Martínez Lucio**, *Leeds University [now University of Bradford School of Management]*
Miguel Martínez Lucio is a senior lecturer of Industrial and Labour Studies, Leeds University Business School. He obtained his PhD from the University of Warwick. Miguel's research interests include the changing nature of European industrial relations, and the relationship between new forms of workplace organisation and management and trade union strategies. He is currently working on a range of related projects, including a collaborative project with Mark Stuart on the development and politics of partnership in the UK (funded by the Manufacturing Science and Finance Union). Miguel has published over 50 articles and book chapters.

**Noah M. Meltz**, *Netanya College (Israel) and University of Toronto*
Noah M. Meltz was a professor of business at Netanya Academic College in Israel, and Professor Emeritus, University of Toronto. At the University of Toronto, he served as the Principal, Woodsworth College, and Director, Centre for Industrial Relations. He received his PhD from Princeton University. He served as past president of the Canadian Industrial Relations Association, and received the Gerard Dion Award for outstanding contributions to Canadian industrial relations. He was also named Chair of the Editorial Board of the journal, *Relations Industrielles/ Industrial Relations*.
(*Editors' note*: Professor Noah Meltz died on 29 January 2002 in Israel. He contributed significantly to the development of themes of several papers in this volume.)

**Sian Moore**, *CEP London Metropolitan University*
Sian Moore is Senior Research Fellow at the Working Lives Research Institute, London Metropolitan University. Following her doctorate at the University of Essex (in Social History), she has worked in local government, the trade union, NALGO, in Labour Research Department, an independent, trade union-based research organisation, and in the Leverhulme Foundation Future of Trade Unionism Programme, at the Centre for Economic Performance, London School of Economics. Her main research interests are the impact of the UK statutory recognition legislation of 2000, trade union organisation and mobilisation, and historical analysis of women's consciousness and organisation.

**Paul Osterman**, *Sloan School of Management, MIT*
Paul Osterman is Professor at the Sloan School and the Department of Urban Planning, MIT. Osterman is the author of many books including, *Securing Prosperity* and *Employment Futures*. He has co-authored, *Working In America; The Mutual Gains Enterprise; and Change At Work*, and edited two books, *Internal Labor Markets*, and *Broken Ladders*. Osterman has been a

senior administrator of job training programmes for the Commonwealth of Massachusetts and consulted widely to government agencies, foundations, community groups, and public interest organisations. He received his PhD in Economics from MIT.

**Michael Piore**, *Sloan School of Management, MIT*
Professor Piore is a labour economist, best known for the development of the concept of the internal labour market and the dual labour market hypothesis, and more recently for work on the transition from mass production to flexible specialisation. He has worked on a number of labour market and industrial relations problems including low income labour markets, the impact of technology upon work, migration, labour market segmentation, and the relationship between the labour market, business strategy and industrial organisation. The central theme in Piore's work is the social, institutional, and cognitive dimensions of economic activity.

**Chris Riddell**, *University of Toronto*
Chris Riddell is a post-doctoral fellow with the Team for Advanced Research on Globalisation, Education and Technology, based in the Department of Economics at the University of British Columbia. Research interests span the fields of compensation and industrial relations as well as labour and health economics. Current research includes the effect of pay-for-performance contracts, union organising and management tactics, the long-run effect of unemployment insurance on labour supply, and the interaction between social assistance and health outcomes.

**W. Craig Riddell**, *University of British Columbia*
Craig Riddell is a Professor, Department of Economics, University of British Columbia, and an Associate of the Canadian Institute for Advanced Research. His research interests are focused on unemployment and labour market dynamics, the role of human capital in economic growth, experimental and non-experimental approaches to the evaluation of social programmes, unionisation and collective bargaining, and gender differences in labour market behaviour. Professor Riddell has served as Academic Co-Chair of the Canadian Employment Research Forum, and Past-President of the Canadian Economics Association.

**Reuben Roth**, *Trent University*
Reuben Roth teaches sociology at Trent University, is a project coordinator at York University's Centre for Research on Work and Society, and a Senior Research Officer at the Ontario Institute for Studies in Education at the University of Toronto. He is currently completing his doctoral dissertation, which examines working-class consciousness among unionised autoworkers at General Motors' (GM) assembly facility in Oshawa, Ontario, Canada.

This research is informed in part by his employment on the GM assembly lines from 1984–1991.

**Glenda Strachan**, *University of Newcastle*
Glenda Strachan is an Associate Professor, School of Management, University of Newcastle. Research interests are contemporary and historical workplace change, with a special emphasis on women's employment and gender equity policies. Glenda is the co-editor of the Journal of Interdisciplinary Gender Studies, member of Labour History editorial board and on the board of the Employment Studies Centre, University of Newcastle.

**Mark Stuart**, *Leeds University*
Mark Stuart is a senior lecturer in the Industrial and Labour Studies Division of Leeds University Business School. He holds a PhD from the University of Leeds. Mark's prime research interests focus on the industrial relations of skill formation and social partnership. He is currently working on a large research project in collaboration with Miguel Martínez Lucio, that investigates the development and politics of partnership in the UK. This project is funded by the Manufacturing, Science and Finance Union.

**Michael Terry**, *Warwick Business School*
Michael Terry is Professor of Industrial Relations at the Industrial Relations Research Unit, Warwick Business School, UK. He has worked with and studied trade unions in the UK for many years and has published extensively on the subject. He is the author of Redefining Public Sector Unionism: UNISON and the future of trade unions.

**C. S. Venkata Ratnam**, *International Management Institute, New Delhi*
Professor Venkata Ratnam specialises in topics such as International Labour Standards and Trade and Diversity Management and Negotiation Skills. He has served as a consultant to the International Labour Organisation and Asian Productivity Organisation. He is also the Director of the GITAM Institute of Foreign Trade. He has conducted extensive longitudinal research studies integrating behavioural sciences and industrial relations in ports, shipping, refineries and engineering industries and state electricity boards. He has been a Visiting Professor at the International Institute of Management, Graz, Austria. He has published several books and papers and is the Editor, Global Business Review.

**Anil Verma**, *University of Toronto*
Anil Verma is a Professor at the Centre for Industrial Relations and Joseph L. Rotman School of Management. He received his PhD from the Sloan School of Management, Massachusetts Institute of Technology. Anil has

served as President, Canadian Industrial Relations Association; Member of the Executive Board, International Industrial Relations Association; Member; and, Member of the Advisory Committee on Labour Statistics at Statistics Canada. He has co-edited several books including, *Contract and Commitment: Employment Relations in the New Economy* and *Industrial Relations in Canadian Industry* (with Richard Chaykowski).

**Pat Walsh**, *Victoria University*
Pat Walsh is Professor of Human Resource Management and Industrial Relations and Head of School at the School of Business and Public Management, Victoria University of Wellington, New Zealand. Dr. Walsh holds a PhD from the University of Minnesota and MA (First class honours) from the University of Canterbury. Along with Professor Raymond Harbridge, he is a joint leader of the Employment Institutions Project, a major project which for the last decade has been analysing the structure and operation of employment institutions in New Zealand with particular reference to changing patterns of workplace employment relations.

**David Wilkinson**, *La Trobe University*
Dr. David Wilkinson is Deputy Head of School and Programme Director at the Graduate School of Management. He has worked as a labour market economist for the both State and Federal governments, as well as an economist in the private sector. He has written for the OECD on regulatory issues and has undertaken extensive consulting with public sector organisations, presented papers at a number of international conferences and has a number of refereed journal articles. Dr. Wilkinson's current research interests include government regulatory issues, trade union legislation and cost-benefit analysis.

**Geoffrey Wood**, *Conventry Business School*
Geoffrey Wood currently lectures at – and is Director of the Human Resource Management Research Group – Coventry Business School, Coventry University, England, and is a Fellow of Rhodes University, South Africa. Previously he was Associate Professor in Industrial Sociology at Rhodes University, and has also served as Commissioned Researcher for the South African Truth and Reconciliation Commission. He is the author of over 50 peer reviewed journal articles (as well as author/co-author/editor of several books) on subjects ranging from trade union organisation, to contemporary HR practice, to structural adjustment and democratisation in lusophone Africa.

**Stephen Wood**, *University of Sheffield*
Stephen Wood is Research Professor and Deputy Director, Institute of Work Psychology and Co-Director, Economic and Social Research Council Centre

for Organisation and Innovation, University of Sheffield. He is also a Research Associate at the Centre for Economic Performance at the London School of Economics. He gained his PhD from the University of Manchester and worked at LSE from 1974–99, where was an Institute of Personnel and Development Fellow during 1992–96. Currently he is Chief Editor of the British Journal of Industrial Relations.

# 1

# Unions in the 21st Century: Prospects for Renewal

*Anil Verma and Thomas A. Kochan*

## Introduction

Trade unions have occupied a central place in industrial relations research since the beginning of this field of study. With the well-documented decline in union membership that occurred around the world in the latter half of the 20th century, research on this topic has taken on a tone of heightened concern and urgency. Once again, fundamental questions about the role of unions as institutions in the labour market and society are being raised. Are unions outmoded institutions that arose out of the industrial revolution and grew to prominence and power in response to the economic and social conditions of the industrial economies of the 20th century but ill-suited to the economies, societies, and workers of today? Or, is the decline in unions likely to be reversed in the near term? If so, how? And, perhaps more fundamentally, if so, will the unions of the future be mirror images of those of the past and will the processes by which unions reverse their declines mirror the organising models and histories of the past? Or will the organising processes and organisational forms, strategies and roles of unions also change in significant ways? Finally, what is at stake in these debates? That is, should others outside the labour movement care whether or not unions rebuild their membership and regain their lost power and status as labour market institutions?

These are central questions facing industrial relations theory, research, policy, and practice today.[1] They are the questions that motivate this volume of research papers. In this essay, we summarise the lessons that we take from these papers and from the larger collection of research that speaks to these questions. Our goal is to sharpen the debate over the future of unions, and to identify issues we believe need greater attention by the industrial relations research and policy communities.

In what follows we first briefly review the data on union membership decline around the world. This is not new information. It is presented here simply to document the breadth and depth of decline in this labour market

1

institution and to set the context for the discussion that follows. Then we take up the question of whether, or more precisely, why researchers, policy makers, and citizens should be concerned about the decline in unions. All this sets the stage for brief comments on the lessons we draw from these papers for the key questions raised above. Our final section lays out a set of propositions that flow from the accumulated studies on union decline and revival that we believe are central to answering the questions raised above.

## Union membership density since 1980

Table 1.1 displays union densities across the globe in the post-1980 era. Although union density data were not always available for the same years, the percentage change in union densities shown in the last column is broadly indicative of the decline unions have experienced since 1980.

There are some exceptions to this general trend. Union densities increased in six countries. Upon closer examination, however, these appear to be special cases. For example, in the case of South Africa, Zimbabwe and Chile, unions had been officially suppressed for a period. When more liberal political and legal regimes were introduced, union densities increased due to a pent-up demand from years previous. Only if these trends are sustained beyond the reference period would they be truly exceptional cases. In the case of China these numbers are not directly comparable because China's trade unions are not independent of Communist Party control. In India's case, density rose marginally between 1980 and 1993. But these data do not capture the full impact of India's economic liberalisation programmes introduced in the early 1990s. According to some reports, trade union density in India traditionally very low, has fallen further as economic reforms take hold (Ratnam, 2001). Hong Kong and Taiwan are the other two countries that report an increase in union density. Taiwan's increase is largely attributed to a social insurance benefit that became available only to union members (Kuruvilla et al., 2002). That leaves Hong Kong as the only case where an independent trade union movement has added to union density within a liberal economic system. In all other cases, independent unions working within liberal economies have declined in density.

The reasons for union membership decline vary by country and by continent but the end result is strikingly similar. This stagnation and decline has attracted wide interest from many quarters, particularly from researchers and social analysts who worry about the consequences of continued union decline.

## What's at stake?

Should society care about the decline of unions and whether or not they will be a significant force in the 21st century? There is no doubt that many

*Table 1.1*    Union densities in selected countries since 1980

| Country | Year | Union density (%) | Year | Union density (%) | Percentage change |
|---|---|---|---|---|---|
| **Africa** | | | | | |
| Egypt | 1985 | 38.9 | 1995 | 29.6 | −23.9 |
| Kenya | 1985 | 41.9 | 1995 | 16.9 | −59.6 |
| Mauritius | 1985 | 34.8 | 1995 | 25.9 | −25.7 |
| South Africa | 1985 | 15.5 | 1995 | 21.8 | 40.7 |
| Uganda | 1989 | 7.8 | 1995 | 3.9 | −49.9 |
| Zambia | 1985 | 18.8 | 1995 | 12.5 | −33.5 |
| Zimbabwe | 1985 | 11.6 | 1995 | 13.9 | 20.1 |
| **Asia** | | | | | |
| Australia | 1980 | 47.2 | 1995 | 28.6 | −39.4 |
| China | 1981 | 55.9 | 1995 | 68.8 | 23.1 |
| Hong Kong | 1980 | 19.0 | 1994 | 21.0 | 10.5 |
| India | 1980 | 18.2 | 1993 | 18.9 | 3.8 |
| Japan | 1980 | 31.1 | 1995 | 23.9 | −23.1 |
| Korea | 1980 | 15.5 | 1995 | 12.7 | −18.0 |
| New Zealand | 1980 | 53.5 | 1995 | 23.2 | −56.6 |
| Singapore | 1980 | 26.8 | 1995 | 15.6 | −41.8 |
| Taiwan | 1980 | 26.2 | 1995 | 50.1 | 91.2 |
| **Europe** | | | | | |
| Finland | 1980 | 69.8 | 1995 | 59.7 | −14.5 |
| France | 1980 | 17.6 | 1995 | 6.1 | −65.3 |
| Germany | 1980 | 35.6 | 1995 | 29.6 | −16.9 |
| Ireland | 1980 | 52.7 | 1993 | 36.0 | −31.7 |
| Italy | 1980 | 44.1 | 1994 | 30.6 | −30.6 |
| Norway | 1980 | 55.7 | 1995 | 51.7 | −7.2 |
| Sweden | 1980 | 78.0 | 1994 | 77.2 | −1.0 |
| Switzerland | 1980 | 31.1 | 1994 | 20.0 | −35.7 |
| United Kingdom | 1980 | 48.6 | 1995 | 26.2 | −46.1 |
| **North America** | | | | | |
| Canada | 1980 | 33.2 | 1993 | 31.0 | −6.7 |
| Mexico | 1989 | 54.1 | 1991 | 31.0 | −42.7 |
| United States | 1980 | 21.1 | 1995 | 12.7 | −39.8 |
| **South America** | | | | | |
| Argentina | 1986 | 48.7 | 1995 | 25.4 | −47.9 |
| Chile | 1985 | 11.6 | 1993 | 15.9 | 37.2 |
| Columbia | 1985 | 11.2 | 1995 | 7.0 | −37.3 |
| Costa Rica | 1985 | 22.9 | 1995 | 13.1 | −42.6 |
| Venezuela | 1988 | 25.9 | 1995 | 14.9 | −42.5 |

*Sources*: ILO (1997–1998); Visser (1993).

observers, some from the union ranks but many others, view this decline with concern. A simple search through a typical university library catalogue turns up more than 25 books published since 1998 alone on the question of the future of unions. In this outpouring it is not always clear if the concern is about the loss of an institution considered vital to the workings of just and fair societies or whether it is just old-fashioned nostalgia.

Chaykowski and Slotsve (2002) document one significant consequence of the decline of unions, namely an increase in income inequality. Using Canadian data, they show that union decline has increased inequality the most in the lower quintiles of the wage distribution. This finding is consistent with earlier economic analyses of union effects on the wage distribution (Freeman and Medoff, 1984) and more recent studies seeking to understand the causes of growing income inequality in North American economies (Card, 2001; DiNardo and Lemieux, 1997; Fortin and Lemieux, 1997; DiNardo, Fortin and Lemieux, 1996; Freeman, 1993, 1996).

Clearly, however, the effects of union decline go beyond these economic considerations. Throughout the 20th century, labour unions have been viewed as important political institutions for enhancing and protecting democracy and pluralism in society. Some have argued that unions make their most positive contributions to society when they are broad-based and representative enough to speak for the workforce and to take an inclusive rather than a narrow perspective in political discourse (Barbash, 1991). The decline in union density, and perhaps of equal importance, the failure of most labour movements to organise the newer and more rapidly growing industries and occupational groups, reduces significantly labour's ability to play this constructive political role. Indeed, there is growing evidence that as unions decline it becomes harder for them and policy makers responsible for labour and the workforce to get these issues on the agenda of government policy makers. This is particularly true in the U.S., regardless of which political party is in the majority (Reich, 1997; Osterman, Kochan, Locke and Piore, 2001).

It is a concern elsewhere as well. In Europe, the decline of national level tripartite consultation at the national level has been well documented. In Britain, while the end of the Thatcher era and the ascendancy of the New Labour Government to power has produced important new labour policies such as a minimum wage statute, a new labour relations recognition statute, and an endorsement of labour-management partnerships, the general consensus is that the labour movement's role and influence in the Labour Party has declined considerably from the pre Thatcher era. The decline in labour's influence at the national level in Europe may in part be replaced by labour's voice in deliberations at the level of the European Community. This however, remains a subject of considerable debate and one worthy of continued research, in the European context as well as in the growing number of other transnational forums affecting economic and labour market policies.

Among developing nations, the traditional role of the International Labour Organisation (ILO) in promoting labour standards and human rights has been overshadowed in recent years by the demands of international financial institutions such as the International Monetary Fund (IMF) and the World Bank for market reforms that reduce the power and role of unions and other labour market institutions.

Protests against the role of the World Trade Organisation and at gatherings of economic policy makers and corporate leaders signal an effort to reverse the decline in labour's political influence. Whether they will have their desired effect, and more generally, what it will take to reverse the longer run pattern of labour's declining political influence is an issue worth serious attention by those who see this as a cause for concern.

Thus, there are sound normative reasons for both industrial relations researchers and other social scientists and policy makers to be concerned over the consequences of the pattern and magnitude of union decline. Yet these concerns need not trigger a simple nostalgic hope for a revival of unions in the mirror image of their past forms and functions. The world today is different than when unions took root in many parts of the world. The composition of industries, their locations and their methods of production have all changed dramatically. More important, the bulk of these changes were concentrated in the last quarter of the 20$^{th}$ century that coincided with the sustained decline in unions. This brings us to the current debates over the causes of union decline and the likely effects of alternative strategies for renewal. The papers included in this volume begin to shed some light on which of these scenarios are playing out at this moment in history and the likely consequences that will result depending on which dominates the future of unionism.

## Looking ahead: the possibility of continued decline

Kaufman (Chapter 4) uses evidence from the 20$^{th}$ century on union growth and decline in the U.S. to forecast the future trend in union density in the early years of the 21$^{st}$ century. He examines key variables influencing union growth and decline: the breadth and depth of labour problems, the effectiveness (instrumentality) of unions in solving these problems, the availability and effectiveness of substitute methods to solve labour problems, the support given by labour law to union organising and bargaining power, and the leadership and organisational structure of unions. In the absence of wartime mobilisation of the economy or major social or economic disruption, he predicts union density is most likely to continue its slow decline in the years ahead.

A large body of research assesses the causes of union decline in different national or institutional settings. While the relative weights assigned to different factors vary across countries, the broad causal categories examined tend to include: (1) structural changes in the economy and labour force, (2) employer opposition either through direct suppression of unions or substitution of the functions unions have traditionally performed, (3) government policies, and (4) union strategies. Studies from various countries (Visser, 2002; Meltz, 1984; Freeman, 1988; Farber and Western, 2001) have documented that each of these factors accounts for varying portions of the decline, depending on the specific setting. The implication is that no single factor can account for it all.

Riddell and Riddell, in Chapter 11, show that the decline in union density in Canada and the U.S. during 1984–98 is comparable, i.e., 8 per cent in the U.S. and 7 per cent in Canada. Moreover, much of the decline remains unexplained by the shift in employment from highly unionised industries towards highly nonunion industries. The sectoral shift in employment explains only 20 per cent of the decline in the U.S. and none of it in Canada. The implication is that workers are less likely to be unionised across all industries and workplaces.

Evidence from other countries also reinforces the notion that something more fundamental than the regulatory regime must change to facilitate union renewal. In Chapter 5, Walsh, Harbridge and Wilkinson examine the case of New Zealand where the legislative regime has changed significantly twice since 1991. The first change saw the introduction of the labour-unfriendly Employment Contracts Act in 1991 followed by the current regime under the more labour-friendly Employment Relations Act in 2000. Despite the fact that current regime is supportive of worker rights to unionise, union density has increased only marginally since 2000. Similarly, Wood in Chapter 16 examines the case of post-apartheid South Africa to conclude that the old organising model for gaining new members will not be enough in the future. He points to the large pool of workers in the informal sector who are unlikely to be responsive to methods of organising used in the formal sector that consists of large-scale organisations.

In Chapter 6, Wood and Moore using data from Britain reinforce the idea that incremental changes in the regulatory regime are unlikely to boost union density significantly. They examine the impact of union recognition procedures in Britain to find that despite being labour-friendly, the Employment Relations Act 2000 that sets up a state-regulated recognition procedure, did not substantially alter the trend in union density decline although it did contribute to a slowing down of the trend.

A number of studies, both in this volume and elsewhere (Visser, 2002; Charlwood, 2002; Gomez, Gunderson and Meltz, 2002), present evidence to come to a similar conclusion: the standard model of union organising that relies on dissatisfaction with current working conditions and the instrumental view that unions can improve these conditions, is far too limited an organising model to entice workers to join unions today. This is especially true in labour law regimes that require a majority of workers in a specific bargaining unit to vote for union representation. While U.S. unions face further handicaps in using this model to organise because of strong employer resistance to unions and demonstrated inequities and failures of labour law to protect worker rights to unionise (Commission on the Future of Worker Management Relations, 1994), the fact that the same conclusions about the limits of this model emerge from studies in other countries (Canada, Britain, and the Netherlands) that vary on both intensity of employer opposition and labour law, suggests that the problem is much deeper.

## Prospects for renewal

Given this evidence, more recent work has begun to focus on what unions might do to reverse their declines. Much of the analysis presented in the published literature can be classified in two groups. One line of investigation builds directly on studies of the causes of union decline and extrapolates to the future relationships observed among past and current union strategies, worker views of unions, and external factors. The bottom line of these studies is that if past cause-effect patterns continue, incremental shifts in union strategies will not reverse the decline. For example, Farber and Western (2002) point out it would take more than a ten-fold increase in organising activity (and the same ratio of organising success) for American unions to rebuild union density to their pre 1980 levels.

Yet a range of studies (mostly done in North America) suggest that there remains a strong demand for union representation of one type or another (Kochan, 1979; Fiorito, 1987; Lipset and Meltz, 1998; Freeman and Rogers, 1999). The bottom line of this work is that in North America perhaps 30 to 45 per cent of the workforce expresses an interest or preference for traditional union representation over non-union status. But twice as many want other forms of voice at work that do not entail the risks of a strike or employer retaliation and resistance encountered in traditional union organising drives. Workers also express strong interest in having a job environment that supports continued learning and development and that allow them the flexibility to integrate or better balance work and family life. Organisations that can meet these expressed interests will be in higher demand than traditional unions. An important research priority would be to test what forms of worker voice and representation workers want in other cultural and national settings.

In this volume, Lockwood, in Chapter 7, investigates the impact of labour-unfriendly legislation in Britain requiring mandatory ballots for a variety of internal union decision-making procedures. Enacted by a Conservative government, the hope was that such ballots will allow 'moderate' union members who would otherwise be intimidated by union extremists, to influence union policy. Contrary to Conservative expectations, Lockwood finds that the legislation did not result in a weakening of unions or a dilution of their activist platforms. In fact, the mandatory voting strengthened the union activist processes by giving them greater legitimacy. The implication is that unions can use such democratic processes to gain greater legitimacy and thereby broaden their appeal to more workers.

One conclusion to be drawn from these studies is that an alternative recruitment model will be necessary that both attracts and retains workers for the long run. The retention problem is perhaps as important as the initial recruitment challenge. Consider two facts. In the U.S., there are currently twice as many former union members as there are current members (see Chapter 3 by Osterman, Kochan, Locke, and Piore). That means many workers pass through a phase of union membership at some point in their careers but do not retain their membership over their life course. Visser (2002) documents the magnitude of this organising challenge. For every ten members recruited into Dutch unions, eight members are lost. This means that to realise a net gain of one new member, unions have to organise or recruit five people! Clearly, strategies that maintain membership through periods of job transition, movements in and out of the labour force or from full-time to part-time status would pay handsome dividends to union growth (Horowitz, 1997). A shift to a model of life-long membership that provides services and benefits to workers as they move through their full life course is one way to rethink the process of organising and recruiting.

Few unions currently provide this type of continuity, however, and this makes it difficult to test these ideas with traditional field based research methods. Yet some broad international comparisons are suggestive. As Visser (2002) points out, the union movements that come the closest to providing incentives for workers to retain their membership when they move between jobs, namely unions in countries such as Denmark and Sweden that deliver unemployment benefits to people between jobs, are also the labour movements that have done better in limiting union membership decline. This question needs to be explored in more depth in different occupational and national settings. Indeed examples can be found of unions in various countries (e.g., the Association of Professionals, Engineers, and Scientists of Australia, the Communications Workers of America, etc.) that are experimenting with these types of recruitment and retention strategies. More micro analyses of these experiments and their results would be extremely useful.

Hyman, in Chapter 2, argues that union renewal may require unions to focus on internal union processes that feed into the choices they face in terms of who they represent, what interests they emphasise, and how they are constituted as organisations to mobilise resources in action. Possible groups to target include the elite workers, the core workforce, the peripheral workers, the unemployed and those out of the workforce who could be potentially employed. Choices in the area of interests include bread-and-butter issues, voice and fairness, macroeconomic and social policy, and community-wide interests such as environmental protection. Lastly, Hyman suggests that unions in the past have been generally strong at the national level. Now they face pressures pulling them down to the enterprise level on the one hand while global pressures are pulling them in the international arena.

In considering new roles for unions within the context of a service and information economy, Marsden examines evidence from Britain to suggest ways in which unions may be able to adapt in the area of pay policies in Chapter 10. Traditionally, unions have taken the 'common rule' approach to pay policies which results in uniform pay for all workers in a given job. This approach appears increasingly out of date in today's context where both employers and workers want some monetary incentives built into the pay structure. Marsden suggests that unions can switch their role from being the guarantor of uniform pay to becoming the gatekeeper on procedural fairness in determining pay. Evidence shows that employees regard unions as effective vehicles for procedural justice. If unions substitute a procedural justice role for their traditional reliance on establishing a 'common rule', management can achieve better operation of their incentive schemes, and employees may experience less unfairness and poisoned work relations.

A change in roles needs to be coupled with a strategy to broaden the union reach outside its historical membership profile. Several chapters in this book and elsewhere suggest areas where unions may focus their efforts at recruiting new members: Gomez, Gunderson and Meltz focus on youth (Chapter 17) while Strachan and Burgess examine the potential in recruiting women (Chapter 12). Others such as Erickson et al. (2002) have studied the potential for signing up low wage workers who also frequently happen to be immigrants (Reitz and Verma, 2004). Another group of authors explore renewal prospects that lie latent in new technology (Diamond and Freeman, 2002), new internal union structures (Hyman in Chapter 2), and new external collaborations (Osterman, Kochan, Locke, and Piore in Chapter 3). Similarly, Gumbrell-McCormick (Chapter 13) examines the role of the ICFTU in fostering international collaboration within the global labour movement, Carmichael (Chapter 8) investigates the strategic use of pension funds by unions, Ratnam and Verma (Chapter 18) examine the potential for unions to collaborate with NGOs and Livingstone and Roth (Chapter 9) look at tapping workers' knowledge for union renewal. Lastly, Lucio and Stuart (Chapter 14) and Terry (Chapter 15) examine the prospects for unions to enter 'partnerships' as a strategy for renewal.

Gomez, Gunderson and Meltz in Chapter 17 suggest that the biggest payoffs lie in wooing young workers who are about to enter the labour market. Young workers are not less interested in joining unions than older workers, even though it is well documented that they are less likely than their older counterparts to be union members. Both papers argue that social capital factors – influence of family members, peers, and co-workers – have big effects on views of unions of young workers. Visser (2002) also comes to a similar conclusion: either unions organise workers within the first five years of their job experience or they are likely to lose them for the rest of their careers!

Strachan and Burgess, in Chapter 12, analyse the relationship between declining trade union density and the growing feminisation of the Australian workforce. They examine the extent to which trade unions have accommodated the interests and needs of women workers to conclude that unions have changed dramatically in the past 20 years in their attitudes towards and policies about women workers, however, these policies are still not regarded as mainstream issues. Often women's issues are treated as special interest topics within the union. If unions have to broaden their appeal they need to give women's issues a more central place in their affairs.

Apart from the need to focus on attracting new labour market entrants into unions and providing a range of services, benefits, and organisational experiences needed to retain these members, unions also need to examine a social capital strategy for its renewal. That is, what linkages among workers and institutions in their environment domestically and internationally need to be forged to build the networks and social capital needed for sustainable union renewal?

In Chapter 9, Livingstone and Roth argue that underestimation of the current range and depth of workers' knowledge and skills by union leaders represents a significant barrier to further growth of the labour movement. Using findings from a national survey and case study they find that unionised and non-unionised industrial and service workers in Canada are increasingly highly educated, increasingly participating in adult education courses and devoting substantial amounts of their time to informal learning activities. In light of both the rapid expansion of formal schooling and the massive amount of informal learning among working people, it is imperative for unions to address the growing learning interests of workers with more responsive and inclusive educational programmes and strategies in order to enhance membership solidarity and attract new members.

Ratnam and Verma in Chapter 18, open up an important line of analysis by describing the roles played by a number of non-governmental organisations (NGOs) in India. This chapter raises several questions: will NGOs become significant instruments for employee voice and representation in developing countries? Should NGOs be considered part of the labour movement of the 21st century? Should existing unions build coalitions with the NGOs and support their efforts or see them as competitors? Clearly some of the most successful NGOs have demonstrated how to use information to expose exploitation of children and adult workers in contractors tied to transnational firms. In doing so they demonstrate the potential of information and transparency as a source of power for workers and their advocates. Whether NGOs can translate episodic exposures and achievements into ongoing institutions and organisations would appear to be the central question in this debate.

In Chapter 13, Gumbrell-McCormick examines the international issues and labour's possible response through its apex body, the ICFTU. She finds that it is a difficult task for the trade union movement, whatever its espoused policies, to escape the heavy weight of inequality between the rich and poor countries. The ICFTU has supported major initiatives in favour of debt relief and other measures to equalise trading relationships, and has opposed colonialism and exploitation; but as the influence of the trade union movement has waned in the industrialised countries over the past 20 years of neo-liberalism, so has its ability to affect the crucial decisions involving world trade and global inequality. In recent years, a more critical appreciation of the dynamics of trade liberalisation, and the growth of a more robust trade union movement both in the developing and the industrialised countries, have encouraged new ways of thinking within the international movement. There have been recent examples of international trade union solidarity, where unions from the south have given their assistance to unions in the north. Furthermore, the emerging leaders of the international movement in such countries as Brazil and South Africa are establishing close links among themselves, and may be leading the way to a more egalitarian international structure and greater autonomy and initiative from the trade unions of the developing world.

In Chapter 8, Carmichael describes new directions being taken by the trade union movement in Canada through control over investment of pension funds and through social investment strategies. This chapter presents evidence from case studies, to conclude that joint trusteeship of pension funds and social investment strategies may offer labour a strategic advantage in the economy. By taking into account the interests of society as well as union members in investment of pension funds, unions may gain access to new union organising constituencies and broaden their appeal.

These and other such examples suggest that the 21st century labour unions may take a variety of organisational forms, some of which identify themselves as 'unions' and some of which perform some of the functions or provide some of the services of unions without adopting the name or the on-going structures of 20th century unions. That is, we may be witnessing the early stages of a metamorphosis in which the institutions that represent workers in the 21st century differ significantly in form, function, and identity than the labour unions of the 20th century. Indeed, we believe industrial relations researchers need to give a high priority to analysing the roles played by alternative models of worker voice and representation that can be observed in different settings. Part of the evolutionary process by which a metamorphosis occurs involves increased variation as species try different approaches to adapting to a changed environment. Some of these succeed and survive; others do not. We may be observing this process unfold as 20th century unions seek to adapt to 21st century conditions.

## Conclusions: tracking alternative scenarios for the future

The purpose of this research volume is to draw implications from current research about the future of unions and to identify directions for future research on this question. No responsible social scientist can make a firm prediction about the future of unions given the data available at this time. Instead, we will offer a set of alternative scenarios that could play out differently in different parts of the world. In doing so, we will offer predictions on the factors that might influence whether, or under what conditions, each scenario is likely to be forthcoming. Testing these propositions, we believe, would both sharpen the debates over the future of unions and help to identify which, if any of these scenarios will dominate in the years ahead.[2]

*Past Trends Predict the Future.* Perhaps the clearest prediction that can be drawn from research on unions is that if unions do nothing to change their approach to organising, or make only modest changes at the margin such as investing more resources in current strategies, the trends of the past two decades are likely to continue. Unions, at least as we knew them in the 20th century, will continue to decline in membership density. Although density is not a perfect predictor of power and influence, it is perhaps the strongest correlate of the ability of unions to perform positive political and economic functions for their members and their societies.

History, however, teaches us that such predictions are seldom borne out completely. Conditions change, pent up demands for institutions produce innovations either within or outside existing organisations to meet these demands. So while steady-state predictions hold if the environmental trends of the past continue into the future, the *ceritas paribus* conditions here are the controlling factor.

*Powerful Niches.* There is another scenario which follows the extrapolation of the current situation and relationships but one which differentiates more sharply between union membership size or density and union power and influence. This is the possibility of a labour movement in the future that is numerically strong in a limited number of sectors within individual economies. Such an existence in particular niches is highly compatible with ecological theories of social and economic institutions. The labour movement could maintain its current base and, with continuous adaptation, become stronger and more effective in some sectors with little growth or even presence in others. The same could be true across countries. For example, one could imagine that unions in Scandinavian countries in particular, and perhaps in Europe more generally, will maintain their membership and perhaps expand from their current base more successfully than unions in other parts of the world. Labour in Europe continues to be more fully integrated into social and political affairs, accepted as a key institution for a democratic society, and, in some countries, delivers key labour market services to members that create incentives to maintain membership over one's full life cycle. Where these conditions pertain, unions are likely to remain at least as strong as they are today.

*Waiting for the Crisis: Events will Create a Revival.* Another view suggests there is no reason to be too concerned about some decline in union ranks. Historically, unions have grown in spurts during periods when unique combinations of social, political and economic forces have created a positive climate for union growth. The current period, although unfavourable to unions, is unlikely to last forever. Eventually a traumatic economic or social crisis, similar to the Great Depression in the United States, the fall of the Berlin Wall in Europe, or the defeat of Nazism and Fascism in World War II would produce a resurgence in unions.

In our view, this interpretation places too much reliance on some invisible or natural swing of history without asking what factors affect whether or not unions have grown in past periods of economic or political crisis or change. Consider the three examples mentioned above. Unions in the U.S. did grow rapidly after the Great Depression. But they did so because they adopted a new form and organising strategy under a new labour law. Industrial unionism was born out of the failure of craft unions to organise the growing numbers of unskilled and semi-skilled workers in manufacturing. At the end of World War II, unions in Japan and in Germany reemerged and grew to positions of significant influence in their societies with the active support of the occupation governments. Both German and Japanese labour movements adapted their structures and processes to fit the economies and societies of that era. Enterprise unionism, for example, grew out of a political struggle in Japan and fit well with the culture and industrial organisation of the post war Japanese economy.

The fall of the Berlin Wall demonstrates that unions do not emerge as a natural response to a liberal economy and democracy. Union membership has not spread to large numbers of workers in the former East Europe economies. Where it has grown the most, as in the former East Germany and, briefly, in Poland, it did so because unions had strong support from the government and other actors and institutions in civil society. So even those waiting for some crisis need to ask what new strategies and structures for unions will gain this type of support when and if a crisis occurs. Crisis may be a necessary condition for non-incremental union revival. But history suggests it is not sufficient.

*Metamorphosis to New Forms.* Finally, we come to a scenario that, based on our reading of the papers in this volume, the works of other union researchers, and our own views, is most likely to produce a revival and a renewal of unionism. This scenario envisions unions going through a metamorphosis during which by trial and error a variety of new organisational forms emerge, are tested, and coexist. This introduction and the papers that follow provide hints at what some of these new forms and strategies might involve. At the micro level unions would meet the pent up demands for union representation by recruiting members early in their careers and adapt strategies and organisational structures that allow them to retain members as the move across jobs and through different stages of their life cycle. This will require unions to form network like structures that connect workers and perhaps their family members to different organisations that provide the specialised representation and/or labour market services needed at different points in time and life experience. At more aggregate levels, this type of labour movement would take on the features of a web of related yet differentiated organisations and institutions, some of which identify themselves as unions and some of which call themselves something else but perform important functions for workers and labour markets. Whether these differentiated forms coalesce to amass political influence on behalf of the workforce similar to or greater than that achieved by 20th century unions at their pinnacle will be another interesting and important issue to track. Much remains to be understood regarding whether the isolated innovations that can be observed within unions, NGOs, and other groups and organisations that are attempting to speak for workers today will grow in number, find their appropriate niches in which they can function successfully and contribute to a revival of worker representation, and be a part of the 21st century labour movement. Clearly, exploring these questions could keep labour scholars busy for a long time. Our hope is this research volume will stimulate and encourage researchers to take up these important issues.

## References

Barbash, J. (1991) 'American Trade Unionism: The State of the Art', in G. Strauss, D. G. Gallagher, and J. Fiorito (eds) *The State of Unions*. Madison, WI: Industrial Relations Research Association, 347–52.

Card, D. (2001) 'The Effect of Unions on Wage Inequality in the U.S. Labor Market'. *Industrial and Labor Relations Review*, 54: 296–315.

Charlwood, A. (2002) 'Why do Non-union Employees Want to Unionize?' *British Journal of Industrial Relations*, 40(3): 463–92.

Chaykowski, R. P. and Slotsve, G. A. (2002) 'Earnings Inequality and Unions in Canada'. *British Journal of Industrial Relations*, 40(3): 493–520.

Commission on the Future of Worker Management Relations, (1994) *Fact Finding Report*. Washington, D.C.: U.S. Department of Labor and Department of Commerce.

Diamond, W. J. and Freeman, R. B. (2002) 'Will Unionism Prosper in CyberSpace?'. *British Journal of Industrial Relations*, 40(3): 569–98.

DiNardo, J. and Lemieux, T. (1997) 'Diverging Male Wage Inequality in the United States and Canada, 1981–1988: Do Institutions Explain the Difference?' *Industrial and Labor Relations Review*, 50: 629–51.

DiNardo, J., Fortin, N. and Lemieux, T. (1996) 'Labor Market Institutions and the Distribution of Wages, 1973–1992: A Semiparametric Approach'. *Econometrica*, 64: 1001–1044.

Erickson, C. L., Fisk, C. L., Milkman, R., Mitchell, D. J. B. and Wong, K. (2002) 'Justice for Janitors in Los Angeles: Lessons from Three Rounds of Negotiations'. *British Journal of Industrial Relations*, 40(3): 543–68.

Farber, H. S. and Western, B. (2001) 'Accounting for the Decline in Unions in the Private Sector', *Journal of Labor Research*, 22: 459–85.

Farber, H. S. and Western, B. (2002) 'Ronald Reagan and the Politics of Declining Union Organization', *British Journal of Industrial Relations*, 40(3): 385–402.

Fiorito, J. (1987) 'Political Instrumentality Perceptions and Desires for Union Representation', *Journal of Labor Research*, 8: 271–89.

Fortin, N. and Lemieux, T. (1997) 'Institutional Changes and Rising Wage Inequality: Is There a Linkage?' *Journal of Economic Perspectives*, 11: 75–96.

Freeman, R. B. (1988) 'Contraction and Expansion: The Divergence of private sector and public sector Unionism in the United States', *Journal of Economic Perspectives*, 2: 63–88.

Freeman, R. (1996) 'Labor Market Institutions and Earnings Inequality'. *New England Economic Review*, (May/June): 157–68.

Freeman, R. (1993) 'How Much Has De-Unionization Contributed to the Rise in Male Earnings Inequality?' In Danziger, S. and Gottschalk, P. (eds), *Uneven Tides: Rising Inequality in America*. New York: Russell Sage Foundation, pp. 133–63.

Freeman, R. B. and James, L. Medoff (1984) *What Do Unions Do?* New York: Basic Books.

Freeman, R. B. and Rogers, J. (1999) *What do Workers Want?* Ithaca: Cornell University ILR Press.

Gomez, R., Gunderson, M. and Meltz, N. (2002) 'Comparing Youth and Adult Desire for Unionization in Canada'. *British Journal of Industrial Relations*, 40(3): 521–42.

Horowitz, S. (1997) '*A New Labor Structure for a Transient and Mobile Workforce*'. Perspectives on Work 1: 50–52

Kochan, T. A. (1979) 'How American Employees View Unions', *Monthly Labor Review*, 104(4): 23–31.

Kuruvilla, S., Das, S., Kwon, H. and Kwon, S. (2002) 'Trade Union Growth and Decline in Asia'. *British Journal of Industrial Relations*, 40(3): 431–62.

Lemieux, T. (1993) 'Unions and Wage Inequality in Canada and the United States'. In Card, D. and Freeman, R. (eds), *Small Differences That Matter: Labor Markets and Income Maintenance in Canada and the United States*. Chicago: University of Chicago Press, pp. 69–108.

Lipset, S. M. and Meltz, N. M, (1998) '*Canadian and American Attitudes toward Work and Institutions*'. Perspectives on Work, 1: 14–19.

Meltz, N. M. (1984) 'Labor Movements in Canada and the United States', in T. A. Kochan (ed.) *Challenges and Choices facing American Labor*. Cambridge, MA: MIT Press, 315–34.

Osterman, P., Kochan, T. A., Locke, R. M., and Piore, M. J. (2001) *Working in America: A Blueprint for the New Labor Market*. Cambridge, MA: MIT Press.

Ratnam, Venkata, C. S. (2001) *Globalization and Labour-Management Relations: Dynamics of Change*. New Delhi: Response Books (a Division of Sage Publications).

Riech, R. M. (1997) *Locked in the Cabinet*. New York: Knopf.

Reitz, Jeffery and Anil Verma. Forthcoming (2004) 'Immigration, Ethnicity and Unionization: Recent Evidence from Canada'. *Industrial Relations.*

Verma, A., Kochan, T. and Wood, S. (2002) 'Editors' Introduction'. *British Journal of Industrial Relations*, 40(3): 373–84.

Visser, J. (2002) 'Why Fewer Workers Join Unions in Europe'. *British Journal of Industrial Relations*, 40(3): 403–30.

# 2
# The Future of Trade Unions

*Richard Hyman*

## Introduction

For some 20 years now, it has been common to refer to a crisis of trade unionism; as one recent survey puts it (Martin and Ross, 1999: 368), 'unions are under siege'. What the future holds for labour movements – or indeed, whether they still have a future – seems increasingly uncertain. To pose the issues slightly differently, should unions be viewed as the subjects or objects of history? For many critics (trade unionists themselves as well as academic observers), unions in most countries appear as victims of external forces outside their control, and often also of their own conservative inertia. Or do they still hold the capacity to shape their own future as strategic actors? In all countries, trade unions possess powerful traditions and inherited structures; these all to frequently can constitute a straitjacket, but potentially can provide a resource for creative initiative.

Envisaging the future is, in large measure, a matter of interpreting (and extrapolating) the trajectory from past to present. Such exercises are doubly hazardous. First, it is all too easy to counterpose an idealised conception of the past to the stark empirical reality of the present; not least because labour movements themselves typically draw inspiration from myths of a golden age of commitment and solidarity. Second, human causalities are always contingent: self-consciousness – learning from history – can generate new options. A crisis (literally, a moment when a patient hangs between death and recovery) can provide a shock which compels the abandonment of once comfortable routines and the search for new directions. How far does this provide grounds for optimism?

In this contribution I will explore, schematically and with incautious generalisations, the pathways from past to present to future. The authors of the following chapters provide more detailed maps of the road ahead.

## Unions in the past

The history of trade unionism can be traced back more than two centuries, and the dynamics of unions' formation and consolidation reflect the multiple differentiations of context and of the ambitions of their creators. What common themes can be identified from among the immense historical diversity? There are five which I consider both plausible and relevant to the understanding of current predicaments and future possibilities.

First, unions in the past were built in the main on pre-existing solidarities: they gave institutional form to a prior consciousness of collective interests and collective identity. This is not to deny that forging unity in union was often an uphill struggle; but collectivism had firm supports. In some cases (notably, craft unionism) the principles of collective identity had an institutional foundation pre-dating capitalist employment relationships. In others, the displacement of traditional norms of moral economy by the ruthless logic of wage-slavery fired spontaneous collective resistance to exploitation (Thompson, 1968). In more settled times, when the capital-labour relation had attained a largely unquestioned normality, collective experience at work was complemented by domestic life in a contiguous residential community and by shared recreational, cultural and sometimes religious pursuits; the union was an institution embedded in an encompassing social landscape. Later still, in the context of recognised union status within a 'Fordist' production regime, the employer functioned as recruiting agent; the union was an extension of the company community.

Second, trade unions in their evolution from outlaw status to respectability displayed a persistent tension between the roles of 'sword of justice' and 'vested interest' (Flanders, 1970): on the one hand fighting for all those oppressed and underprivileged, on the other defending the particular interests of the relatively advantaged sections of the working class who in most countries disproportionately filled the ranks of union membership (an issue to which I will return). This tension, it should be added, was historically mediated by distinctive union ideologies and identities both within and between countries. This is evident to any student of European trade unionism, almost certainly explains some of the contrasts between Canada and the USA, and is certainly of crucial importance if we consider trade unionism in a broader global perspective.

Third, most unions were traditionally founded, at least in industrialised countries, on what has often been termed the 'normal' employment relationship. Those whose situation was seen as most evidently appropriate for collective organisation and representation, and certainly as providing the most favourable support for union recruitment and retention, were employed full-time on more or less permanent contractual terms; typically also in larger organisations and in occupations where collective withdrawal of labour could have a persuasive impact. The stereotypical trade unionist possessed 'industrial muscle'. He (in trade union iconography it was almost always a 'he') was identified above all else with his work, and this identification was carried over into his allegiance to his union.

Fourth, this core constituency could be regarded in most countries where unions first emerged as (almost) a popular majority. Even if the manual industrial working class was in few countries numerically the dominant segment of the population, it was the most visible and could plausibly be regarded as the face of modern society. Even if union membership largely excluded workers who were female, insecure, transitory, unions' pretensions to represent a general working-class interest were rarely questioned.

Fifth, and framing all these other characteristics, was the fact that unions – even those professing inter- and anti-nationalism – were embedded in national societies. Their world-views were coloured by national cultural assumptions (or less politely, prejudices); and crucially, their regulatory capacity was conditioned by their adversaries and interlocutors – employers and political authorities – who likewise operated on a primarily national terrain. The industrial relations systems of which unions became components and ultimately defenders were by the same token nationally bounded and nationally distinctive.

## Unions in the present

These features of the past construction of trade unionism deserve emphasis if we are properly to understand unions' current predicaments and future options. The changes since the 'heroic' years of union expansion are by now all too familiar, and require only brief recapitulation.

The stability of national industrial relations systems founded on the triangular relationship of unions, employers and governments has been undermined by a series of external challenges, usually identified under the label of 'globalisation'. In part this involves the intensification of cross-national competition, as new competitors make inroads in product markets once dominated by a small number of European and North American economies. Another aspect is the internationalisation of production chains within multinational companies (MNCs) detached from the regulatory frameworks of national industrial relations systems and increasingly assertive in redefining the industrial relations agenda, whether through policies of union exclusion or through clawing back (in 'concession bargaining') many of the gains won by organised labour in earlier decades. The visible hand of the MNCs interacts with the increasingly coercive invisible hand of finance capital. The last three decades have seen a radical transformation: the liberalisation and deregulation of international capital and currency markets; the acceleration of transactions through advances in information and telecommunications technologies; and the breakdown of the American-dominated post-war system of international monetary stabilisation. The resulting volatile pattern of capital flows is translated into disruptive instability in the physical economy. Deprived of much of their previous room for manoeuvre in shaping macroeconomic policy, governments too (even when notionally of the left) have typically embraced policies of 'deregulation' in support of supply-side flexibility in labour markets. While the extent of such challenges varies substantially cross-nationally, universally the foundations of the Fordist industrial relations compromise – and the status of unions as its ambiguous beneficiaries – are significantly weakened.

What may be termed the internal challenges to trade unionism stem from transformations in the unions' own constituencies: the changing world of work and, as part of this, the erosion of the 'normal' employment relationship of the past; and also more extensive social and generational changes. The male, manual industrial worker whose nine-to-five job was central to his existence has become a declining species: the world of work now manifestly has two genders, is occupationally and often ethnically diverse, and involves highly differentiated patterns of activity over the day, the week and the lifetime. The dense (and often oppressive) bonds between workplace and community have disappeared. Class boundaries have become more diffuse, and there seems less willingness than in the past to submerge particular interests within a more broadly defined class identity. To the extent that trade unions still represent primarily their old core constituencies, they suffer declining membership and face the threat of increasing marginalisation. To the extent that they succeed in extending their boundaries of organisation (usually very partially at best), the consequence is often internal division and the loss of capacity to constitute an integrated movement. Partly in consequence, unions' image as a 'sword of justice' defending the weak and disadvantaged is easily tarnished, facilitating an ideological offensive presenting them rather as vested interests at least in part responsible for economic adversity. Or else they become widely perceived as tired, archaic bureaucracies, largely irrelevant to the major issues of the contemporary world: a view particularly common among those in their 20s and younger, who virtually everywhere are far less unionised than their parents.

Almost universally, the consequence of these trends has been a serious decline in union membership and – though measurement is here more difficult – in power and influence. The severity of this decline has however varied substantially across countries, and this variation is one explanation of qualitative differences in reactions (another, certainly, is the unevenness of strategic capacity within national movements).

One response has involved the proliferation of individual services (for example, cut-price banking, insurance, travel) as selective incentives to membership. While often presented as a (post-) modern adaptation to more individualistic and consumerist worker orientations, it has affinities with the portfolio of individual benefits offered to their members by early craft trade unions. There is little evidence however that such services have contributed significantly to membership recruitment and retention. What does appear more effective, however, is enhanced advice and representation in the case of employment-related grievances and problems (Leisink, 1997; Waddington, 2000; Waddington et al., 1997: 467–8).

Organisationally, hard times have precipitated a wave of union mergers (Chaison, 1996; Streeck and Visser, 1997). While at times rationalised as a proactive strategy to facilitate recruitment in the new growth sectors of the economy, more typically these have been defensive reactions to membership loss and the shrinkage of traditional recruitment bases. Often the pattern of amalgamations has owed more to inter- and intra-union politics than to any clear labour market rationale. Certainly the outcome has at times brought advantages from economies of scale (or at least counteracted the diseconomies resulting from membership decline); but often also has generated structurally complex conglomerates riven with barely concealed internal tensions.

A very different organisational response is the rediscovery (or reinvention) of the principles of active recruitment and representation. Pioneered in North America, further developed in Australia and latterly adapted in Europe, the struggle for an 'organising culture' involves a focus in particular on groups of workers traditionally underrepresented by trade unions, building a cadre of recruiters (both paid and volunteer) with whom the target groups can identify, and giving their specific concerns a higher priority on the union agenda. In the abstract this can appear straightforward; in practice their are many difficulties. Active organising is expensive, both in simple balance-sheet terms and in its demands on the time and energies of those involved. Crucially, there are choices to be made between an emphasis on recruitment, and effective representation of existing members (including new recruits). Again in theory, the dilemma may be resolved by 'empowering' members to constitute the front line of their own self-representation; again in reality, the effort to construct and sustain a structure of workplace activism can be a thankless labour of Sisyphus. The vicious circle of membership loss, declining efficacy of representation and demoralisation is not readily transformed into a virtuous circle of recruitment, representation and empowerment.

In some cases – strikingly apparent in my own country – a response is the pursuit of 'partnership'. This can be directed at different levels. In Britain (there are analogies here to the idea of 'mutual gains' in North America) an important focus has been the company. Here, the emphasis is on a joint interest of employer and employees in workplace competitiveness and survival: expressed in union agreement to changes in the production regime (reduced numbers of employees, more flexible working-time arrangements, interchangeability of jobs) in return for management commitment to (more or less bounded) guarantees of continued operation. Such deals have become quite widespread: for example, in the German notion of *Stand-ortsversicherungsvereinbarungen* (agreements to safeguard the production location). The problem here is the implication of a *de facto* variant of company unionism in a context where intensified competition implies that not all companies will compete successfully, however much their respective workforces agree to abandon previously sacrosanct conditions of employment. The role of unions as supra-company-level organisations fighting for minimum standards across a far broader constituency is thereby put in question.

'Partnership' is also a factor at this higher level. For example, in much of Europe from the 1990s there has been an emergence of 'social pacts' involving trade union cooperation, not simply as in previous decades in wage restraint but also in concessions to relax the restrictions on employers contained in labour law regimes, and in acquiescence in cutbacks in state welfare provision, in return for (typically imprecise) commitments to employment-creating policies on the part of governments and employers (Fajertag and Pochet, 1997). Here too there is a collective actor problem: unions (and to a large extent also governments) address the problem of intensified competitiveness at national level; MNCs are happy to accept the concessions but as a precedent for more ambitious demands in other juris-dictions. In Europe, this process has notoriously been described as 'social dumping'.

A final response has been to turn (or return) to a conception of unions as organisations campaigning for rights. Unions raise their profile by engaging in 'contentious politics' (Tarrow, 1998). This involves an assertion of unions' identity as 'sword of justice': contesting oppression, inequality and discrimination. It can also imply cooperation, often uneasy, with other social movements which have never acquired the respectability gained by trade unions in most countries. Potentially it redefines unions as outsiders in a terrain where until recently the role of insiders was comforting and rewarding.

Five responses: and no doubt there are many more. Are these comple-mentary or contradictory? To greater or lesser degree there are surely choices to be made: the 'composite resolution' through which unions have declared their commitment to incompatible objectives is surely no longer a productive option. Some of these choices, often difficult, are explored in my concluding section.

## Unions in the future

Trade unions in the 21ˢᵗ century confront old dilemmas, but in new forms. Most fundamentally, these can be described as the who, the what and the how of trade union representation.

*Whose* interests do trade unions represent? In simple terms one may define four categories: the qualified elite, the core workforce, peripheral employees and those outside employment. Historically, unions in many countries emerged on the foundations of a segment of the labour force with scarce skills, relatively high pay, and often either considerable job security or else a favourable position in the external labour market. Subsequently the 'mass' trade unions of the 20th century tended to find their strongholds among the 'core' workforce of large-scale industrialism: workers whose labour market strength as individuals was often limited but who collectively could impose effective sanctions against recalcitrant employers. Unions which embraced socialist or communist (and sometimes also christian) ideologies typically claimed to extend their concerns to the peripheral workforce or to those outside employment altogether. Such claims in many countries have been more rhetorical than real. And even in representing the core workforce, union priorities have usually been biased in favour of certain group interests to the detriment of others.

The second issue is *which* interests of those represented are of primary relevance for trade unions. Simplifying again, we may identify four main constellations of interests. The first constitutes the traditional core agenda of 'bread-and-butter' collective bargaining over wages and other conditions of employment. The second relates more to procedure, status and opportunity: rights limiting employers' arbitrary authority and underwriting employment protection, 'fair' mechanisms for promotion and career advancement, training opportunities and so on; and the regulation of production, the allocation of work and the determination of workloads. The third addresses the role of the state: the constitution of the social wage (hence concern with social welfare provision and taxation policy), the politico-legal framework of trade union organisation and action, the macroeconomic policies which shape the circumstances of the labour market. Finally there is an agenda not directly linked to the worker's status as employee but addressing other facets of personal and social existence: the environment, the sphere of consumption, the institutions and facilities of the local community.

*How* are interests represented? This requires more detailed discussion; and again, a fourfold classification may be presented, involving a set of organisational choices to which unions and union movements have historically given different (and often contradictory) responses. They may be termed the issues of structure, capacity, democracy and activism. The first relates to the earlier question of constituencies, and concerns the organisational form of interest aggregation. The two main lines of inclusion (and hence also, typically, exclusion) are horizontal and vertical. Horizontal structures integrate workers according to labour market status (professional, other white-collar, craft, non-skilled manual); vertical structures according to sector or employer (industrial or company unionism). Despite the existence of few pure models, most national labour movements have tended to reflect one or the other form of integration (and separation). The implications for solidarity are complex: occupational forms of unionism may privilege a narrow repertoire of craft or professional interests, but may avoid the risks of too close an identification with 'their' employers which some industrial unions display. We should also note the existence in some countries of general unions which both occupationally and sectorally are broadly encompassing. Elsewhere (as noted earlier) the creation of multi-industrial unions through amalgamation has similar effects. In addition, a key factor in organisational form is the degree of articulation *between* unions (for example, through an authoritative central confederation) which may help transcend sectional divisions and integrate diverse membership interests.

The question of organisational capacity involves vital but complex issues: the ability to assess opportunities for intervention; to anticipate, rather than merely react to, changing circumstances; to frame coherent policies; and to implement these effectively. It is not easy to theorise or to specify concretely the components and causal dynamics of organisational capacity, but it is obvious to any informed observer that some trade union movements possess this quality to a far greater degree than others. Perhaps we may define the key elements as *intelligence, strategy* and *efficacy*. Intelligence is in part an organisational matter: the extent to which unions and confederations possess specialist expertise in research, education and information-gathering, and the means to disseminate knowledge throughout the organisation (which is to some degree a question of resources); but it is also (and perhaps more importantly) a matter of the degree to which, at all levels within union movements, knowledge is seen as an essential component of union power. Strategy depends on organisational structures and organisational traditions which link knowledge to action through analysis of circumstances, evaluation of alternative options and planning of objectives and forms of intervention. It links closely to that much abused concept, leadership. Finally, efficacy is in part a question of the attainability of union policies within the objective context; in part, of the overall coherence (notably, between and within unions) of aims, which is more easily achieved where a reasonable degree of centralised authority exists; in part, of the degree to which union members (and non-union workers) 'own' the strategic priorities and are willing to take action in their pursuit, which calls for scope for decentralised initiative.

This links to the third issue, the complex dialectic between leadership and democracy – which should certainly not be regarded as simple opposites. The question of democracy might be posed as follows: how much scope do members have in shaping the priorities and programmes of their unions (and do some groups have greater scope than others?). In part, democracy clearly requires significant structures for participation, involvement and self-activity at rank-and-file level. Yet localised autonomy alone is a recipe for fragmentation of policy and action and is unlikely to lead spontaneously to inter-group solidarity. To be effective, rank-and-file democracy requires centralised co-ordination and articulation: in other words, processes of leadership.

Finally, how do unions balance two contradictory (but usually combined) modes of action: mobilisation and struggle on the one hand, concertation and compromise on the other? Unions have been eloquently described as 'managers of discontent' (Mills, 1948): to win workers' allegiance they must identify and articulate unresolved grievances, unmet needs and unrealised aspirations. Yet to the extent that they are accepted as interlocutors of employers and governments, and wish to justify and maintain this intermediary role, they are constrained to select and prioritise workers' discontents in forms which admit (at least temporary) compromise. To some extent, unions' ideological orientations – their conceptions of capitalist society and of their own role within it – have encouraged more oppositional or more conciliatory conceptions of the management of discontent. This connects in turn to the extent that unions embrace the role of labour market actors, and the degree to which they define their role in broader social (and societal) terms: the familiar distinction between 'business' and 'social movement' unionism. As suggested earlier, a narrow conception of trade union functions (which certainly facilitates the status of 'social partner' pursuing compromise agreements with employers and governments) makes a broad achievement of worker solidarity less possible and probably less necessary.

This schematic discussion points to many of the key choices which will determine the future of trade unions. In some cases, the line of least resistance may be to consolidate organisation around traditional core constituencies, or to seek to compensate for the decline in former strongholds by appealing to the distinctive interests of the new elite sections of the changing workforce. Inevitably this will confirm unions' status as a vested interest defending the position of the relatively advantaged. The alternative is to reassert trade unions' role as a *popular* movement, which means developing the capacity to represent the *losers* as well as the beneficiaries from economic restructuring. The peripheral workforce has in most countries proved painfully difficult to unionise, if indeed unions have even made the attempt; but there have been sufficient success stories to show that the task is not impossible. Yet to persuade the stronger sections of the labour force to lend their resources to such an effort is indeed an enormous challenge, and certainly one which cannot be addressed on the basis of narrow business unionism.

Traditional trade unionism, in most industrialised countries, reflected (and often reinforced) a compartmentalisation between work and the broader experience of life. This tendency was indeed counteracted to varying degrees in labour movements explicitly committed to a broader social project (whether socialist or confessional); but the ideological roots of classic social unionism have withered. In any event, these former linkages of work and life were essentially mechanical, centred around the conception of a 'normal' employment relationship explicitly or implicitly the preserve of the male worker. If trade unionism in the future is to appeal to a broader constituency, its agenda must reflect the far more differentiated ways in which work connects to life – or in which workers would *wish* it to relate. Here, a crucial question is that of individual choice. This is a concept which has usually proved difficult for trade unionists. The principles of unity and solidarity have traditionally been interpreted as requiring that individual preferences be subsumed within a collective interest. The natural corollary is that individualism and collectivism are mutually antagonistic principles. This can indeed be the case, and many of the ideologues of individual choice are undisguised enemies of trade unionism and of collective regulation in general.

Yet it is doubtful if real solidarity was ever possible on the basis of the suppression of individuality; and it is certain that in today's societies, with their diversities of cultures and life-styles, this is altogether impossible. One reason for unions' loss of popularity is that they have often given their enemies grounds for the claim that trade union regulation typically involves the bureaucratic imposition of standardised modes of conduct. Choice and opportunity have become key slogans of the anti-union right; yet could, and should, they be reclaimed by the labour movement? For most of the 20th century, the core workforce which formed the main basis of trade unionism achieved their employment status through the dull compulsion of circumstance; whereas career advancement and self-directed occupational mobility are aspirations increasingly salient for unions' actual and potential constituencies today. The weakening of the ties to the existing occupation and employer is however emancipating only to the extent that real and preferable alternatives are open. The choice among alternative options is an individual project, but one which is illusory unless a genuine and favourable *structure of opportunities* exists. To enhance the opportunity structure is necessarily a collective project, one which challenges both employers' discretion and the anarchy of market forces. In many ways a redefinition of the traditional function of trade unionism, this is but one key dimension of a union agenda, which can appeal to diverse constituencies in solidaristic fashion.

Another instance is the issue of flexibility, which is of course a familiar slogan of those who wish to weaken and restrict labour market protections, making workers more disposable and more adaptable to the changing requirements of the employer. Yet flexibility can have alternative meanings. The 1970s demand for 'humanisation of work' was in essence a claim for flexibility in the interests of workers through the human-centred application of technologies, the adaptation of task cycles and work speeds to fit workers' own rhythms, the introduction of new types of individual and collective autonomy in the control of the labour process. This agenda was in large measure hi-jacked as part of the new managerialism of the 1980s and 1990s (with its mendacious rhetoric of 'empowerment', 'teamwork' and 'human resource development'). Can unions recapture the initiative? A key issue in the contemporary world of work, in addition to those raised by industrial workers and their unions a quarter-century ago, is that of time-sovereignty: the temporal linkages between employment, leisure and domestic life; the ability to influence the patterns of the working day, week, year and lifetime. There is a worker-oriented meaning of flexible working time which can directly confront that of the employers, and which offers new potential for integrating very different types of employee interest. So too with other dimensions of flexibility. Rigidity and standardisation were impositions of a particular model of capitalist work organisation; to the extent that some of the features of Taylorist-Fordist systems have lost their attractions to employers, space exists for unions to mobilise support for radical alternatives which transcend some of the divisions within the working class.

For example, changes in the organisation of production and the employment relationship (such as team-working, quality circles, performance related pay, personalised contracts) are often accompanied by a managerial propaganda offensive in which 'empowerment' is a central rhetorical device. Typically this is a crude deceit, providing a 'democratic' gloss to employer efforts to intensify production pressures, cut staffing numbers and undermine traditional forms of collective regulation. The 'new workplace' is one in which employees often have increased responsibilities but always with reduced power. By focusing their own demands and activities on this contradiction, trade unions have the potential to address current worker discontents in ways which generalise fragmented experiences and permit new forms of solidarity in the pursuit of *genuine* empowerment.

This leads to the *how* of trade union organisation and action. In most countries the classic organisational form was centred around the *national* union. This centrality has been eroded from below, with the increasing shift towards company-specific employment regimes; and from above, as economic internationalisation constraints the scope for effective regulation on a purely national basis. Twenty-first century trade unionism has to be local, national and international at one and the same time. This in turn imposes immense challenges if unions are to sustain adequate organisational capacity: requiring both effective decentralised activism and new levels of strategic leadership.

Compounding such dilemmas, old questions of modes of action assume new characteristics. Unions in the past have often assumed a demarcation of arenas of engagement, between 'industrial relations' and 'politics'. If this distinction was ever plausible it is no longer so. Trade unionism is today inescapably political, not least because those who shape the political agenda have defined trade unionism and industrial relations as key political 'problems'. But traditional modes of political engagement have lost much of their relevance; in the conventional sphere of party politics, unions can no longer hope to find reliable allies. In part this is because for so long trade unions in most countries have responded to political attack by reasserting ancient rhetorics and ideologies which no longer resonate with any but a dwindling committed minority. Here indeed there is a sharp contrast to be drawn between long-established union movements and those (in such countries as South Africa, Brazil, Korea) which are less weighed down by historical baggage. Such instances suggest that unionism can still stake a claim to constitute a popular movement, by imaginative engagement in a *battle of ideas*. Trade unions have to discover a language which can express aspirations, projects, even utopias which are consistent with the principles which inspired the movement in the past but which address the very different world in which we live today. And as part of this process they have to recognise – as many unions indeed have done, often painfully – that there are other social movements which have captured the enthusiasm, particularly among the young, that unions have largely lost; and that it is necessary to seek common ground with these.

If I can end with a note of relative optimism, there are two points which I would emphasise. The first is that the crisis which I invoked at the outset has shaken the complacency of many sclerotic trade union movements. Even if the 'modernisation' of trade unionism for which many have called has rarely advanced very far, unions are increasingly asking the right questions; and this is the necessary precondition of finding adequate answers. The second is that current information technology offers dramatic possibilities if seized imaginatively. Traditional multi-layered hierarchies can give way to more open, interactive and democratic communication, opening the scope for rapid and participative decision-making in a manner unimaginable just a few years ago. Solidarities can be built in ways which transcend organisational, national and linguistic barriers (as the Australian dockers recently demonstrated, for example). Public campaigning can take new forms, potentially far more effective than in the past. Can trade unionism in the 21ˢᵗ century succeed by re-inventing itself as a virtual social movement?

## References

Chaison, G. (1996) *Union Mergers in Hard Times*. Ithaca: ILR Press.
Fajertag, G. and Pochet, P. (1997) *Social Pacts in Europe*. Brussels: European Trade Union Institute and Observatoire social européen.
Flanders, A. (1970) *Management and Unions*. London: Faber.
Leisink, P. (1997) 'New Union Constituencies Call for Differentiated Agendas and Democratic Participation', *Transfer*, 3(3): 534–50.

Martin, A. and Ross, G. (1999) *The Brave New World of European Labor: European Trade Unions at the Millennium.* New York: Berghahn.

Mills, C. W. (1948) *The New Men of Power.* New York: Harcourt, Brace.

Streeck, W. and Visser, J. (1997) 'The Rise of the Conglomerate Union', *European Journal of Industrial Relations*, 3(3): 305–32.

Tarrow, S. (1998) *Power in Movement* (2nd edn). Cambridge: Cambridge UP.

Waddington, J. (2000) 'Towards a Reform Agenda? European Trade Unions in Transition', *Industrial Relations Journal*, 31(4): 317–30.

Waddington, J., Hoffmann, R. and Lind, J. (1997) 'European Trade Unionism in Transition? A Review of the Issues', *Transfer*, 3(3): 464–97.

# 3

# Extended Networks: A Vision for the Next Generation Unions[1]

*Thomas A. Kochan, Richard Locke, Paul Osterman, and Michael Piore*

Union membership and collective bargaining coverage have declined dramatically in the U.S. to the point where there is a serious question of whether unions can now, or in the future, serve the functions American workers and society expect of them. Yet, most of us who are grounded in the values and traditions of the field of industrial relations continue to believe in the need for and value of unions. So do 75 per cent of the American public[2] and at least some thoughtful leaders in the business community.[3] History tells us, however, that unions are only successful when they adapt to and match up well with the structure of the economy, employer organisational forms, and the preferences and needs of the workforce. Given the significant changes in these features of the economy and society, it is obvious that unions have a tall order in store. This paper develops a view of what we believe American unions need to do if they are to be significant players in today's and tomorrow's labour markets and economy. We propose that the next generation unions[4] view and position themselves as networked institutions that enroll, represent, and provide services to workers on a continuous life-long basis beginning when they are in school and about to enter the labour market, throughout their careers, and into their retirement years.[5] This view of unions is part of a larger set of institutional changes we see as necessary for updating America's labour market institutions and policies to catch up with changes in the workforce, nature of work and economy.

To adapt to the changing industrial structure and varied circumstances and needs of workers, unions will need to represent worker interests in a variety of ways inside firms, in local areas and labour markets, in professional communities, and in political affairs.[6] They will need to use multiple methods and tools, grounded to be sure in collective bargaining, worker participation, and broader labour-management partnerships, but supplemented by making full use of modern communications technologies and personal networks to provide information, education, technical advice and assistance to individuals and groups, and to articulate and communicate worker concerns and perspectives to the public and to political leaders. They will need to be open organisations, with blurred and porous boundaries between 'unions' as they have been traditionally organised in industrial or craft jurisdictions and local, national, international, and federated structures and various coalition partners in the religious, nongovernmental, government, educational, research, and even employer communities. Linking together unions and coalition partners at the community level in particular will take on significantly greater importance in the future than in the recent past. Individuals will need to be able to move across these boundaries shifting their 'primary membership' from one to another at different stages of their careers and family lives. But once they join the extended network, they should be considered a member for life, just like once a student is accepted by a college, he or she becomes part of that school's extended family for life.

In our view, the central challenge facing unions and other forms of employee voice is the incredible diversity/heterogeneity of the American workplace. As a consequence of this diversity unions, and other representatives of employees, need to experiment with and adopt a range of organisational forms. Four segments of the labour market require distinctive approaches towards enhancing employee voice. These are (1) the industrial and craft sectors where unions have had long term strength; (2) professionals and managers; (3) contingent workers; and (4) employees trapped in low income labour markets.

## What employees want

Before turning to the question of how unions might represent these different workers' interests, we might first ask a more basic question: Do Americans still believe unions are needed and, if so, what forms of representation do they prefer? The consistent findings from studies dating from the 1970s to today are that (1) workers want a direct and influential voice in decisions affecting their work and employment conditions, (2) a substantial number of unorganised workers want to address many of these issues through either unions or some other form of group or collective effort, and (3) there is an upward trend in both of these preferences over the past two decades.

The 1977 'Quality of Employment' conducted for the U.S. Department of Labor by the Survey Research Center at the University of Michigan clearly documented that workers wanted more of a say over how to do their work, what kinds of training opportunities were available to them, how new technologies would affect their work, and an array of 'bread and butter' issues like wages, safety and health, and job security.[7] Other studies conducted in the early 1980s showed that workers' expectations exceeded the actual amount of say or influence they experienced on their jobs.[8] These basic findings applied to all demographic groups – blue collar, white collar, men, women, whites and people of colour.

The percentage indicating a preference for joining a union has gone up since the 1970s. The 1977 survey found about 30 per cent of non-union workers would join a union while recent surveys report numbers in the 43–47 per cent range and as high as 57 per cent for young workers.[9] Thus, the constituency for a traditional union as envisioned in the eyes of non-union American workers when asked this type of question is larger today than it has been in the past. However, it is still a minority of the workforce, and given American labour law that requires a majority of a specific unit or group of workers to vote to unionise before any single worker gains representation, sole reliance on this core constituency will produce a labour movement composed of the most disenfranchised members of the labour force – those with few alternatives. Moreover, as long as unfair treatment is the primary motivator, who gets unionised is more in the hands of employers than unions.

Recent surveys have also probed more deeply into the forms of representation and participation workers prefer and in doing so document significant variation in these preferences. This was one of the key findings reported in the recent Worker Representation and Participation Survey (WRPS) conducted by Richard Freeman and Joel Rogers.[10] Like earlier surveys, it showed that the vast majority of employees want more involvement and greater voice in company decisions affecting their workplace

How should this voice and participation be expressed? On some issues, like harassment and training, workers prefer to express themselves as individuals. But on others, like workplace health and safety, pay and benefits, workers prefer to speak as a group. Moreover, workers want cooperative relations with management. Although about one-third of all employees surveyed in the WRPS reported that management mistreats employees and is not trustworthy, few workers believe that the solution to these problems is to institutionalise labour-management conflict. Instead, the vast majority believe that the more effective workplace organisation is one that is independent but that also enjoys management participation and support. Finally, the vast majority of workers reported that management resistance is the primary reason they do not have their desired level of influence at the workplace.

Similar findings were reported in a March 1999 survey commissioned by the AFL-CIO. When asked 'if an election were held tomorrow to decide whether your workplace would have a union or not', 43 per cent of the respondents reported that they would either definitely or probably vote for forming a union. Seventy-nine per cent of these same respondents reported that they would probably or definitely vote to form an employee association. Again, employees believe that unions and other forms of collective representation would enhance not only their salaries and benefits but also provide them with voice on the job.[11] Thus, American workers have strong preferences for representation and participation, but widely varying views on the forms that best suit their situations and needs.

## Responding to the new labour market

The labour movement has in recent years engaged in a series of organisational and strategic innovations that have sought to rekindle its vitality and re-connect with workers, employers, and local communities. One of John Sweeney's first policy initiatives after being elected President of the AFL-CIO in 1995 was to allocate 30 per cent of the federation's resources to union organising, an unprecedented amount of money given that in the past union organising was viewed as primarily the responsibility of the separate national unions not the overall Federation. He also urged individual unions to make similar allocation of their resources to organising and some have since done so. A new Organizing Institute was also created to train staff in how to undertake this difficult process. In an effort to build support among college students a 'Union Summer' programme was initiated to provide students with opportunities to learn about and try first-hand at organising workers. A 'Union Cities' initiative was introduced to rejuvenate central labour councils in recognition of the increased importance of the community as an arena for coalition building, political activism, and union organising. A new unit was created to explore how unions should address issues of corporate strategy and governance and to foster workplace democracy. These initiatives are very important. Unfortunately, they have yet to produce a reversal of union membership declines. Something more is needed.

## Innovating at the core

The Communications Workers of America (CWA) is a prototype of the industrial union that grew out of and prospered in the old economy under the auspices of the New Deal labour legislation but has been severely threatened by the changing competitive environment and technology that have altered the telecommunications industry in fundamental ways. The CWA was formed in the 1940s by merging a number of older company and regional telephone unions and gradually developed a more centralised structure culminating in national bargaining with its dominant employer, AT&T, in 1970. Since 1984, however, the year that AT&T was forced to begin divesting its regional phone operations, bargaining gradually became more decentralised. Then, as new entrants into traditional telephone markets (e.g., Sprint and MCI) took market share from AT&T and later in the 1990s as cable TV and the wireless and internet portions of telecommunications exploded on the scene, union membership plummeted.

With deregulation and technological innovation, the industry has changed to include not only new, non-union wire-line companies but also wireless, cable, and TV firms. Moreover, the changing boundaries of the industry has led to a proliferation of new occupational groups employed within it. In addition to traditional occupational groups like network technicians, repairmen, splicers and customer service workers, new kinds of workers like computer programmers are now employed in the broader information services industry. As a result of these changes in both the contours of the industry and the composition of its workforce, the CWA has struggled to transform itself from a 'telephone' union to the 'union of the information age'.[12]

This transformation, however, has created several challenges for the union. The first challenge concerns the size of the labour force. Whereas before the divestiture roughly one million people were employed in the telephone industry, today over six million people work in the broader information services sector. Thus, although the CWA's membership of 650,000 is more or less what it was in the early 1980s, union density in this sector has fallen precipitously, from approximately 67 per cent in 1982 to 27 per cent in 1997.[13] Even within AT&T, union membership has fallen dramatically in absolute numbers from over 200,000 to approximately 40,000, or from essentially 100 per cent of the non-exempt labour force to about 50 per cent today. Second, many of the new workers in the industry are quite occupationally different from the union's traditional base of craft and service workers and a significant number are employed in non-standard work arrangements like independent contractors, temporary workers and freelancers. Finally, not only the workers but also the employers have changed in this industry. Whereas before the break-up, the CWA had a longstanding relationship with a handful of companies and bargained a national collective agreement across the entire Bell system, today the union faces not only the reconfigured (and downsized) 'RBOCS' (Regional Bell Operating Companies such as Bell Atlantic, Bell South, Ameritech, etc.) but also myriad other firms, small and large alike, in other segments of the industry that are non-and/or anti-union.

The CWA has responded to these challenges in a variety of ways, including using collective bargaining and its influence among government regulatory boards to extract neutrality agreements with AT&T and the traditional RBOCS. While the implementation of these agreements has not been entirely smooth (both the union and the companies have argued that negative campaigning and other practices that violate the agreed upon norms and procedures continue to occur), the agreements are beginning to payoff in terms of union growth.

This example demonstrates the pivotal role of management resistance or neutrality in determining the ability of private sector unions to organise successfully. In contrast with the small successes at AT&T and in the

RBOCS, the CWA has not been able to penetrate the newer non-union companies either in the core telephone line of business, or in the newer wireless, cable, and internet segments of the industry. These companies have vigorously and largely successfully fought union organising efforts.

The CWA also provides associational membership to individual workers employed in either non-union enterprises or in non-standard employment arrangements. Its best known example is WashTech (the Washington Alliance of Technology Workers), an organisation of software professionals at Microsoft and other high tech companies, affiliated with the CWA through The Newspaper Guild.

In an effort to build a presence outside of its traditional wireline telephone base, the CWA has merged with a variety of unions representing workers in the broader information services industry. In 1987, the CWA merged with the International Typographical Union (ITU), in 1994 with the National Association of Broadcast Employees and Technicians (NABET), in 1995 with The Newspaper Guild (TNG) and in 1998, 2,500 workers at Dow Jones joined the CWA along with 40,000 members of the International Electrical Workers in 2000. In addition to boosting membership, these mergers have strengthened the union's presence in the content side of the information industry as well as among white collar technical and professional employees. For example, NABET includes engineers, news writers, announcers, and directors who work at ABC, NBC, and over 100 private radio, TV, and film companies. The Newspaper Guild represents journalists, photographers, translators and interpreters, as well as on-line writers and designers. These new members have facilitated the CWA's efforts to reach out to unorganised white collar and professional workers in the new (and growing) sectors of the industry. As a result of these past successes, the CWA is now exploring mergers with the Association of Flight Attendants as well as other unions.

Thus, CWA is an industrial union that is attempting to adapt to the reconfiguration of its industry – an industry with an expanded array of older unionised firms and newer non-union competitors operating in traditional and new lines of business. The union has used the collective bargaining process to negotiate limits on employer opposition to new union organising wherever it could and these have begun to produce some union growth. It has attempted to organise other more traditionally anti-union employers with traditional approaches through the NLRB election process but has not been able to overcome employer resistance. It has experimented with selected use of association membership strategies outside of collective bargaining and has attracted small numbers of new members through these approaches. And it has stabilised and broadened the base of its membership through absorption and merger of smaller unions representing various technical and professional occupations. Still, despite this range of strategies, the vast majority of workers in today's telecommunications and information services industries are not represented.

Turning from telecommunications to construction is valuable because in many ways construction unions have represented the stereotypical (negative) image of American unionism. They were seen and at times even behaved as highly exclusive, bureaucratic, and conservative organisations. Where these unions were strong, they controlled access to the high-wage work. Entry into the unions and their apprenticeship jobs was difficult. Often, women and minority workers were excluded. Today, construction trade unions are among the most innovative organisation in the U.S. labour movement. Having suffered dramatic losses in membership and influence in the industry – an industry that has actually experienced a significant increase in employment growth in recent years – the various construction trade unions have embarked on a series of experiments that are redefining their relations with employers, non-union workers, and even their own membership.

From a high of 80 per cent union density in the 1940s, construction unions today represent less than 20 per cent of the workforce in the industry. The decline in membership in the last 25 years has been steep. Both the carpenters and the painters have lost over half of their membership. Membership in the construction trades overall has declined by one-third. The residential part of the market is almost completely non-union; light commercial (small office buildings and apartment complexes) is largely so.

In response to this dramatic decline in both influence and membership, the building trades unions have engaged in a series of organisational and strategic reforms aimed at revitalising their structures and regaining centrality in the industry. These reforms include: Creating innovative new strategies for organising workers; forging new relationships with contractors and owners; revitalising their training and apprenticeship programmes; and engaging in significant structural changes within the unions themselves.

For example, in recent years, several building trades unions have launched initiatives in training and skill formation. Training and apprenticeship programmes have traditionally been among the most important tools in the construction trade unions' ability to recruit new workers and defend themselves against assaults by non-union (open shop) employers. Despite efforts on the part of the open shop to usurp the union's position, the trades maintain clear dominance over the propagation of the most highly skilled workers in the market. Throughout the worst days of the 1980s, all of the trades ensured that their training and apprenticeship programmes remained strong. Open shop advocates admit that non union firms do a poor job of developing and funding training programmes for skilled workers in the industry.[14]

## Organising professionals and managers

In 1997, the Committee of Interns and Residents (CIR), which represents 9,000 medical interns and residents in six states, affiliated with the SEIU; recently, it joined with other physicians' unions to form the National Doctors' Alliance, which bargains collectively for 15,000 doctors. The CIR represents an important example of how professional workers and their associations are evolving towards collective bargaining.

As doctors have felt increasingly pressured by HMOs and insurance companies, physician unions have grown in appeal. The organising of interns and residents seems less unusual, given the limited control they have over their work and working conditions. According to Sandra Shea of CIR, 'Many of their concerns are basic trade union issues like making a living wage to put food on the table and to pay back enormous student loans, dealing with unusually long working hours and poor working conditions. They walk a fine line between the really hard work it takes to learn this profession and outright exploitation and misuse of their time and concern for humanity'.

Most unionised interns and residents are found in the public sector, where public labour boards tend to grant them the status of employee. In the private sector, where the majority of interns and residents work, a ruling by the NLRB 20 years ago denied these same young doctors that same status, labeling them as students instead. However, in 2001, the CIR was able to overturn this decision by bringing a case against the Boston Medical Center. With this victory, the CIR will be able to engage in collective bargaining for significantly larger numbers of people.

We mentioned elsewhere the example of the American Federation of Teachers initiative to recruit and provide representational and other professional services to psychologists, many of whom are independent contractors. This approach recognises that many professionals today, or over the course of their careers, will move in and out of different types of employment arrangements – sometimes being classified as independent contractors or consultants, sometimes working part-time for multiple employers, and sometimes perhaps employed full-time for a single, clearly defined employer. The task of organisations that want to represent these types of workers is to stay with them through these changes in their employment status over the full course of their career.

As the National Education Association sees it, the task is to represent professionals like this for 'employability' rather than for 'employment security' in any single job they might hold at a particular point in time. A big part of the NEA strategy involves creative use of Web, CD ROM, and related interactive technologies to provide professional services to current and future members.

The NEA or other American unions that seek to represent professionals might learn a great deal from the efforts of the Association of Professional

Engineers, Scientists, and Managers of Australia (APESMA) to use cyber-space and other services to recruit and serve its members. This association represents a mix of professionals in these different occupations both through collective negotiations, and a variety of membership services. Among other things, it adopts a full career life-cycle approach by offering university students free affiliate membership, career advice, and placement assistance. When these students graduate and enter their professional careers, APESMA offers the range of services such as job market information, salary surveys and personalised comparison, and continuing education degree programmes linked to a major university.

## Organising in low income labour markets

One of the truly fascinating cases of union innovation concerns the Service Employees International Union's (SEIU) successful organising campaign of new kinds of workers, at both the top and bottom of the labour market. One of these efforts is their organising of homecare workers in Los Angeles county.

Homecare workers are prototypical examples of the difficulties encountered in organising low wage workers today. In addition to being poorly paid, many are minorities and/or immigrants, a majority are likely to be women with children and are employed in highly atomised worksites – the homes of their clients. SEIU's successful organisation of 75,000 homecare workers in Los Angeles county illustrates the importance of forging lasting coalitions between the union movement and other organisations in the local community as well as constructing entirely new institutions to govern work and employment relations in the new economy.

Organising these workers required considerable use of political power, both at the state and local government levels and an organising strategy capable of reaching and communicating with a multi-cultural labour force in workers' homes, churches, community centers, etc. rather than at their place of work. This is symptomatic of the types of efforts that will be needed to reach and attract other low wage workers.

Increasingly, community groups are organising around issues of work and economic development – offering representation, training, and organising assistance to low-income and immigrant workers across employers and industries. Some of these efforts are done in coalition with unions, but some are formed and operate on their own. These groups organise across territorial and industrial communities and take into account the diversity of worker identities and interests. Their collective activity has led to a new thrust in the labour movement, what Janice Fine calls 'community unionism'.[15]

Examples of community organising around labour market issues are proliferating. National organisations like the Industrial Areas Foundation and

ACORN have partnered with local community groups to mount living wage campaigns across the country. Project QUEST in San Antonio, Texas, joined with the national Industrial Areas Foundation (IAF) to establish a community training and employment center for low-income workers. In Long Island, the Workplace Project's immigrant worker center passed a statewide unpaid wages law. The Baltimore organisation BUILD has worked for the enactment of a series of city-wide labour market ordinances, including living wages, right-to-organise, and right to first refusal ordinances, as well as a 'school counts' law that allows mothers moving off welfare to count education towards their work requirement.

## Organising contingent employees

One of the characteristics of the new labour market is the increased use of contingent employees. This is a group of workers in need of representation but are hard to organise because they are scattered among many work sites and because their employment tenures are so short.

One strategy rests on revitalising the Central Labor Councils (CLCs). One such effort is the South Bay Central Labor Council in San Jose, California. Located in the heart of Silicon Valley – considered a harbinger of the economy of the future – the South Bay Labor Council created a number of corollary, non-profit organisations aimed at rebuilding its own capacity and organising workers in the new, traditionally unorganised information economy. For example, in 1995, the South Bay Labor Council, in partnership with various local organisations, created Working Partnerships, an organisation seeking to promote local economic development and enhance union strength. One of the partnership's programmes, Together@Work is an initiative aimed at making systematic changes in the region's temporary employment industry. A membership-based organisation that provides pension and heath benefits as well as financial services, this labour-led temporary employment agency meets regional skill standards set by an employer advisory committee. The ultimate goal of this agency is to increase the wage floor for lower-paid temp work, and to help ensure greater employment stability for its workers.

Another innovative organisation is Working Today, a national organisation based in New York City, that has been promoting the concerns of self-employed media workers since its founding in 1995. Working Today has both individual members and serves as a link to a network of associations, including the Newspaper Guild, the Translators and Interpreters Guild, and the New York Foundation for the Arts. The central benefit available to members is health insurance, although Working Today also provides a range of other network-like functions and benefits. The organisation operates a website and publishes a newsletter that informs members both of its expanding services and of recent developments in laws and programmes.

## Other instruments for employee voice

Many workplaces in America now have some form of employee participation in place. While these range considerably in their influence and effectiveness, on average, the data presented earlier in this chapter indicate that the majority of employees like these arrangements and want to see them grow in number and in influence. They are not substitutes for independent representation and they are restricted by law from being used to negotiate over wages or other terms and conditions of employment. But the reality is that some employers use these informal participation processes as part of their union avoidance efforts, and the evidence suggests that they are quite successful in serving this function. The challenge is for unions to figure out how to turn these from competitors to complements of other forms of representation that they provide.

In addition to these employee participation and partnership efforts, other groups have been organising employees across firms, within local communities, occupations, and according to different social identities. These groups tend to represent women, African-American, Asian-American, gay/lesbian/bisexual, or aging employees. While there is little empirical evidence regarding the effects of these groups, one study of identity groups in a high technology firm found that their primary accomplishments included: increasing awareness of diversity issues as a necessary step towards change in the workplace; mobilising around specific events to make the work environment more comfortable for traditionally marginalised and less powerful employees; improving retention and promotion opportunities; and changing the style of working and the allocation of power.[16] These groups have grown in number and variety. One estimate suggests that about one-third of Fortune 500 firms have such groups. Even IBM, a company that is well known for avoiding any form of group or collective process that might serve as an incubator for union activity, now reports having over 70 identity groups in place, 30 of which are local area women's networks.[17]

## Conclusion

As these examples suggest, there is a renewed vigor and a great deal of experimentation with new approaches underway within unions and professional organisations and in other groups not directly affiliated with the labour movement that serve some (but not all) of the functions of traditional unions. Notwithstanding the notable achievements of these and other organising efforts, however, it is important to recognise their limited impact to date in reversing organised labour's decline in this country. For example, even though 73,000 new members were recruited into the building trades unions in 1997, union density in this sector only increased by

0.1 per cent. In 1998, construction unions lost 11,000 workers or one per cent of their total membership. Likewise, although the CWA has gained new members by diversifying into other white-collar occupations, its membership continues to be concentrated in the traditional (and shrinking) wireline segment of the industry, particularly among traditional craft workers and service and sales workers in local exchange carriers. Finally, even though the SEIU has been making strides in organising new kinds of workers (homecare workers, doctors, etc.) it too has been unable to reverse the trend of union decline and weakness. The SEIU in recent years has spent considerable sums of money organising (combined spending by SEIU locals and the International grew from under 20 million dollars in 1995 to over 60 million dollars in 1998) and it has also recruited record numbers of new members (38,000 in 1996, 81,000 in 1997, 185,000 in 1998). But given that a significant number of these 'new' members resulted from mergers with already existing unions (144,000 in 1997 and 1998 alone) we need to treat even these successes as further indications of the difficulties American unions face in reversing their decline.

Each of the innovative efforts described here can contribute to building the next generation unions. But so far these examples are all independent, isolated efforts. As far as we know, there is no effort to think about how they might be linked together to create a network of opportunities for representing workers over their full working lives. This, we suggest is a challenge that needs to be taken up at some point in the future. But if the labour movement doesn't do it, other organisations will likely step in and fill the void that may or may not be linked to or sympathetic to labour's broader objectives and role in society.

If it is to do so, the labour movement will need to do a number of things simultaneously. First, it will need to continue to serve its traditional constituency. That is, it will need to continue to organise workers who are mistreated on their jobs and distrust their employers and see collective bargaining as a way of achieving improved employment standards and justice. This is the bedrock responsibility of any labour movement, and the American labour movement has clearly signaled its continued commitment to doing its best to serve this constituency.

Second, to meet the preferences and needs of a more representative cross section of the workforce unions must move to an organising and recruiting strategy and image that reaches those outside of this core constituency – those who are not necessarily locked in a low trust relationship with their employer and who still want and would benefit from an independent institution that strengthens their voice and helps them achieve the dignity, opportunity to learn and develop new skills, and enhance their sense of professionalism at work. Becoming a champion for these outcomes will require some changes in both labour law and in the mentality that unions now view employee participation. Instead of seeing it as a competing force for worker loyalties and as a union avoidance tactic on the part of employers, unions will need to appropriate the power of this tool and become both visible champions and skilled facilitators of employee voice at work. Taking this approach will open up a large, new 'market' for union membership and services.

Third, the next generation union will need to address the needs of workers in jobs of uncertain duration and workers who expect to move across firms multiple times over the course of their careers. This means adapting the occupational/craft/professional models of organising and viewing union membership as a life-long commitment and relationship in which the union provides services aimed at maintaining members' employability and access to changing job opportunities. Many workers flow through union membership at some point in their work lives. Yet each time a worker leaves a union job, chances are that he or she will have to be organised again in future jobs. Indeed, national surveys report that there are nearly twice as many former union members in the labour force as there are current union members! Imagine the numbers and power labour would gain if these could be retained for life by providing a set of services tailored to their changing needs.

In summary, the next generation unions will need to employ a variety of different, but complementary and linked strategies to recruit, organise, represent and retain their members. Unions will not, however, be able to do this alone. They will need to be skilled in forming and maintaining coalitions with community groups and other worker advocacy groups. They will need to work to reduce the costs of organising to employers and in return, (or for some employers through the use of their power) employer opposition to organising will need to be neutralised. And from the government, unions will need to achieve economic, regulatory, and labour policy changes that give unions and their future members access to the jobs of the new economy.

These different functions may not necessarily be performed by the same organisations. There might be specialisation – core competencies if you will. Some unions may choose to organise in traditional ways relying on traditional employee motivations while new organisations, professional associations, networks, etc. grow up that recruit, represent, and service members in new ways. We believe this would be a second-best solution. But if this is the case, then there must be active strategies for linking and cooperating across these different boundaries and mutual respect among and support among the different organisations in the network – unions, professional organisations, others yet to be named or invented. Or we might see the labour movement as the hub of a wheel that coordinates the work of different groups. That is why we see the next generation unions as extended networks of groups and organisations through which individuals flow over the course of their working lives.

For this vision of the next generation unions to become a reality at least three things need to change. First, unions need to expand the ways they recruit and retain members. They need to recruit individuals and stay with them over the course of their careers rather than limit their organising to the high stakes, all or nothing 50 per cent majority it now takes to get one new member. Second, substantial change in labour law will be needed to make it possible for unions to play these different roles effectively. Third, American management culture will need to change significantly to accept the simple idea that workers should have the same freedom of association at work as they have in civil society. This may be the biggest hurdle of all to overcome.

# 4
## Prospects for Union Growth in the United States in the Early 21<sup>st</sup> Century

*Bruce E. Kaufman*

### Introduction

At we progress into a new century it seems particularly appropriate to ponder on the future of one of America's most important social and economic institutions – the organised labour movement. Recent years have been hard on American unions. Union density has suffered a slow but cumulatively significant decline, falling from 34 per cent in the mid-1950s to 13 per cent today. In the U.S. private sector, where the great bulk of jobs are, union density has fallen even lower (9%). Certainly the old century did not end, and the new century begin, on a very auspicious note when the *New York Times* (January 21, 2001: 18), in reporting on the Department of Labour's survey of union membership, led off the article with this title: 'Unions Hit Lowest Point in Six Decades'.

Given the long and uninterrupted decline in union density in the United States, a reasonable, low-risk forecast of future union prospects in the years ahead would be 'more of the same'. Such a verdict is made even more sensible by a recent careful statistical analysis of union growth by Henry Farber and Bruce Western (2001) who conclude, based on past employment and organising trends, that the steady state level of union density is two per cent.

Two things keep me from immediately opting for this forecast, however. The first is the specter of George Barnett. Barnett, in his presidential address to the American Economics Association in late 1932, predicted that American unions would decline further in the years ahead (Barnett, 1933; Kaufman, 2001a). Unfortunately for Barnett, union organising exploded less than a year later and by the end of the decade union density had more than doubled, making his prediction look spectacularly misinformed. The second is a recent paper by Richard Freeman (1998). In it he argues that union growth over the 20<sup>th</sup> century has been dominated by sudden large-size 'spurts' in new organisation, followed by longer periods of consolidation and decline. One of these spurts caught Barnett by surprise, and the modern-day forecaster of union growth has to be concerned that another such spurt may lie just over the horizon.

What, then, does the next decade hold for American trade unionism? To an economist, this question is not any different in principle than forecasting the future course of stock prices, interest rates, or employment. The value of these variables at a point in time is determined by the intersection of their respective demand and supply curves and their time series behavior is likewise explained by shifts in these curves. In what follows, I utilise this demand/supply perspective as a forecasting tool for predicting the likely course of American union density for the early part of the 21st century. I note, however, that the analysis is historical and qualitative, not econometric, and a broad range of non-economic factors, such as political events and social attitudes, are introduced.

To begin this exercise, in the next section I provide a brief overview of the pattern of union growth in the 20th century in the United States. I then describe the demand/supply model of union growth, giving special emphasis to key determinants of union demand as identified in the writings of early 20th century institutional labour economist John R. Commons. In the remainder of the paper I use this model to draw inferences about union growth in the early 21st century, based on trends and developments in the past century.

Perhaps tempting fate, my forecast is similar to that made by Barnett in 1932: continued slow decline in union density. Unlike Barnett, however, I remember to say the economist's most important caveat, 'other things equal'. In particular, my forecast assumes the nation's basic legal and policy stance toward collective bargaining remains unchanged – an assumption Barnett did not make and that caused his forecast to go badly awry with the advent of the New Deal in 1933. Whether this assumption holds true for the early part of the 21st century rests largely on the nation's ability to avoid the two exogenous shocks that have in past years caused the government to substantially expand legal protection and encouragement of trade unionism: economic depression and wartime mobilisation and wage/price controls.

## The 20th century pattern of union growth

The pattern of union growth in the United States over the 20th century is depicted in Figure 4.1. Shown in the figure is union density for the years 1900–2000. Union density is calculated as total union membership as a per cent of nonagricultural employment.

Several aspects of the pattern of union growth stand out. First and foremost is the inverted V shape union density tracks over the century. In 1900 union density was quite modest – only 7 per cent. Then over the next five decades union density gradually rose in an irregular fashion, peaking-out at

46

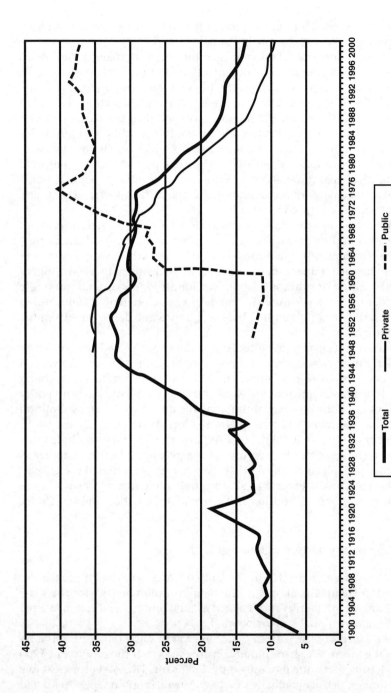

*Figure 4.1* Union Density, 1900–2000.
*Source:* Bennet and Kaufman (2002).

34 per cent in 1954. Then for the rest of the century density slowly retraced its steps, falling more or less steadily for 45 years until in 2000 it stood at 13 per cent. In the private sector density in 2000 was 9 per cent, a level quite close to that 100 years earlier.

Two other aspects of the pattern of union density deserve brief mention. The first is the large degree of volatility in density in the first half of the century, which largely collapses around the long-term trend in the second half. The second is that much of the increase in union density occurs in massive surges or 'spurts', such as centered around World War I (1917–1920), the years of the New Deal (1933–39), and World War II (1942–1945).

Union density is not, of course, the only way to measure union growth. The other approach is to look at the change in union membership itself (not shown in Figure 4.1). The two series tell much the same story for the first half of the century, but diverge in the second half. While density shows marked union decline, the number of union members shows long-term stability. In the mid-1950s, for example, union membership was roughly 16 million, which is where it was when the century ended in 2000. Since nonagricultural employment expanded by 240 per cent over this period, density naturally nose-dived. I focus on density in this paper, since the economic and political power of unions rests to a significant degree on the proportion of the workforce that is organised. But all discussions of union decline have to be qualified with the recognition that in terms of absolute numbers the union movement in the United States remains large and has fairly well managed to hold its own.

## An explanatory model

Forecasting requires a model, or at least an analytic framework, if the exercise is to be more than *ad hoc*. Sketched below is a framework I find useful for thinking about future union growth. The basic structure of the model involves demand and supply functions for union services. After sketching the model, I examine the determinants of union demand in more detail, drawing largely on the earlier writings of Commons.

### Demand/supply model

Forecasting future union growth can be considered akin to forecasting other economic phenomena, and the economist's natural inclination is to frame the issue in terms of a model of demand and supply. Such a framework has been developed and applied to unions by Pencavel (1971), Farber (1983), and Hirsch and Addison (1986), among others, and I follow in their footsteps.

The basic idea is to treat union membership as determined in a market, with the demand of individual workers for union representation on one side and the supply of union representation by trade unions on the other. At a point in time the level of union membership is determined by the breadth/depth of worker demand and the willingness and ability of unions to supply representation services; while over time variations in union membership is a function of shifts in the demand and/or supply functions. Statements about union membership translate into equivalent statements about density, assuming the size of the labour force is held constant.

On the supply side of the market, the level of union membership and density is determined, in part, by the cost, quality, variety, and availability of the representational services unions provide. These factors are determined, in turn, by variables such as the organisational structure of unions, their goals, organising and bargaining strategies, quality of leadership, the size and geographical dispersion of work sites, and (importantly) the laws and regulations that govern the union-joining process and the practice of collective bargaining.

The demand for union services at both the level of the individual worker and the nation state turns on a comparison of benefits and costs. I note that although the penchant of economists is to portray benefits and costs in rationalistic terms, in the case of union-joining they are often significantly influenced by emotions, such as feelings of injustice and fear (Wheeler and McClendon, 1991). Given this caveat, it is assumed that workers compare the benefits they get from union representation, such as higher wages, increased job security, and protection from termination, with the costs of obtaining such representation, where these costs take the form of union dues, time lost to strikes, possible job loss, and other such things. Just as government laws and regulations affect the supply side of the union representation market, so too do they play an important role on the demand side. Stronger government protection of the right to organise, for example, reduces worker fear of job loss and increases the demand for union services, while rulings that restrict the range of issues that unions can negotiate over or the pressure tactics they can use in bargaining reduce the appeal of union representation. Finally, as with other goods, the demand for union services also depends on the price, availability of substitutes, and the tastes and preferences of the employee 'consumers' regarding collective approaches to solving workplace problems.

The product price plays a key role in microeconomic theory as a determinant of both the demand and supply functions, and as the device that coordinates a balance between the two. When applied to unions, however, problems arise. It is not obvious what the price is (union dues?), nor that this price is flexible enough to equilibrate demand and supply. A number of authors (e.g., Farber, 1983) assume that the price mechanism in this particular market is largely non-operational and thus a divergence between demand and supply can persist for a lengthy period and is rationed through some non-price method (e.g., a queue of workers waiting to he hired into union jobs). I follow this approach, subsuming union dues and other aspects of price as part of 'cost' of union services.

## The nature of union services

To make the demand/supply model operational, the determinants of demand and supply have to be specified. In thinking about this issue, I am drawn to the title of Freeman and Medoff's (1984) well-known book: *What Do Unions Do?*. It seems to me that this question of 'what do unions do?' gets to the heart of the matter because it defines in large part the nature of the services unions provide, which in turn impacts both the benefits and costs of union services on the demand side and the goals, organisational structure, and tactics of unions on the supply side.

Freeman and Medoff examine this issue using an 'exit/voice' model of unions, which they adapted from the earlier work of Albert Hirschman (1970). I think additional insights are available, however, by going back much further in the literature. In particular, I have in mind the writings on unions by Commons – the person most frequently viewed as the father of the American industrial relations field. It turns out that the Freeman and Medoff's 'exit/voice' model can be viewed as a much later and more narrowly conceived version of Commons' model.

Commons argues that unions play two important roles, one economic and the other non-economic. Consider first the economic.

The economic function of unions, he said in 1906 (reprinted in Commons 1913, p. 121), is 'wealth redistribution', 'joint aggrandisement', and 'protection' (WRAP). Unions accomplish these goals by acting much as a cartel of firms in the product market – they organise as many of the sellers of labour as possible, establish rules that allocate the available work among the members, and use their market power to set a common price for all sellers that is above the prevailing market rate. By doing so, they redistribute income from capital to labour, increase the wage bill for labour ('aggrandisement'), and shield workers from adverse consequences of market competition, such as wage cuts, speed-ups, and long hours. The union function of WRAP has both microeconomic and macroeconomic dimensions and a good deal of the debate about unions centers on the benefits and costs of each. I also note that the economic function of WRAP broadly corresponds to the 'monopoly face' of unions developed by Freeman and Medoff.

The non-economic function of unions, according to Commons (1905, p. vii), is to provide what he called 'constitutional government in industry' (CGI), or what the Webbs' (1897) called 'industrial democracy'. According to Commons, every organisation is a form of 'government' in that each is a product of collective action, is governed by working rules that specify authority relations and the distribution of rights, liberties, duties and exposures, and employs sanctions to enforce the working rules. In the work world, the most important organisation is the business firm and, parallel to modern writings of new institutional economists such as Oliver Williamson (1985), Commons suggests that we view firms as a form of industrial government or a 'governance structure'.

Looked at from the vantage point of the early 20th century, the governance structure of most firms was closely akin to that of 14th century England, which is to say a system of unvarnished autocracy in which a monarch rules with largely undisputed authority (Kaufman, 2000). Commons thought this system of industrial government to be obviously despotic (but perhaps benevolently so), and thus favoured trade unions as a way to introduce democracy or representative government into the workplace. By 'democracy' he did not necessarily mean majority voting, but he did envision representation of workers' interests, the substitution of 'rule by law' for 'rule by men' in the governance of the workplace, and due process and impartial adjudication in the resolution of disputes. This noneconomic function of unions subsumes the 'collective voice' face of unions later developed by Freeman and Medoff.

### Substitutes for union services

The demand and supply of union services is also affected by the range and quality of substitutes available in the worker representation market. Obviously, if there is some other way to deliver at lower cost or with greater effectiveness the things workers want from unions, the demand and supply of union services will be correspondingly reduced. Commons also offers useful insight on this matter.

Unions arise, according to Commons (1905), as a response to various 'labour problems'. These labour problems take the form of low wages, long hours, unsafe working conditions, insecurity of employment, arbitrary and capricious management decisions, lack of dignity and respect in the workplace, and other such factors. The more widespread or grievous are these labour problems the greater will be the demand for union WRAP and CGI (other things equal).

Labour problems, in Commons' view, originate from characteristics and conditions of the employment relationship and the market system in which the employment relationship is embedded. In the world of neoclassical economic theory few, if any, labour problems exist. In this schema, 'perfect' people (rational, maximising individualists) trade goods and services in 'perfect' (purely competitive) markets, leading to maximum economic efficiency, a 'just' set of economic rewards, and absence of exploitation or abuse by management (since workers can costlessly quit one employer and find work at another). The greater the degree, however, to which real world people and labour markets are imperfect the more pronounced will be labour problems and, hence, the demand for unions.

Thinking about substitutes for unions, therefore, the first to be listed is 'perfect markets'. Good markets, like good bosses, reduce the demand for unions because workers get more of the things that lead to individual well-being and sense of satisfaction at work – wages that are as high as the worker's education and skill can command, hours and conditions of work that are 'optimal' in terms of worker preferences and relative prices, and opportunities for advancement and skill development.

To the extent that markets (and people) are not perfect, labour problems will arise. But even in this case there are other solutions besides unions to these problems. Commons (1921) identifies two such substitutes.

The first is what at that time was generically called the 'employer's solution' to labour problems (Kaufman, 2003). Another name would be 'good management'. The employer's solution endeavours to solve labour problems through effective organisational structures and human resource policies and practices that foster a unity of interest, satisfaction with wages and employment conditions, and a culture that emphasises fair dealing and respect. Tools that employers can use to accomplish these objectives include employment security, above-market wages, gain-sharing forms of compensation, training of foremen and supervisors in 'human relations', employee involvement programmes, and a strong commitment to fairness and equal opportunity in the workplace. These practices today are often associated with a 'high performance' work model, but were originally developed by Commons (1919) as part of what he called a 'goodwill' employment strategy.

The second substitute for unions is government law and regulation. In Commons' time this approach was called the 'community's solution' to labour problems (Kaufman, 2003). Government can help solve labour problems in several ways. One is through protective labour legislation, such as minimum wage and maximum hour laws, safety and health regulation, pension protection, and anti-discrimination statutes. A second is social insurance programmes, such as worker's compensation, unemployment insurance, and government-funded old age and retirement programmes. A third is that government through legislation and court rulings can change property rights and endowments in favour of workers, thus causing market demand and supply to yield outcomes that are more equal or advantageous to labour relative to capital. Examples of the latter include replacement of the 'employment-at-will' doctrine with a 'just cause' standard and free public education and subsidised university training for children from lower-income groups.

## The record of the 20<sup>th</sup> century: lessons learned

I now come to the central question of this paper: what will be the course of union density in the United States in the early part of the 21<sup>st</sup> century? To answer this question I proceed in two steps. In this section I derive a short set of 'lessons learned' from the 20th century experience, based on events and trends and the demand/supply model of unionism just described. In the next section I then use these lessons to project the trend in union density in the 21st century (also see Bennett and Kaufman, 2002).

Here are what I consider the central lessons of the 20th century:

(1)   The base line level of unionisation is low relative to world standards because of the American social ethos of individualism and consumerism, widespread acceptance of capitalism and market competition, a poorly defined and fragmented working class, and lack of a viable labour political party. All of these factors reduce the demand for unionism.

(2)   The level of union density rose in the first half of the century because of favourable structural factors, such as the spread of large-scale industry, growth of a full-time wage earning labour force, and decline in the extent of immigration. These were a positive stimulus to union demand.

(3)   The growth prospect of unions is directly tied to the breadth and depth of labour problems affecting wage earners. Union density rose in the first half of the 20th century because labour problems (on net) remained broad and deep, such as low wages, intensification of work, employment insecurity, and widespread discrimination. The key event was the decade-long Great Depression of the 1930s that not only wiped out the improved conditions gained in earlier years (e.g., the Welfare Capitalism period of the 1920s) but reinforced in workers' minds a psychology of insecurity and need for protection. Their demand for unions was accordingly also heightened.

(4)   Besides the breadth and depth of labour problems, workers' demand for unions is also dependent on their belief that (a) unions can effectively solve or redress these problems and (b) other good substitute methods to improve their position are unavailable. In the context of the first half of the 20th century, the shift in public policy toward support of unions and augmentation of their bargaining power in the New Deal years and World War II led workers to believe unions would indeed be more effective in collective bargaining, thus fueling greater demand for unionism, while union demand was also stimulated by the apparent failure of two substitutes – good labour markets and progressive management – and the relatively modest and incomplete regime of protective labour law and social insurance.

(5)   A final factor fueling expanded union density in the first half of the century were innovations and developments affecting the supply side of union services. Examples include the formation of the Congress of Industrial Organizations (CIO), the spread of industrial unionism,

emergence of a new generation of dynamic union leaders (e.g., Walter Reuther), and new labour law (the National Labour Relations Act) that facilitated union organising and bargaining.

(6) The decline of union density in the last half of the 20$^{th}$ century arose from a reversal in many of the factors promoting increased density in the first half. Structural factors, for example, on net retarded union demand and growth, including the relative spread of non-traditional forms of employment (contingent workers, part-time employment), an employment shift toward occupations/industries that are not union-prone (e.g., information technology, services, retail trade), and much expanded immigration and labour supply in low wage labour markets.

(7) The breadth and depth of labour problems affecting American workers declined over the last half of the century, leading to jobs and work-places that were on net considerably superior to those of several decades earlier. Arduous and dangerous working conditions were gradually reduced, as were hours of work and the extent of arbitrary and insensitive management, while many positive attributes of employment rose, such as real earnings, employee benefits, job security, and equal treatment. To be sure many problems remained and few workplaces were yet 'heaven on earth', but overall the reduction in labour problems led to a concomitant reduction in workers' demand for unions.

(8) Workers' demand for unions also declined because they perceived unions were less effective in winning (and maintaining) improved conditions. Union bargaining power was undercut by increased capital mobility, globalisation, the deregulation of markets, and decline in the effectiveness of striking, making it more difficult to deliver WRAP and CGI. Worker demand for unions was also undercut by much expanded (or renewed) employer resistance, practiced through striker replacement, use of high-powered consultants and attorneys to defeat union organising drives, termination of union activists, and refusal to negotiate first contracts.

(9) The range and effectiveness of union substitutes also increased sub-stantially in the last half of the century. On net, labour markets were much closer to full employment due to the success of Keynesian-inspired counter-cyclical macroeconomic policies, thus allowing workers to find employment protection and opportunities through 'good markets' instead of collective bargaining. Likewise, the practice and effectiveness of personnel/human resource management notably improved, as did the breadth and depth of legal protection through new laws governing things such as civil rights, anti-discrimination, pension protection, portability of health insurance, and family leave. Neither of these substitutes were perfect or complete, but they did

on net contribute to a reduced demand for unions through 'better management' and 'better laws'.

(10) The supply of union services was hindered in the last half of the century by a variety of developments, including a weakening in the effective protection given union organising by labour law, the bureaucratisation of unions, the ossification of their top leadership, and declining union resources. The most positive development was extension of collective bargaining rights to the public sector in the 1960s and 1970s. By the 1980s, however, the force of this factor was largely spent.

(11) The final lesson important to glean from the 20ᵗʰ century experience is that the most pronounced periods of union growth come in a few 'spurts' of sizable, fairly quick surges in membership. In the first half of the 20ᵗʰ century this occurred during the two world wars and the Great Depression. In the last half of the century a 'quasi-spurt' occurred in the 1965–75 period in the public sector. In each case the union spurt happened when government labour policy made a substantial shift toward encouragement and protection of collective bargaining. The preconditions for such a shift in government labour policy seem to be: (a) the government needs union cooperation and/or labour peace, particularly during a crisis situation (e.g., the two world wars), (b) union WRAP is seem as essential to ending an economic crisis and restoring stability and growth (e.g., the Depression), and (c) public opinion becomes much more supportive of union WRAP and CGI.

## Forecast for the early twenty-first century

These lessons provide the input or 'raw data' for my forecast of union density over the early part of the 21ˢᵗ century. In deriving this forecast, I proceed in two steps. The first step is to forecast union growth assuming the basic legal structure and government policy toward collective bargaining remains essentially unchanged. The second step is to then consider the prospects for change in law and government policy and the implications thereof for union growth.

### Status quo in the legal/policy regime

Assuming the present legal and policy regime remains unchanged, all the forces discussed above lead to the conclusion that union density will continue on the same downward trajectory it has been on for several decades. In other words, the forecast is 'more of the same'. There are both positive and negative trends for unions in the forecast, but the negative significantly outweigh the positive. First the positive.

The existence of labour problems is a necessary condition for workers to want unions in this country, and the good news for unions is that the early

21<sup>st</sup> century workplace will continue to have a number of such problems. Indeed, the greater market competition and financial pressure from Wall Street that is sure to continue will no doubt intensify labour problems for some workers, such as longer hours of work, the continual threat of job loss, and reductions in benefits. A significant portion of 21<sup>st</sup> century labour problems will be fairly traditional, such as a desire for higher pay, protection of benefits, fair treatment, greater job security, and obtaining a voice in the workplace, while others will be more non-traditional, such as greater work-family balance and flexible work schedules. The growing income inequality in the United States, stagnation of earnings and economic mobility for the less skilled, and glorification of consumerism also create labour problems as workers at the lower end of the labour market develop a sense of inequity, frustration, and alienation.

Another piece of good news is that a sizable number of 21<sup>st</sup> century workers will also continue to find that these problems are frequently not easily or effectively solved through individual action. Particularly employees who lack education or skill will find they have very modest leverage with employers over basic terms and conditions of employment, and that the exit option is either costly or takes them to another company with similar jobs and similar problems (Appelbaum, Bernhardt, and Murnane, 2003). Likewise, opportunities for effective individual voice will remain stunted at a number of firms with a traditional management style of command and control, while fears of possible retribution for speaking up will remain an ever-present reality.

These labour problems will be severe enough that many workers in the early 21<sup>st</sup> century will express a favourable attitude toward unions and tens of thousands will actively seek union representation. Indeed, surveys (Freeman and Rodgers, 1999) show that today 30–40 per cent of workers, if given the opportunity, would vote for union representation at their workplace.

But now comes the bad news. For a variety of reasons the number of workers unions are able to organise will continue to seriously lag behind labour force growth, while unionised companies will continue to shed thousands of jobs. The result will be a one-two punch to union density.

With respect to new member growth, the problems are several. The first is that the 30–40 per cent of workers who express union interest are scattered across the economy and often cannot get a majority of their fellow workers at particular worksites to vote YES for union representation.

A second factor is that the nature of work and conditions of employment in the 21<sup>st</sup> century workplace will, at least for the majority of workers, most likely continue to improve over the long-term, further reducing the breadth and severity of labour problems and union demand. Yes, labour problems will continue to exist and perhaps worsen in certain respects for some groups of workers, employer and employee interests will remain partially opposed, and to a degree employee dissatisfaction is a matter of relative (not absolute) deprivation. But I nonetheless conjecture that the proportion of employees expressing strong dissatisfaction with their jobs will nonetheless most likely continue to slowly shrink over the long term with ongoing improvements in the nature, organisation, and conditions of work – assuming labour markets do not suffer from a prolonged bout of joblessness and/or rampant job insecurity.

A third 'negative' is that even among those workers with significant labour problems a growing proportion will perceive that unions are not an effective method for solving them. As markets become more competitive, unions have greater difficulty delivering WRAP and making it 'stick'. The threat of striker replacement will also continue to undercut union bargaining power and the ability to deliver WRAP.

A fourth factor diminishing worker demand for unions in the years ahead will be the growing availability and increased effectiveness of substitutes for union WRAP and CGI. I judge the most important of these substitutes to be 'good markets', because bad markets are both a major source of labour problems and a block to one important avenue of individual action. The future course of the economy is obviously unknowable and no doubt future recessions and other macroeconomic maladies lay ahead. Also, the process of globalisation, while a beneficial source of new jobs and rising living standards in the long run, may lead to significant job losses and work insecurity in America in the short run, or even a full-blown world financial crisis. Giving due consideration to these contingencies, it is nonetheless the case that over the last half century the trend has been toward a more stable, low inflation, full employment economy. If this condition of 'good markets' continues into the future, which seems at least a fair bet over the longer term, then I foresee further decline (or at least no major increase) in worker demand for unions.

The other major substitutes for union WRAP and CGI are progressive personnel/HR management and government legislation. Certainly viewed over the long term the HR management function has grown and developed in terms of the quantity and quality of employee relations it delivers to both companies and their workers, thereby taking away a portion of the demand for unions (Jacoby, 2003). I see no reason why this long-term trend should not continue, although it is heavily dependent on a good economy and is at some risk due to management's growing preoccupation with short term financial returns. Another long-term trend has been greater government regulation of labour markets and labour conditions and I also see no reason for this trend to reverse. There is to be sure considerable disenchantment with the large costs, long time delays, and undue litigiousness that arise from using the courts and regulatory agencies to resolve labour problems, but I think the trend will be to reform this process, not cut it back and instead place greater reliance on collective bargaining. While both good markets and HR management depend for their effectiveness on a measure of individual action, government legislation and regulatory agencies provide a collective form of action that is indeed rivalrous of unions (Bennett and Taylor, 2001).

The demand for union representation is a function not only of the benefits but also the costs. The gist of the preceding is that fewer labour problems and the availability of better substitutes has reduced the net benefits. At the same time I think the costs of union representation will continue to rise. One such cost is increased threat of job loss as labour demand curves become more elastic due to greater competition and capital becomes more mobile. A second cost comes from increased management resistance, arising from employers' perceptions that unions impede flexibility and raise cost – burdens that companies are increasingly averse to shouldering in today's more competitive, fast-changing economic environment (Hirsch, 2004). The costs to workers from increased management resistance can take a variety of forms, such as closing the plant and sending production overseas, using replacement workers in a strike, and/or firing union activists. The latter type of action is illegal but the penalties and enforcement procedures in the NLRA are too weak to deter some employers intent on remaining union-free (Flanagan, 2004).

Finally, consideration must be briefly given to supply side considerations. I do not see anything particularly promising for unions in the near-term future. The public sector opened up a 'new frontier' for unions in the 1960s–70s, but now union density there has plateaued and I see no similar new frontier to take its place in the first decade of the 2000s. It is also difficult to detect any major institutional innovation, such as a new form of union structure, that will substantially increase the effective supply of union services. Nor do unions seem able to innovate a more effective organising model, despite a significant increase in resources devoted to organising in the late 1990s.

## A change in legal/policy regimes

The message of the last section is that in the context of the present economic climate, institutional structure, and legal regime it appears highly likely that union density will continue to decline in the years ahead. But the record of the 20th century shows that 'other things equal' is not always a good assumption.

In particular, the three episodes of substantial union growth in the last one hundred years took place during crisis periods – two world wars and one economic depression. In each case conditions were created that made union WRAP and CGI much more attractive to workers. Equally important, in each period the federal government's stance toward organised labour noticeably shifted to greater encouragement and protection of collective bargaining in terms of both overall policy and specific legislative and regulatory actions. The government's pro-labour shift in the two world wars was principally motivated by the need to maintain labour peace and secure organised labour's cooperation in the wartime economic controls programmes, while in the Depression the Roosevelt administration fostered collective bargaining on the belief that union WRAP would help stabilise the wage/price structure and equalise the distribution of income, thereby promoting economic recovery (Kaufman, 1996). The net result, however, was the same in all three crisis periods – a surge of worker interest in unions arising partly as an organic response to much-amplified labour problems and partly as a response to much expanded legal and regulatory protections and encouragements given to collective bargaining.

Any forecast of future union growth must recognise that these kinds of crisis periods can occur at any time, and they can lead to events and developments that cause a pronounced spurt in union membership. Should the nation experience either a major wartime economic mobilisation or a deep and prolonged economic collapse – say due to the instabilities and contradictions of globalisation, conditions would again become far more propitious for union resurgence. Until then, I foresee that public opinion will remain largely indifferent to the union cause and certainly not supportive of any kind of broad-based legal reform that would significantly expand the current scope of unionism in this country. As happened several times during the 20th century, some crisis or social breakdown may so energise workers' desire for independent representation that they organise en masse despite legal and bureaucratic roadblocks, but in today's environment this scenario falls in the realm of the fanciful.

Looking at the matter further, one direction public sentiment seems to be slowly shifting toward with respect to reform of the NLRA concerns the statute's ban on employer dominated labour organisations ('company unions'). Recent legislation called the TEAM Act, for example, sought to relax this ban, but was vetoed by President Clinton. The labour movement regards these nonunion committees as both a direct substitute for independent unions and a powerful tool of union avoidance and, hence, strongly opposed this legislation. My own view (Kaufman, 2001b) is that legalisation of these nonunion employee councils would be the most effective short run method to significantly reduce the representation/participation gap (Freeman and Rodgers, 1999) and could actually lead to greater union organising gains rather than less (because some nonunion employers would mishandle the committees and dissatisfied workers would opt for independent representation). But even this relatively modest change in the NLRA is caught in political gridlock, so the best forecast for the immediate future is a status quo position with regard to labour law.

## Conclusion

If the analysis in this paper is anywhere close to on-target, the growth prospects for organised labour in the United States do not look bright for the foreseeable future. The union movement will do well to maintain its current membership base, while union density will surely continue its long-term decline in the face of stagnant membership growth and a steady expansion in the labour force. 'More of the same' seems a safe forecast, therefore, absent a major deterioration in the economy or other social/political upheaval.

This projected decline in union density in the United States leaves me feeling ambivalent. On one hand, I think every social institution has to pass the 'market test' and if unions cannot attract sufficient members to remain viable then this is unfortunate but not necessarily a cause for public concern. Also, union 'decline' has to be put in perspective – even if density declines further the union movement remains a strong economic and political force with over 16 million members and each year unions will successively organise tens of thousands of new members.

There are other reasons, however, that make the decline in union density a source of concern. A viable union movement is needed to protect the powerless and voiceless in the labour market, to motivate nonunion employers to maintain competitive labour standards and progressive treatment of workers, and to provide an effective counterweight in the economic and political spheres to powerful business interests.

These positive contributions of unions, and the inability of the current legal and administrative framework to fully protect workers' rights to organise, lead me to believe that modest legislative changes are needed in the NLRA to ensure a level playing field for unions and guarantee that workers are able to exercise free choice in matters of independent representation. My impression, however, is that these kinds of legal reforms – even if they could somehow be accomplished in this adverse political climate – would not alter the fundamental conditions that are leading to union decline. The best hope for unions thus rests on developments of a perversely negative kind – that either the nation experiences some kind of wrenching social or economic crisis that generates large-scale worker dislocation and unrest, or the balance of power in governing the workplace swings too far in employers' favour and they over-reach.

## References

Appelbaum, E., Bernhardt, A. and Murnane, R. (2003) *Low Wage America: How Employers are Shaping Opportunity in the Workplace*. New York: Russell Sage.
Barnett, G. (1933) 'American Trade Unionism and Social Insurance'. *American Economic Review*, 23: 1–15.
Bennett, J. and Taylor, J. (2001) 'Labor Unions: Victims of Their Political Success?' *Journal of Labor Research*, 22: 261–74.

Commons, J. (1905) *Trade Unionism and Labor Problems*, 1st ed. Boston: Ginn & Co.
——. (1913) *Labor and Administration*. New York: MacMillan.
——. (1919) *Industrial Goodwill*. New York: McGraw-Hill.
——. (1921) *Trade Unionism and Labor Problems*, 2nd ed. Boston: Ginn & Co.
Farber, H. (1983) 'The Determination of the Union Status of Workers', *Econometrica*, 51: 1417–37.
——, and Western, B. (2001) 'Accounting for the Decline of Unions in the Private Sector, 1973–1998'. *Journal of Labor Research*, 22: 459–86.
Flanagan, R. (2004) 'Has Management Strangled Unions?' *Journal of Labor Research*, 25: (forthcoming).
Freeman, R. (1998) 'Spurts in Union Growth: Defining Moments and Social Processes'. In Bordo, M., Goldin, C. and White, E. (eds), *The Great Depression and the American Economy in the Twentieth Century*. Chicago: University of Chicago Press.
——, and Medoff, J. (1984) *What Do Unions Do?* New York: Basic Books.
——, and Rogers, J. (1999) *What Workers Want*. Ithaca: ILR Press.
Hirsch, B. (2004) 'What Do Unions Do for Economic Performance?' *Journal of Labor Research*, 25: forthcoming.
——, and Addison, J. (1986) *The Economic Analysis of Unions*. London: Allen & Unwin.
Hirschman, A. (1970) *Exit, Voice, and Loyalty*. Cambridge: Harvard University Press.
Jacoby, S. (2003) 'A Century of Human Resource Management'. In Kaufman, B., Beaumont, R. and Helfgott, R. (eds), *Industrial Relations to Human Resources and Beyond: The Evolving Process of Employee Relations Management*. Armonk: M. E. Sharpe.
Kaufman, B. (1996) 'Why the Wagner Act?: Reestablishing Contact with Its Original Purpose'. In Lewin, D., Kaufman, B. and Sockell, D. (eds), *Advances in Industrial and Labor Relations*, vol. 6. Greenwich: JAI Press.
——. (2000) 'The Early Institutionalists on Industrial Democracy and Union Democracy'. *Journal of Labor Research*, 21 (Spring): 189–209.
——. (2001a) 'The Future of Private Sector U.S. Unionism: Did George Barnett Get It Right After All?' *Journal of Labor Research*, 22: 433–57.
——. (2001b) 'The Employee Participation/Representation Gap: An Assessment and Proposed Solution', *University of Pennsylvania Journal of Labor and Employment Law*, 3: 491–550.
——. (2003) 'John R. Commons and the Wisconsin School on Industrial Relations Strategy and Policy'. *Industrial and Labor Relations Review*, 57: 3–30.
Pencavel, J. (1971) 'The Demand for Union Services: An Exercise'. *Industrial and Labor Relations Review*, 22: 180–91.
Webb, S. and Webb, B. (1897) *Industrial Democracy*. London: Longmans Green.
Wheeler, Hoyt and John McClendon (1991) 'The Individual Decision to Unionize'. In Strauss, G. et al. (eds), *The State of the Unions*. Madison: Industrial Relations Research Association.
Williamson, O. (1985) *The Economic Institutions of Capitalism*. New York: The Free Press.

# 5

# Employment Relations in New Zealand: The Role of the State vis-à-vis the Labour Movement

*Pat Walsh, Raymond Harbridge and David Wilkinson*

## Introduction

The essence of free enterprise is that individual agents are allowed to make their own decisions. Consumers and labourers, for example, choose how much to spend, how much to save, how many hours to work at what wage rate. Firms decide which products to produce, how much to produce, what price to charge, which inputs to use, and how much to invest.

Governments decide on issues such as the income tax rate, the level of expenditure on areas such as defence, and the growth rate of the money supply. These decisions affect both the welfare of agents and how they behave. Economic theory lays down a number of prerequisites for efficient markets. Among these are secure, transferable property rights, a large number of buyers and sellers, each of which has complete information, and no barriers to entry (or exit). Simple observation leads to the conclusion these conditions are rarely (if ever) met in the real world: there is no such thing as a perfect market.

Markets may fail to operate competitively or efficiently for a number of reasons. The most common reasons are (i) the existence of, or requirement for, public goods; (ii) the existence of externalities; (iii) the existence of natural monopolies; and (iv) the existence of information asymmetries.

The presence of these market failures serves as the principal rationale for government intervention in a market economy. With each problem or social objective that arises, a regulator will be faced with the question: can an imperfect regulation improve upon the workings of an imperfect market? For much of the post-Second World War period, the answer to this question was yes. However, the decades of the 80s and 90s saw a complete reversal of this attitude – to a period of deregulation and less government involvement.

The *raison d'être* of deregulation is to increase the degree of competition in an economy. This is achieved by ensuring that an economy becomes less subject to government involvement – indeed less dependent on government. The proponents of 'smaller government' and privatisation argue that it will lead to faster economic growth, higher income and more jobs. This argument held sway in countries such as the UK, USA, Australia and New Zealand, indeed most OECD countries. Such views were bolstered by the arguments put forward by people such as Porter (1990) who argued that firms which developed in a competitive environment were more likely to embody the dynamic understanding of markets essential to success in international markets. By extension, the same logic, if applied internally, was the key to economic development, growth, and jobs.

Unions are a response to market failure. Their essential role is to provide a countervailing force to employers, and thus seek an improvement in the welfare of their members over what would occur in a purely free market environment. However, they depend upon the state for their legitimacy and legal standing – indeed, they may be seen as creatures of the state.

There is, however, a tendency to speak loosely and generally about state regulation of industrial relations. It is seen as something which we either have or do not have. This perspective obscures its associated complexities. States may choose to regulate certain elements of employment relations in particular historical periods but not in others. Equally, a state may disengage from some aspects of employment relations while extending its jurisdiction over other aspects. It is important to consider the modes of regulation open to a state, their scope, and their objectives. At certain times, states may regulate or deregulate as part of a strategy to promote economic development; at other times, regulation or deregulation may be prompted by a desire to restore a balance between employers and employees.

In other words, a range of factors bear upon the state in making its regulatory choices. The varying importance of each set of factors in different periods helps account for the particular and often contradictory mix of policies adopted by the state at different times.

However, states may also be constrained by what they or their predecessors have done before. Current policies reflect a dynamic interplay between what newly fashionable policy diagnoses see as desirable and what is possible within the constraints of existing institutions and procedures. Moreover, the state itself is not a unified structure. The government, the state bureaucracy, and specialist state agencies develop their own, sometimes diverse, interests in industrial relations. The eventual policy mix that is chosen often reflects a compromise among these different structures (Walsh, 1997).

We identify four areas of employment relations in which states must decide whether or not to regulate:

- the representation of employer and employee interests;
- the process by which employment conditions are determined;

- minimum terms and conditions of employment; and
- disputes over the application, interpretation or enforcement of the terms of their relationship.

We analyse the regulatory choices made by New Zealand in these policy areas. The critical issue is the degree to which the regulatory regime legitimises trade unions and facilitates membership recruitment, collective bargaining and union capacity to deliver satisfactory conditions of employment for their members. The other side of this coin is the degree to which a regulatory regime legitimises and facilitates effective employer resistance to the activities of trade unions. To understand this issue, we ask four questions about these regulatory choices:

- what philosophy underpinned the regulatory regime?
- what policy objectives did the state derive from this philosophical underpinning?
- what policies were implemented to achieve those objectives?
- what were the consequences of those policies?

We apply these questions to the four policy areas above in two contrasting regulatory regimes in New Zealand – the long period of the arbitration system which lasted from 1894 to 1991 and the decade of the Employment Contracts Act from 1991 to 2000. We conclude with a consideration of the implications of the current regime established by the Employment Relations Act which began in 2000.

## The arbitration regime

The regulatory system that governed industrial relations in New Zealand for almost a century was the arbitration system established by the Industrial Conciliation and Arbitration Act, 1894 (Holt, 1986). The arbitration system was underpinned by a moral philosophy which held not only that the labour market involves a significant inequality of power between employers and employees and corresponding potential for exploitation, together with an economic logic which held that an economy dependent on the exporting of goods to competitive international commodity markets had an interest in minimising industrial disruption and controlling the rate of wage increases. The policy objective derived from these beliefs was the state's obligation to redress inequality, minimise exploitation and ensure a stable industrial relations system which generated a competitive wage rate. The arbitration system was thus established as a distinctive form of labour market regulation which legitimised trade unions and facilitated their recruitment and negotiating capacity. However, the system imposed extensive constraints on the scope of trade union activity, thus reducing employer dissatisfaction. To ensure an acceptable level of wage increases, the system assigned responsibility for wage determination to a Court of Arbitration. This regulatory regime was not fundamentally challenged until the final quarter of the 20<sup>th</sup> century. The Act regulated employer and employee representation and the negotiation of employment conditions. The most important concession to unions was a guarantee of institutional security. The Act did not make union membership compulsory. Nor did case law permit the negotiation of closed shops. Rather, the Act encouraged the formation of trade unions by giving them a privileged role in the industrial relations system. The Act established a system of union registration and gave a registered union the exclusive right to bargain on behalf of workers. The Act required the formation of unions, required employers to negotiate with registered unions and provided compulsory arbitration by a Court of Arbitration to resolve unsettled negotiations. These constituted strong incentives for unions to be formed and for workers to join them, and the number of unions and their total membership grew sharply in the years following the passage of the Act (Holt, 1986).

The first Labour government, elected in 1935, further enhanced union institutional security. It made membership of a registered union compulsory for any worker covered by an award negotiated by the union. Union membership trebled between 1936 and 1938 as a direct result of compulsory membership. In 1961, a conservative National government abolished statutory compulsion, but permitted the negotiation of what were called unqualified preference clauses in which a worker was required to join the relevant union. This provision became negotiated in all awards and remained in place until 1991.

The second major concession to unions concerned bargaining. Registered unions secured exclusive rights to represent workers covered by their membership rule. They also gained exclusive access to compulsory bargaining forums (conciliation councils). An unsettled dispute was referred from the conciliation council to the Court of Arbitration which issued binding awards. Through this process, the state effectively guaranteed that union members would receive at least minimally acceptable conditions of employment. The third major concession to unions was a guarantee by the state that an award would apply to all employers of workers covered by the award. By virtue of this 'blanket coverage' provision, an award prescribed minimum employment conditions for all workers and employers in the occupation or industry concerned. This constituted one of the arbitration system's great attractions for unions since it meant they did not have to negotiate separately with each employer. In addition, the state not only required the universal application of an award, it also accepted responsibility for its enforcement.

The representation and negotiation systems established by the arbitration system constituted substantial concessions for unions. But they came at a high price (Walsh and Fougere, 1987). Compulsory membership and compulsory arbitration robbed many unions of their organisational vitality by eliminating the recruitment and negotiating challenges faced by union movements elsewhere. Unions were able to obtain a legally binding award, no matter how organisationally weak. Other aspects of the system reinforced their relative lack of vitality. The system of union registration set strict limits on a union's occupational and geographical jurisdiction and on the fees they could charge. This ensured that the New Zealand union movement was made up of hundreds of small, weak unions. Union dependence on the protections of the arbitration system meant that high levels of union density and collective bargaining coverage sat alongside relative industrial weakness on the part of the majority of unions.

The nature of this regulatory regime meant that the state was much less active in the other two key areas – the regulation of minimum conditions of employment and industrial disputes. It was expected that unions and employers would negotiate satisfactory employment conditions in their awards – and if they failed to do so, the Court of Arbitration would impose them. Consequently, for most of the twentieth century, only a limited range of legislation was enacted to prescribe minimum employment conditions. The state had accepted responsibility for occupational safety and health legislation from the 1890s, and during the 1930s and 1940s enacted legislation governing hours of work, holidays and the minimum wage. Even with as central an issue as the statutory minimum wage, successive governments believed that it was the responsibility of unions and employers to negotiate appropriate minimum rates in awards. In the 40 years following its enactment, the statutory minimum was rarely adjusted, and by the 1980s was considerably below the rates prevailing in awards.

During the 1960s and 1970s, the state's role in prescribing minimum employment conditions began to change. A new focus emerged on the provision of anti-discrimination legislation, while other legislation provided unpaid maternity leave with a guaranteed right of return to the workplace. These changes reflected an emerging social emphasis on individual rights and the development of feminism.

The arbitration system paid little attention to procedures to resolve employment disputes until the latter part of the twentieth century (Anderson, 1988). From 1905, all strikes and lockouts were illegal in the arbitration system and successive governments took the view that disputes procedures were therefore unnecessary. Instead the focus was on measures to punish unions for unlawful industrial activity. Penalties were increased over the years and the definition of strikes broadened to include progressively more forms of collective action. From 1939, the state also had the power to deregister a union. A deregistered union lost all its rights under the arbitration system, its awards and agreements were cancelled and a replacement union could be registered. Deregistration was applied sparingly, but was a highly effective weapon when it was used or threatened. Not until 1949 did the state accept the need for statutory procedures to resolve disputes, and those that were introduced were only *ad hoc* and not required to be included in awards. By the 1970s, however, industrial disputation had grown to an alarming degree, resulting in procedures being established to resolve employment disputes.

Thus, for nearly three quarters of a century, the regulatory regime established by the arbitration system achieved its objectives to a degree which successive governments found broadly satisfactory. The protections afforded to union activity and their high level of legitimacy meant that union members enjoyed acceptable conditions of employment while ensuring the worst forms of exploitation were prevented. Equally, the constraints imposed on which unions ensured a considerable degree of industrial stability, with intermittent but exceptional outbreaks being dealt with by the system's punitive measures (Bassett, 1972; Olssen, 1988). Employers were unhappy with the system. In an ideal world, they would have made significant changes to the system, but they were broadly, albeit grudgingly, satisfied (particularly the moderate levels of wage increases generated and the overall levels of industrial stability).

However, support for the arbitration system declined for a number of reasons in the latter part of the century. Of crucial importance was the loss of employer faith in the system and their growing willingness and capacity to challenge its legitimacy. As reluctant supporters, they did not relish the protections enjoyed by unions, but accepted them so long as the system delivered what it promised. By the 1970s and 1980s, it did not (Harbridge and Walsh, 2000). Those unions whose size and membership solidarity would have allowed them to succeed without the protections of the system capitalised on the long period of post-war prosperity to negotiate directly with employers. The result was a steep rise in industrial conflict, high levels of wage inflation and industrial disorder. Two other significant developments signalled the death-knell of the system.

A radical programme of economic deregulation initiated by the Labour government of 1984–90 generated even more pressure for the abolition of the arbitration system (Bollard and Buckle, 1987). The failure to deregulate the labour market was seen as inconsistent with the broader programme and as having the capacity to undermine it. In particular, it was argued that the continued determination of wages on an occupational basis without regard for the economic circumstances facing particular industries and firms was untenable in a deregulated economy. It was claimed that this limited the capacity of firms to respond flexibly to changing market conditions and that the industrial relations system was a key contributor to low productivity and high unemployment (New Zealand Business Roundtable, 1987).

Alongside economic deregulation, the rise of individualism and associated values challenged the continued existence of the arbitration system.

This was particularly focussed on opposition to compulsory union membership, but it extended to most of the collectivist principles inherent in the system. The Labour government made a number of changes in an effort to ensure the system's long-term survival. These included the abolition of compulsory arbitration but retained most key features (Walsh, 1989). The election of the conservative National government in 1990 heralded a radical shift.

## The contracting regime

Rarely has one labour market regulatory regime been replaced by another so fundamentally at odds with its predecessor. In 1991, the National government enacted the Employment Contracts Act (Anderson, 1991; Hince and Vranken, 1991). It and associated legislation formed a regulatory regime based on contracting. The philosophy underpinning it was that the labour market involves equal and freely contracting individuals and that the potential for exploitation is relatively low. The policy objectives derived from this philosophy were that the labour market should only be regulated to the extent necessary to provide an efficient contracting regime and to protect the capacity of individuals to operate effectively in the labour market. Antagonism to collective organisation and activity was central to this analysis. It is often claimed that this regime constituted total and unrelenting deregulation of the labour market. In fact, one regulatory regime replaced another. The new regime did remove the state from its regulation of some key features of the former regime and, in this sense, the new regime included deregulation. Equally, the state continued and extended its regulatory role in other areas. Accordingly, the 1990s saw a regime which removed the state from the regulation of representation and the negotiation of employment conditions, but extended the state's regulation of minimum conditions of employment and of disputes over the terms of employment contracts (Walsh and Ryan, 1993).

The vital shift from one regime to another was, firstly, that the new regime denied unions the legitimacy they had enjoyed under the arbitration system and, secondly, placed significant obstacles in the path of collective organisation and practice. The consequence was greatly heightened employer resistance to all aspects of union activity (Dannin, 1997). The denial of union legitimacy and the obstacles to collective organisation and practice were explicit in the ECA: unions no longer had official status in the industrial relations system. The premise of the Act was that the activities of trade unions had no greater public policy significance than those of any other voluntary society. The Act abolished the system of union registration and made the negotiation of any form of compulsory membership unlawful. By making union membership voluntary, the Act struck at the historical basis of union power in New Zealand. Employers were given the right to veto union access to a workplace for the purpose of recruiting members, although rights of access to discuss negotiations with members for whom the union had established authority to recruit were retained. Secondly, the Act abolished the complex regulatory web around the negotiation of employment conditions. No statutory procedures governed the negotiation of any contracts of employment. The blanket coverage provision was abolished, requiring unions to negotiate separately with individual employers. The Act gave employers the capacity to veto any attempt to negotiate multi-employer contracts by outlawing strikes to support multi-employer bargaining.

These legislative provisions posed significant difficulties for unions. These difficulties were compounded by the development of case law under the Act which allowed employers to pursue aggressive de-unionisation strategies (Dannin, 1997; Harbridge and Honeybone, 1996). Importantly, the Act imposed a higher standard for the courts to set aside employment contracts than for any other commercial contract. The normal contractual test of 'unfair' or 'unconscionable' contractual behaviour was replaced by the requirement that the contract must have been procured by 'harsh and oppressive behaviour'. The combined effect of legislative and judicial sanctioning of these approaches made for a bleak industrial landscape for unions and imposed severe impediments to effective collective organisation.

The consequences for unions were profound. With the shift from multi-employer to enterprise bargaining, they struggled to negotiate many times more separate contracts on behalf of fewer members and with less resources, against employers emboldened by the new legislative regime to seek harsh changes to employment conditions. Union membership fell precipitately (May et al., 2002). Total membership fell from 603,000 in 1991 to 302,000 in 1999 while union density fell from 52 per cent of wage and salary earners to 21 per cent. Union membership became heavily concentrated in a few industry sectors, with 74 per cent of members in public and community services, and manufacturing. Collective bargaining coverage fell from 50 per cent of the labour force to 25 per cent during the decade. Multi-employer bargaining which had dominated under the arbitration system collapsed. The consequences for workers of a gravely weakened union movement were equally profound. Unions were unable to resist employer determination to downgrade employment conditions. Radical changes were made to a wide range of employment conditions (Harbridge et al., 2001).

It was not only in representation and negotiation that the employment contracts regime differed. The new regime changed regulatory choices with regard to minimum employment conditions and the resolution of disputes. A pure application of a contracting model, in which free and equal individuals negotiate their employment conditions, would have led to the repeal of all existing legislation governing employment conditions. However, the National government did not do this. Instead, it continued and then extended the statutory regulation of minimum conditions of employment. A number of considerations influenced this. Firstly, recognising the inevitability of a significant fall in union membership and the associated potential for exploitation, the Government was unwilling to take the electoral risks associated with a pure contracting approach. Secondly, the Government placed great weight on the need to establish the appropriate framework for an efficient contracting regime. This required that the rules of engagement in the labour market gave individuals the security to operate effectively. The Government justified this as similar to the regulations governing the contracting regimes in other markets. Thirdly, the Government's commitment to individualist values led it to extend the trend towards the statutory provision of individual rights in the workplace.

At the enactment of the ECA, the Government placed great public emphasis on the existence of a minimum statutory code of employment which provided all workers with a range of entitlements that could not be undermined in any contract. The minimum code was not new, consisting almost entirely of existing legislation. The most important development in the statutory regulation of employment conditions lay in the provision of rights for individuals. The Health and Safety in Employment Act, 1992, while continuing an historical responsibility for workplace health and safety, had as an underlying philosophy the right of individual workers to a safe workplace. The Human Rights Act, 1993 considerably extended anti-discrimination legislation to prohibit employment discrimination on the grounds of age, political opinion, sexual orientation and family or employment status. The Privacy Act, 1993 established a set of principles governing the rights of individuals with regard to the use of information collected about them in the course of their employment (Crawford et al., 1998).

The employment contracts regime made radical changes in the fourth policy area under consideration – the resolution of employment disputes. As with the statutory provision of employment conditions, a pure contracting model would argue that no statutory disputes procedures were necessary and that the contracting parties would decide these for themselves. This was the position forcibly advocated by the major employer organisations and supported by the Treasury (Walsh and Ryan, 1993). This was rejected by the National government for the same reasons it rejected a purist model for the legislative provision of employment conditions. However, this left it with the question of the criterion to govern access to these procedures. Under the arbitration system, disputes and personal grievance procedures had been available only to union members employed under an award or collective agreement negotiated by a union. This could not be the criterion governing access to these procedures as the Act made no reference to the existence of unions. Since the Act applied to the negotiation of all employment contracts, its logic demanded its procedures for the resolution of disputes and personal grievances apply to all employment contracts. Consequently, the ECA required that all employment contracts must contain effective procedures to settle disputes. Thus, for the first time, all employees in New Zealand had access to compulsory state arbitration to resolve any dispute that arose in connection with their employment relationship. By any standard, this was a remarkable extension of the role of the state in industrial relations.

## The employment relations regime

The election of a Labour government in 1999 led to the introduction of a new regulatory regime in employment relations. Determined to do away with what it saw as the worst excesses of the employment contracts regime and to restore some balance to the industrial relations system, the new government enacted the Employment Relations Act in 2000 (Walsh and Harbridge, 2001). The focus is on employment relationships rather than employment contracts. The philosophy which underpins the new regime contains an important continuity with that of the arbitration regime by accepting that labour markets contain inherent potential for exploitation. However, it departs from both the arbitration and contracting regime by asserting that productive employment relationships can only be built on good faith behaviours. This imposes on the state an obligation to create a regulatory environment which promotes good faith behaviour in all aspects of the employment environment and by addressing the inherent inequality of bargaining power in employment relationships – by establishing an appropriate balance between the promotion of collective bargaining and the protection of the integrity of individual choice.

The new regime has made changes to the regulation of representation and negotiation, but few changes to the legislative provision of employment conditions or to the resolution of employment disputes. Regarding the resolution of employment disputes, the Act has made mediation the primary dispute resolution process while not changing the rules governing access. That the Labour government did not consider restoring the earlier provision whereby only union members had access to these provisions is an indication of the degree to which the climate of public opinion had shifted during the last decade.

The most important changes made by the ERA are with regard to representation and negotiation. The Act retains the voluntary membership provisions of the ECA. Labour judged that the decade of voluntary membership had established public opinion irrevocably in opposition to compulsion. It restores a system of union registration and confers upon registered unions the exclusive right to negotiate collective agreements. Those agreements cover union members only. The employer's veto right over union access to the workplace is eliminated. However, the blanket coverage bargaining provisions of the traditional award system are not restored, and there is no return to compulsory arbitration nor any compulsion to settle a collective agreement. The obstacles to multi-employer bargaining in the ECA are removed.

A key to the new regime is that unions are seen as legitimate, significant and positive institutions which can contribute to the achievement of important public policy objectives. The Act starts from the premise that employment relationships involve inherent inequality and that collective organisation by trade unions is the most effective way to redress this inequality. However, while removing many of the obstacles to effective collective organisation and practice, the new regime does not restore anything resembling the full range of protections unions enjoyed under the arbitration regime. Instead, the Act aims to level the industrial playing field and give unions the opportunity to repair some of the damage done to their movement during the last decade.

The available evidence suggests that unions have had only limited success in achieving this objective. Union membership has risen slightly from 302,000 to 330,000 but as a proportion of wage and salary earners, the increase is only from 21 to 22 per cent (May et al., 2002). Collective bargaining coverage has actually decreased, falling from 399,000 to 340,000 (Thickett et al., 2003). There is no evidence of unions restoring conditions of employment lost during the 1990s. Although it is less than three years since the enactment of the Employment Relations Act and a longer review period may see different trends, there is no doubt that unions would have expected to have achieved more in this period. It was also clear at the time of the Act's passage that employers had similar expectations. Their strong opposition to the Act is now considerably muted.

What accounts for the lack of change? With regard to union membership, some of the explanation lies in the continuing legacy of the employment contracts decade. The huge loss of membership has driven the resources of many unions down to a level where maintaining current levels of activity exhausts all available resources. Secondly, a decade has passed in which a generation of new workers entering the labour force simply did not consider joining the union, while a generation of new firms have been established without a union presence. Thirdly, more sophisticated human resource management has softened the edges of management practice and for many workers has weakened their sense of needing union protection. One consequence of the ERA has been to reduce free-riding. Under the previous ECA, by 2000, 27 per cent of those covered by a collective contract were not union members (Harbridge et al., 2002). The ERA seeks to prohibit this by assigning the exclusive right to negotiate collective agreements to registered unions and by limiting coverage to union members only. The intent behind this was to encourage non-members to join unions. The Act has been successful at reducing free-riding, not so much through increasing union membership but through reducing collective bargaining coverage.

## Conclusion

Different regulatory regimes in employment relations reflect a rethinking of the relationship between the state and civil society. Regulatory decisions pose sharply the most durable question of political economy, namely the relationship between states and markets. States and markets operate as two alternative, albeit almost always overlapping, modes of regulation. They are not mutually exclusive. At any one time, certain aspects of the employment relationship may be regulated by the state, while other aspects may be open to market influence. States do not decide to regulate or deregulate all aspects of employment relations. Instead, they make regulatory choices in certain policy areas which shape subsequent choices in other areas.

Our analysis suggests that in the New Zealand case, the principal driver of this process has been decisions about how to regulate representation and negotiation. Choices in these two areas are inextricably intertwined and make more likely certain choices in other areas. The highly prescriptive choices made under the arbitration regime with regard to representation and negotiation led the state to be far less prescriptive over minimum employment conditions and the resolution of industrial disputes. Regulation of these areas was considered to be less necessary since unions and employers were expected to resolve employment conditions in negotiation, while the unlawful status of industrial disputes encouraged a focus on penalties rather than resolution. In contrast, under the employment contracting regime, the absence of regulation of representation and negotiation encouraged the state to be more prescriptive in employment conditions and dispute resolution. The regulation of representation and negotiation under the employment relationship regime has so far been considerably less prescriptive than under either of its predecessors. As a result, it has not yet had to grapple with the need for fundamental change in the other two policy areas.

This analysis also shows the degree to which the emergence of different regulatory regimes in employment relations is grounded in wider social and economic changes. These give rise to different philosophies from which states derive new policy objectives. However, each regime grows out of its predecessor. Even as a new regime is established, the legacies of the earlier regime constrain present and future options. This, and the fact that regimes are designed by politicians mindful of the next election and not social or economic theorists, means that it is rare to encounter a regime driven by a wholly consistent set of principles. In New Zealand, the arbitration system tolerated a significant degree of bargaining outside the formal system while the contracting regime incorporated considerable state regulation of employment conditions and dispute resolution. The relationship regime continues almost unchanged key features of the employment contracts system, despite their radically different philosophical bases.

The fundamental issue in any employment relations regulatory regime is the degree to which it legitimises unions and facilitates collective organisation. The more it does this, the less the capacity of employers to resist union activity. The arbitration and contracting regimes adopted radically different systems of representation and negotiation. The arbitration regime legitimised unions and greatly facilitated their operation; the contracting regime did the reverse. The employment relationship regime does not go as far in either direction as its predecessors. It offers unions a degree of legitimacy and support for collectivism which was lacking under the employment contracting regime. However, it has not yet achieved the same degree of change that the other two regimes did in their early years.

Under both arbitration and contracts, the industrial relations landscape was recast in a very short period of time. Under the employment relationship regime, change has been much less dramatic in its first few years. This suggests that patterns of behaviour in industrial relations can become heavily embedded and resistant to change. Regardless of the degree of opposition to a regime when it is introduced, the impact on resources and, as a result, the strategic options open to the parties mean that the parties adjust to a new regime and map their structures and modes of operation onto it even while some continue to express their opposition to it. The introduction of a new regime does not change behaviour unless it also reallocates resources and thereby changes power relations to a degree that opens up new options.

In this lies the explanation for the limited change wrought under the employment relationship regime. By steering a middle ground between the arbitration and employment contracting regimes, the new regime does not effect the shift in resource allocation and power relations that is needed to make possible radically different strategic options for the parties. The issue for the current government is whether it is willing to contemplate the degree of change in its regulatory regime that would be required to achieve this.

Can New Zealand unions recover from their decimation of the last decade? While the re-legitimisation of unions, together with the reinstatement of institutional protection of collective bargaining, may contribute to some reversal in the rate of decline, it is unlikely to lead to any major reversal of the decline experienced over the last decade.

## References

Anderson, G. (1988) 'Strikes and the law: the problems of legal intervention in labour disputes'. *New Zealand Journal of Industrial Relations*, 13(1): 21–32.

Anderson, G. (1991) 'The Employment Contracts Act 1991: An Employer's Charter?' *New Zealand Journal of Industrial Relations*, 16(2): 127–142.

Bassett, M. (1972) *Confrontation '51: the 1951 Waterfront Dispute*, Reed, Wellington.
Bollard, A. and Buckle, R. (1987) *Economic Liberalisation in New Zealand*, Wellington, Allen and Unwin/Port Nicholson Press.
Crawford, A., Harbridge, R. and Walsh, P. (1998) 'Privacy legislation and its impact in the New Zealand workplace'. *Canadian Labour and Employment Law Journal*, 6(3): 387–420.
Dannin, E. (1997) *Working Free: The Origins and Impact of New Zealand's Employment Contracts Act*. Auckland: Auckland University Press.
Harbridge, R. and Honeybone, A. (1996) 'External Legitimacy of Unions: Trends in New Zealand'. *Journal of Labor Research*, 27(3): 425–444.
Harbridge, R. and Walsh, P. (2000) 'The Evolution of Collective Enterprise Bargaining in New Zealand'. *Labour and Industry*, 11(1): 1–22.
Harbridge, R., Thickett, G. and Kiely, P. (2001) *Employment Agreements: Bargaining Trends and Employment Law Update 2000/2001*, Wellington: Industrial Relations Centre, Victoria University of Wellington.
Harbridge, R, Walsh, P. and Wilkinson, D. (2002) 'Re-regulation and Union Decline in New Zealand: Likely Effects'. *New Zealand Journal of Industrial Relations*, 27(1): 65–77.
Hince, K. and Vranken, M. (1991) 'A Controversial Reform of New Zealand Labour Law: The Employment Contracts Act 1991'. *International Labour Review*, 130(4): 475–493.
Holt, J. (1986) *Compulsory Arbitration in New Zealand: The First Forty Years*. Auckland: Auckland University Press.
Hughes, J. (2000) 'Good faith and collective bargaining under the Employment Relations Bill'. *Butterworths Employment Law Bulletin*, April, pp. 53–60.
May, R., Walsh, P., Harbridge, R., and Thickett, G. (2002) 'Unions and union membership in New Zealand: annual review for 2001'. *New Zealand Journal of Industrial Relations*, 27(3): 307–322.
New Zealand Business Roundtable (1987) *Freedom at Work: Why New Zealand Needs a Flexible, Deregulated Labour Market*, Wellington, New Zealand Business Roundtable.
Olssen, E. (1988) *The Red Feds: Revolutionary Industrial Unionism and the New Zealand Federation of Labour 1908–1913*, Oxford University Press, Auckland.
Porter, M. (1990) *The Competitive Advantage of Nations*, Free Press, New York.
Thickett, G., Harbridge, R., Walsh, P. and Kiely, P. (2003) *Employment Agreements: Bargaining Trends and Employment Law Update 2002/2003*, Wellington: Industrial Relations Centre, Victoria University of Wellington.
Walsh, P. (1989) 'A family fight? Industrial relations reform under the fourth Labour Government'. In Easton, B. (ed.) *The making of Rogernomics*, Auckland: Auckland University Press, 149–170.
Walsh, P. (1997) 'From arbitration to bargaining: changing state strategies in industrial relations'. In Rudd, C. and Roper, B. (ed.) *The political economy of New Zealand*, Auckland: Oxford University Press, 183–201.
Walsh, P. and Fougere, G. (1987) 'The unintended consequences of the arbitration system'. *New Zealand Journal of Industrial Relations*, 17(3): 187–197.
Walsh, P. and Harbridge, R. (2001) 'Re-Regulation of Bargaining in New Zealand: the Employment Relations Act 2000'. *Australian Bulletin of Labour*, 27(1): 43–60
Walsh, P. and Ryan, R. (1993) 'The Making of the Employment Contracts Act'. In Harbridge, R. (ed.) *Employment Contracts: New Zealand Experiences*. Wellington: Victoria University Press.

# 6
# Crafting a Statutory Union Recognition Procedure that Works for the UK

*Stephen Wood and Sian Moore*

At least 700 Union recognition agreements were signed in the UK between 2001 and 2002, according to the records of the Trade Union Congress (TUC). This contrasts starkly with the 1990s, when throughout the whole decade the number was less than 100 per year. The signs of a reversal of fortunes for the trade unions became apparent in 2000 when the TUC recorded around 150 new agreements. This rise in voluntary recognitions suggests that the Labour Government's statutory recognition procedure, introduced under the Employment Relations Act in 2000 (ERA), is stimulating recognitions as the trade unions had hoped it would. The Department of Trade and Industry (2003: 28) in its Consultative Document on the Review of the Employment Act, which it published in February 2003, in fact used the evidence of a general rise in voluntary recognition agreements as the main support for its claim that 'the procedure is, overall, working well'. In this chapter we review the operation of the system in order to assess this conclusion.

We firstly introduce the procedure's objectives and background to it. Secondly, we outline the main features of the procedure; thirdly we describe key features of its operation so far, concentrating particularly on how employers have intervened in this; fourthly we discuss how far the statutory recognition process is being used as a last resort and is encouraging voluntary recognitions outside of the procedure. Finally, we assess how the intended changes outlined in the Government's review may help to overcome any problems.

## Introduction

The explicit objective of the Labour Government was not to promote recognition *per se*. It was in fact keen to appear not to be prejudging the value of trade unions, but rather to be seen to be allowing businesses choice in how they conduct employment relations and ensuring recognition is based on the preferences of the workforce. Its objectives were to design a procedure that would firstly 'provide for representation and recognition where a majority of the relevant workforce wants it' (Department of Trade and Industry, 1998: 23) and secondly encourage 'the parties to reach voluntary agreements wherever possible' (ibid.: 25), so that it would be used only when all attempts to reach a voluntary agreement had failed. The introduction of a statutory recognition procedure may nonetheless facilitate this if employers become more willing to sign agreements knowing that the alternative is union recognition imposed by the state.

The Government also had an explicit design objective that the procedure 'would work'. This reflected its concerns to avoid the failings of two earlier attempts at a statutory procedure (both in the 1970s), and particularly the problems that beset the second attempt under the Employment Protection Act (1975). Here the Arbitration and Conciliation Advisory Service (ACAS), the agency for implementing the recognition procedure, was given wide discretion over the criteria that it used to define bargaining units and award recognition, but had limited powers to test the workers' preferences or to force employers to cooperate with the procedure and bargain once an award of recognition had been made. This meant ACAS was unable to counter employer resistance to the procedure and was subject to judicial reviews that added to the employers' belief that they could, if they wished, successfully resist recognition. In the light of this, the reference to a procedure that 'would work' appears to mean a procedure that is acceptable to both sides of industry and robust against judicial review or employer tactics designed to undermine trade union support.

The design of the ERA procedure reflects lessons learnt from ACAS's involvement in the Employment Protection Act (EPA) procedure. Above all, it gives responsibility for the procedure to a revamped Conciliation and Arbitration Committee (CAC), with tighter specification of its powers and the criteria for making its decisions. In so far as the CAC is managing a procedure that is working, it shows that the regulation of employment relations can be improved by 'conscious' learning (Department of Trade and Industry, 2003: 27). The Government intends to continue this process by making some changes to the procedure in the light of experience thus far, as well as responses to their public consultations.

The Government also had aspirations that the Employment Relations Act – of which, the review tells us, the recognition procedure is the centrepiece – would 'change the culture of relations at work' (ibid.: 27). It was seen as 'part of the Government's programme to replace the notion of conflict between employers and employees with the promotion of partnership' (ibid.: 3). It is, however, one thing to design a procedure with the intention of minimising the parties' antagonism towards it; it is another to design one that can effect a qualitative change in the level of cooperation between employers, unions and workers. Union recognition procedures are dispute resolution methods, which take on relevance precisely because some employers are hostile to unions. Some commentators have even argued that they are unlikely to work in these terms and moreover, rather than reduce conflict, they will increase it. Adams (1993: 8), for example, has argued that their very existence generates adversarial relations, since union recognition is viewed as a vote of no confidence in management which heightens employer opposition towards unions and makes employees reticent about seeking recognition.

The main influence on the design of the procedures, however, was the desire to learn from other (past and present) systems, including North American ones, rather than the fostering of partnership. Key aspects of the design – particularly the involvement of employers in the process, the lengthy time periods to allow the parties to agree, and the rather minimal scope of bargaining that can be legally imposed – can be attributed to the desire to encourage voluntary settlements (Godard and Wood, 2000). The parties may even agree a voluntary arrangement whilst the claim is in the CAC procedure, and the union can withdraw it at any time up until the CAC has ordered a ballot. But the exercise of such 'voluntarism' is no guarantee of partnerships (Wood and Godard, 1999: 238–9). The ERA alone could not increase employer commitment to partnerships either with their employees directly or with unions. Nonetheless, at the time the ERA was introduced the possibility that the UK might be pioneering a genuine al-ternative to the antagonistic Wagner-based US system did not seem im-plausible. One of the authors, along with Godard (Godard and Wood, 2000: 68–9) offered this as one of four possible scenarios that followed from their analysis of the procedure prior to its implementation. The other three were (1) the legislation simply fails, as past attempts in the UK have done, because employer opposition to unions intensifies, (2) employers, through playing an active part in the recognition process, perceive unionism as less of a threat, but once recognition is imposed or even agreed they dilute the scope and impact of bargaining; (3) the law is sufficient to induce some marginal employers who are not strongly opposed to unionism to recog-nise a union and bargain meaningfully, but its impact is confined as those opposed to unionism will resist or continue to ignore it.

Our assessment will be aimed at whether the ERA procedure can be said to be achieving the Government's three core objectives and to have overcome the problems of other systems, and we will speculate about which of the above four scenarios seems to fit the UK experience thus far. The analysis will be based on the first three years of the procedure's operation (June 2000–May 2003), which is too short a period to judge fully the effects of the legislation. The number of applications has not been large, and it is in particular too soon to assess either the nature of the collective bargaining emerging from statutory recognition or the effectiveness of the procedure's enforcement mechanisms. But there have been sufficient cases – 233 distinct applications in the first three years – to give some indication of how employers are reacting to it, how the CAC is exercising its discretionary power, how the procedure is faring in the courts and against hostile employers, and whether it is stimulating voluntary recognition of unions.

Our study is based mainly on information on the cases that have gone through the ERA procedure. This has been gained from a survey of union officers about specific CAC cases (just under half of those so far), using both postal questionnaires and interviews, documents made publicly available on the web site of the CAC, observations of CAC hearings, and interviews with CAC officers and General Secretaries of major unions about details of the ERA procedure.

### The Statutory Trade Union Recognition Procedure under the Employment Relations Act: 2000–3

The key features of the ERA procedure, relative to the EPA procedure, are (a) the use of the CAC as the agency responsible for handling recognition claims and (b) its unambiguous criteria for the acceptance of applications and the subsequent granting of recognition. (For a full comparison between the two see Wood, 2000: 141–6.)

To trigger the new procedure, a trade union must formally approach the employer for recognition; if the employer rejects the request or fails to respond, the union may refer the case to the CAC. For such an application to be valid it must be made in writing, the union must be independent and the employer must employ at least 21 workers. The criteria for the acceptance of applications, being much tighter than under the EPA procedure, are that (a) at least ten per cent of the workers in the bargaining unit are union members, (b) there is not already a collective bargaining agreement covering some or all workers in the proposed bargaining unit, and (c) the CAC is satisfied that a majority of the workers in the bargaining unit are likely to be in favour of recognition. The requirement to demonstrate baseline support for the union before a claim can proceed was designed to deter insubstantial claims (Department of Trade and Industry, 1998: 24).

Once the application has been accepted, there is a 20-day period for the employer and union to agree the bargaining unit. If the parties are unable to reach an agreement, the bargaining unit will be determined by the CAC, with the main consideration being the need for the unit to be compatible with effective management. Other factors that the CAC has to consider include the views of the employer and union, existing national and local bargaining arrangements, the desirability of avoiding small fragmented bargaining units, and the characteristics and location of workers. If the bargaining unit decided by the CAC or agreed by the parties differs from that proposed by the union, the application must be reconsidered against the acceptance criteria.

Where a majority of the bargaining unit are not union members, the CAC will order a ballot. If the union has a majority of the bargaining unit in membership, the CAC may grant recognition without a ballot. The CAC may, however, still order a ballot when:

(1) it deems that it is 'in the interests of good industrial relations' (Trade Union and Labour Relations (Consolidation) Act, 1992 (TULR(C)A), Schedule, A1, para 22(4) (a)) to hold a ballot;
(2) it is informed by a significant number of union members that they do not wish the union to represent them for collective bargaining; or
(3) it has evidence that leads it to doubt that a significant number of union members want the union to bargain on their behalf.

Where a ballot is ordered, the union is entitled to have access to the workforce and there are legal duties on the employer to cooperate in the conduct of the ballot. The union must secure a majority in favour of recognition, but also the support of at least 40 per cent of the workers in the bargaining unit. If recognition is granted, the parties are expected to reach agreement on a method for conducting collective bargaining. If they are unable to reach an agreement, the CAC may assist and ultimately determine a legally enforceable bargaining procedure that is limited to pay, hours and holidays. Adherence to this imposed procedure is enforced by an order of specific performance, in which non-compliance means contempt of court with the possibility of unlimited fines and imprisonment.

## The operation of the Statutory Recognition Procedure, 2000–3

### Employer intervention in the Statutory Recognition Procedure

The procedure has scope for employers to influence the outcome of the statutory process and employers have sought to control the CAC's use of its discretion so that the procedure operates to their advantage. There are three points where employers may seek to exert influence; firstly at the admissibility stage, in particular with regard to the demonstration of majority support for recognition; secondly they may contest the bargaining unit; and thirdly they may seek to persuade the CAC that there should be a ballot. Employers may give evidence to the CAC on their perception of the likely support for trade unionism. In some cases, they have organised their own ballots or surveys of the workforce in order to question majority support. Employers have also sought to gain the names of the union members and supporters, the implication being that they would act in some way on this information. The CAC has resisted this and has developed a means of conducting a check on the membership by obtaining the names of union members from the union and of workers in the proposed bargaining unit from the employer (Central Arbitration Committee, 2002: 11).

The CAC has in fact been flexible in its approach to judging the likely support for collective bargaining. It has made its decisions on the basis of the level of membership, letters or petitions by the workers in question, or a recent ballot of the workforce. An application where membership was as low as 16 per cent has been accepted, while one with 67 per cent has been rejected, the latter on the grounds that although ten of a bargaining unit of 15 were union members, seven had written to the CAC opposing recognition for collective bargaining (*GMB and Trafford Park Bakery* TUR1/153/[2002]). Our analysis, however, suggests that applications where existing union membership is less than 35 per cent are not likely to be accepted unless other convincing evidence is provided, and that the CAC has also been flexible in its use of this other evidence, for example by allowing for the difficulty the union has had in gaining access to the workforce.

Another area where there is scope for employer intervention is the determination of the bargaining unit. Here employers have sought to dilute formal support for the union by expanding the bargaining unit into areas where union support is likely to be lower. The CAC has, however, been supportive of the union's proposed bargaining unit in the majority of cases where it has been disputed. The CAC has needed to determine the appropriateness of a bargaining unit in 51 (47%) of the cases that had reached the bargaining unit stage in the first three years, as there was no agreement between the parties on what it should be. It supported the union's proposed unit or a variant of it in 34 (67%) of these. In all but six of the 51 cases (88%) where the employer has attempted to challenge the union's application, it has proposed an expanded bargaining unit based on including either more occupations or sites than were in the original application. Nonetheless, in 23 of the 32 cases where the employer has sought to include more occupations, the CAC resisted this argument on the basis that the terms and conditions of the occupational group proposed were distinctive and accepted the original unit.

Our research suggests that the main problem for unions has been when an employer operating on more than one site has sought to extend the bargaining unit beyond the single site upon which the union's submission is based. In five of 13 cases the CAC has ruled that the bargaining unit should embrace workers sharing the same distinct terms and conditions on all sites in the organisation, while in one other the CAC included another workplace but proposed a new bargaining unit differing in occupational terms. In five of these six cases, the union could not subsequently demonstrate sufficient support for recognition amongst the workers on the other sites that the CAC included in the revised bargaining unit (the sixth had at the time of writing not been revalidated). The application was thus either ruled by the CAC as no longer valid; withdrawn by the union; or failed, as a majority did not vote for recognition in a ballot. In the one case where the union supported a company-wide bargaining unit but the company argued for fewer sites to be included, the CAC ruled in favour of the union. In these multi-site cases the difficulties for unions could be insurmountable, with the result that the procedure is confined in practice to employers operating in a single location where bargaining units remain as now, small.

Since ballots represent an area of uncertainty for unions there is an incentive for the employer to attempt to persuade the CAC to use its discretion to order a ballot where the union has a majority in membership, or to undermine the union's majority while a case is in the procedure so the CAC is bound to order a ballot. Ballots have been held predominantly because the union did not have a majority of the bargaining unit in membership on application. Nonetheless, 18 of 64 ballots (28%) have been held in cases where the union was verified by the case manager through a membership check as having a majority in membership on application to the CAC (Table 6.1). Of these, four were ordered because changes to the bargaining unit (either agreed or determined by the CAC) meant that membership was then below 50 per cent. In three other cases, the union submitted that it did not want to claim recognition without a ballot.

The first criterion ('in the interests of good industrial relations') has been invoked in five cases. For example at *GPMU and Red Letter Bradford Ltd*, TUR 1/12[2000], where relations between the union and the employer had been poor, a ballot was justified as an opportunity to

*Table 6.1*   CAC ballots and reasons for balloting where Union had more than 50 per cent on application

| Reason for ballot | Ballot won | Ballot lost | Total |
|---|---|---|---|
| **Union had 50 per cent plus on application** | | | |
| In the interests of good industrial relations | 4 | 1 | 5 |
| CAC was informed by a significant number of union members that they did not wish the union to represent them | 0 | 1 | 1 |
| CAC has evidence which led it to doubt that a significant number of union members want the union to bargain on their behalf | 1 | 0 | 1 |
| Union agrees to a ballot | 1 | 2 | 3 |
| Change to bargaining unit means union membership fell below 50 per cent | 1 | 3 | 4 |
| Union membership fell below 50 per cent | 1 | 3 | 4 |
| Total | 8 (44%) | 10 (56%) | 18 |
| **Union did not have 50 per cent on application** | 33 (72%) | 13 (28%) | 46 |
| TOTAL | 41 (64%) | 23 (36%) | 64 |

*Source*: CAC web site, www.cac.gov.uk.

'clear the air'. The second criterion (that a significant number of union members inform the CAC that they do not want the union to represent them in collective bargaining) was invoked in *UNIFI and Türkiye IS Bankasi A.S.*, TUR1/90[2001], when three members of the union wrote to the CAC stating that they did not want the union to conduct collective bargaining on their behalf, although the union alleged that this was done under pressure. The third criterion has been invoked in two cases, where the CAC did not consider that the evidence of membership confirmed that a significant number of workers in the bargaining unit wanted recognition.

In four cases, the CAC has ordered ballots when there has been an apparent decline in the number of union members from the time when the application was made to a level below 50 per cent. The reasoning is that the requirement for the CAC to be satisfied that a majority of the workers in the bargaining unit are members of the union (paragraph 22(1)(b) of the Schedule) is worded in the present tense. Thus what matters for the CAC is whether the union has a majority in membership at the time it takes the decision on whether to hold a ballot or grant recognition without a ballot.

When ordering a ballot where 50 per cent of the workforce is in membership, the CAC also appears to have been influenced by the employer's arguments. In *TGWU and Economic Skips Ltd*, TUR1/121[2001], one of the reasons for ordering a ballot was 'the sincerely held view of the employer that the majority of the workers in the bargaining unit did not want recognition'. Ordering a ballot gives the employer an opportunity to influence its outcome that it would not otherwise have. Ballots have been lost in 56 per cent of all the cases where the union had a majority of members when the case entered the procedure, which compares with a 28 per cent failure rate for those where the union did not have the majority.

Finally, we have also observed tactics that suggest a strategy of opposition to the spirit of the process. Two stand out:

(1) legalism, whereby the employer – with legal assistance, in some cases from US-owned legal firms – identifies and exploits technical legal points as a strategy of opposition;
(2) litigation, whereby the employer challenges the CAC at every step, from the judgement about admissibility to the form of the ballot.

The minimum effect of these approaches is to lengthen the case and to add to the costs for the union (for more detail see Ewing et al., 2003: 42–9). The maximum effect is that the union is defeated on some technicality, as in *GPMU and Keeley Print*, TUR1/98[2001], where it was ruled as a matter of law that a director is not a worker with the result that the employer did not have 21 workers. The CAC is relatively powerless to do anything about such tactics: there is little that it can do but deal with the points raised if employers (or unions) who have chosen to be represented by counsel raise technical arguments about the meaning of a 'worker', of a 'trade union member', or of an 'associated employer'. This is even so when these points may result in the termination of an application that, if tested, would have the support of the majority of the workforce.

The extreme of litigation is when the employer challenges the CAC's decision in the courts and seeks a judicial review (there is no appeals procedure). Four applications for judicial review were made in the first three years, and, of these, employers made three and a trade union the other one (CAC, 2002: 18). Two cases were refused leave to be heard and two were heard.

The first judicial review to be heard, *Fullerton Computer Industries Ltd v CAC* [2001] IRLR 752, dealt with several concerns, including the refusal of the CAC to order a ballot where the union had only a slender majority of the bargaining unit (51.3%) in membership – this being done on the grounds that a ballot 'would engender further antagonism and divisiveness detrimental to developing good industrial relations' (TUR1/29[2000]). The court did not challenge this decision, despite the fact that it recorded that it 'would have been inclined to take the view that a ballot has a stabilising influence and might well improve industrial relations rather than to cause them to deteriorate' (p. 745).

The second case involved the CAC's determination of a bargaining unit. In this case, *Kwik-Fit* challenged the CAC's rejection of its proposal for a single unit covering the whole country in favour of the union's proposal for a unit defined as being within the boundary of the London orbital road (the M25). In reaching this decision, the CAC drew attention to the fact that, under the legislation, it is 'not required to decide on the most effective form of management, merely that what we decide is compatible with effectiveness' (TUR1/126 [2002]). This latter approach was endorsed by the Court of Appeal which pointed out that in determining the bargaining unit, 'the statutory test is set at the comparatively modest level of appropriateness, rather than the optimum or best possible outcome' ([2002] IRLR 396). But the appeal judgement stressed that this does not mean that the CAC can confine itself to the union's arguments since it has to consider alternative bargaining units to the extent that these are a part of the employer's argument. But once the CAC decides that the union's proposed unit is appropriate, 'its inquiry should stop there'.

The two judicial cases that have been heard have endorsed the way that the CAC has been operating. The Court of Appeal in *R (Kwik-Fit (GB) Ltd) v CAC* [2002] IRLR 395 approved in 'strong terms' the view that 'the CAC was intended by Parliament to be a decision-making body in a specialist area, that is not suitable for the intervention of the courts' (p. 396), a view which is very different from the unsympathetic response of the courts to the EPA procedure.

## Employer behaviour in the workplace

The procedure also allows employers to put their case against the union to the workforce in order to influence the outcome, and places few constraints on this. A Code of Practice outlines the employer's general duty to cooperate with the union during the ballot period and the minimum provisions for access during the ballot, encourages the parties to avoid acrimonious situations, and explains the kind of behaviour that is not acceptable. In two cases that we observed where the ballot was lost, an oppositional employer was able to limit the access that the union actually had to the workforce during the balloting period relative to what was agreed ahead of it. The CAC can impose recognition where the employer has failed to comply with its duty to cooperate during the ballot, without the need for a ballot to be held. But no such order has been either granted or contemplated.

There are also provisions in Part VIII of the statutory procedure that make it unlawful to subject workers to detriment or employees to dismissal for recognition-related activities. Beyond this there is no regulation of employer behaviour before the ballot period, and while the employer has access to the workforce at all times, unions have access to the workforce only during the balloting period.

In a number of cases, it appears that the employer has genuinely wanted to test majority support for recognition through the procedure and not to interfere with the process. In contrast a minority of employers have invested substantial resources to defeat union support in the workplace. In the first three years of the procedure unions lost over a third of ballots (36%). In just under a third of ballots, (20 of 64), union support was lower than union membership was at the outset and, in some of these cases, this may have been accounted for by employer behaviour after the application was made or in the ballot period. Employers in CAC ballots have used the type of anti-union tactics reported in U.S. National Labor Relations Board elections (see for example Bronfenbrenner and Juravich, 1998: 22–3), including the use of supervisors to convey employer opposition; one-to-one communication between managers and employees about the implications of recognition; captive audience meetings; victimisation and dismissals of activists; redundancies involving union members; and threats to relocate production or close the workplace.

In our survey of CAC cases, we found that, where there have been ballots, 51 per cent of employers used at least two of these anti-union tactics and that there is a significant relationship between the use of these tactics and the outcome of the ballot. In 86 per cent of unsuccessful ballots employers had adopted at least two tactics compared to under a third of successful ballots. The dismissal of union activists has an especially strong impact on union campaigns; unions won only one of the eight ballots where this occurred. In some cases unions have sought redress, but any resolution has come long after the recognition campaign was dead. Similarly employer one-to-ones and captive audience meetings have significantly lowered the proportion voting for recognition in ballots. Threats to relocate or close the workplace do not have a significant effect on ballot outcomes, but case studies of a number of the ballots suggest this is because there is variation in how explicit and how credible workers perceive such threats to be (Moore, 2004). In the case of broadcasting union BECTU and Sky Subscriber Services the threat to relocate production was extremely credible and was key to the union losing the ballot.

## The results of the Statutory Recognition Procedure: voluntary and CAC-ordered recognition

Our research suggests that the CAC procedure has encouraged the voluntary resolution of disputes and has been used as a last resort. First, unions have carefully managed CAC applications, and our two surveys of union headquarters in both 2000 and 2003 confirmed that they do not intend to submit them without first having secured a base of members and exhausted all attempts to reach a voluntary agreement. The union's approach is reflected in the high proportion of voluntary settlements relative to CAC cases. TUC data (Table 6.2) shows that the number of new voluntary recognition agreements from 1995 to 2000 was never above 100 per year, while after the ERA it was at 443 in the year November 2000–October 2001 with a further 264 between November 2001 and October 2002.

The pattern of ACAS conciliation cases involving recognition disputes shows a similar picture. The number of cases peaked in 1979 at 697 and declined steadily to a low of 93 in 1994. There was a gradual increase from then on, with a substantial increase in 2000, taking the figure

*Table 6.2*  Voluntary recognitions: 1995–2002

| Period | Number of new agreements | Average/month |
|---|---|---|
| July 1995–December 1995 | 54 | 9.0 |
| January 1996–June 1996 | 54 | 9.0 |
| July 1996–December 1996 | 56 | 9.3 |
| January 1997–June 1997 | 26 | 4.3 |
| July 1997–February 1998 | 55 | 6.9 |
| March 1998–November 1998 | 34 | 3.8 |
| December 1998–October 1999 | 75 | 6.8 |
| November 1999–October 2000 | 159 | 13.3 |
| November 2000–October 2001 | 443* | 36.9 |
| November 2001–October 2002 | 264* | 22 |

* Excludes all cases that either were decided by the statutory procedure or through voluntary means having been initially in the procedure.
*Source*: TUC (2002).

beyond 200 for the first time since 1985, followed by an even greater increase in 2001, when 339 cases were recorded, a figure that was maintained in 2002 when there were 330 cases. Moreover, the proportion of ACAS cases where recognition for collective bargaining was achieved has increased substantially since the early 1990s. From a low of 21 per cent in 1992 (when ACAS handled 148 cases) the proportion of ACAS's conciliation cases that involved recognition was around 50 per cent each year between 1996 and 1999; in 2000 it was 70 per cent; in 2001, 66 per cent, and in 2002, 57 per cent.

While the TUC and ACAS data suggest that the ERA has stimulated voluntary recognition agreements, the key question for evaluating the ERA procedure is whether the voluntary route has dominated over the statutory so *de facto* the CAC is being used as a last resort. The number of applications to the CAC made in the first three years of the procedure has been small. Of the 233 distinct applications, 205 cases have been decided or withdrawn; of these 64 resulted in statutory recognition and in a further 59 cases the application was withdrawn at some stage because the employer and the union reached a voluntary agreement or desired to enter into voluntary discussion. A comparison of this use of the CAC procedure with that of the ACAS facilities confirms that the voluntary route has been used more than the legal route and this suggests that the latter has been used as a last resort. We can conclude that overall CAC cases represent no more than 21 per cent of all recognition disputes that involved a government agency. Similarly, we estimate that CAC cases represented 12 per cent of new recognitions reported to the TUC during the two-year period between November 2000 and October 2002.

## The consultative document on the review of the Employment Relations Act

In the Government's review of the ERA no changes were envisaged to the basic approach and key features of the procedure. So calls from trade unions, for example, to allow workers in small firms access to the procedure or to eliminate the thresholds in ballots have been rejected. The Government will clarify that pensions shall not be regarded as 'pay' for the specific purposes of the procedure for the present time; but the Government will add pensions to the three core topics when there is evidence that they are typically included as a bargaining topic in recognition agreements.

The main problems that we have identified – the issue of bargaining units in multi-site firms, the CAC's use of its discretion to order a ballot even though 50 per cent of the workforce is or was in union membership, and employer influence over both the CAC and workers' decisions – were discussed in the Consultation Document. First, in the light of the *Kwik-Fit* judicial review the Government proposes to clarify the statute to make clear that the employer's comments on the union's proposed bargaining unit and any counter proposal are taken into account in determining whether the union's proposal is compatible with the statutory criteria. On the one hand, this change could be viewed as simply formalising the current CAC practice since the judicial review judgement made it clear it could not confine itself to the union's arguments. On the other hand, it could be seen as tightening the procedure by making it clear to the CAC that it has to consider the employer's views when assessing compatibility with business necessities. The former may suggest that the CAC may not be so inclined to extend the bargaining unit if the employer seeks it in a 'multi-site' case. While the latter may mean that the arguments about the 'multi-site' nature of the business may still hold sway in gauging compatibility with 'effective management', so the CAC decisions in 'multi-site' cases may not change greatly. Since the *Kwik-Fit versus CAC* judgement, the picture has been mixed. The CAC has upheld three bargaining units based upon one region of companies with wider geographical bases (*GMB and Volvo Truck and Bus*, TUR1/223/[2002]; *TGWU and Grosvenor Casinos Ltd*, TUR1/188/[2002] and *TSSA and Culina Logistics*, TUR1/236[2002]). In another case (*TSSA and Airmiles Travel Promotion Ltd*, TUR1/195[2002]), it determined that the bargaining unit include two call centres, rather than the one that formed the basis of the union's application.

Second, the possibility of abandoning the qualifications which allow the CAC to order ballots in cases where the union has over 50 per cent of the membership was discussed but rejected by the review. So too was the employers' suggestion that there should be a ballot whenever the employer requests one. The review gauged that the existing discretion that the CAC has in this area has value and has been exercised appropriately. There was no mention, however, of the key problem that we have identified: the way the CAC has ordered ballots when there has been an apparent decline in the number of union members from the time when the application was made to a level of below 50 per cent. This is an area of concern for trade unions, since union membership can be fragile and sensitive to labour turnover, redundancies, and employer pressures and intimidation. In Canada votes are expedited to avoid this, and a union may be legally recognised if it is determined that employer intimidation prevented a union from reaching or maintaining majority support. There is a similar provision in the USA, although labour unions must establish that they did at some point have majority support. Since the reasoning of the CAC is that its requirement to be satisfied that a majority of the workers in the bargaining unit are members of the union (paragraph 22(1)(b) of the Schedule) is worded in the present tense, what matters for the CAC is whether the union has a majority in membership at the time it takes the decision on whether to hold a ballot or grant recognition without a ballot. It would be helpful if the statute were rephrased to allow for the final membership check to be at an earlier point, e.g. at the time of acceptance of the application. The continuation of the 'in-the-interests-of-good-industrial-relations' qualifying condition (on granting recognition without a ballot) would still permit the CAC to order a ballot were it to consider that union membership had fallen significantly.

Third, the Government made one proposal that has some bearing on the problem of employers being able to influence employees' choices throughout the process. It proposes to give the union a legal right to access to the workers at an earlier stage than the ballot. The proposed access is from the day the CAC accepts the union's application but it will be only through a postal communication mediated by a third party such as a Qualified Independent Person, the designation of the agent who supervises the ballot. The review did, however, invite views on whether communication should be extended to include electronic systems. While the current provision of union access to the workforce only during the balloting period is widely seen by unions as restrictive, the proposal to allow them access through a postal communication, via a third party, is minimalist. A communication via e-mail would extend it. But access, whether via the post or e-mail, through a third party gives little opportunity for dialogue between the union and workers or for the union to understand the workers' desires.

Our analysis of ballot results demonstrates the influence that employers can have on workers either through direct contact or through their supervisors, and that such personal contact can begin well before the official balloting period. In fact the impact of the employer's behaviour prior to the ballot period may be such that the employer is in a position to appear relatively neutral in the balloting period and to step back from engaging in anti-union campaigns. The current access arrangements allow the parties to develop their preferred methods and the same principles which underlie them might be extended to any access arrangements beyond the ballot period. Consideration should be given to bringing forward the timing of the negotiations on access to the point when the application is accepted.

Extending the access arrangements does not, however, go far enough in meeting directly the problems of employer intimidation and other practices designed to reduce support for the union. This was to some extent recognised in the review (Department of Trade and Industry, 2003: 56) when it acknowledged that the TUC has proposed defining unfair labour practices and ensuring that they are outlawed. The review did not dismiss this completely but noted that there are difficulties defining 'unfair labour practices in such as way as to allow the employer to undertake reasonable campaigning activity in favour of its preferred solution' and that there are questions about whether workable sanctions can be devised.

If consideration were to be given to an unfair labour practice provision, which we concede is probably the only way of addressing this problem, the code of practice already provides some basis for defining these practices. In effect making the provision would be largely a matter of transforming the code into a statutory regulation. However, the provisions would need to extend beyond the balloting period to apply from the time the application is made. We are unsure why the existing sanction for non-cooperation with the procedure – i.e. the CAC's ability to impose recognition on an employer – was not deemed appropriate. The North American experience may again be relevant here as in both Canadian and US jurisdictions, unfair labour practices are defined in statutory and case law and are normally subject to either a 'cease and desist' or a 'make whole' order, the violation of which may ultimately lead to a contempt of court finding, with possible criminal remedies. In Canada, unfair labour practices may, in extreme cases, also be subject to criminal prosecution without a contempt finding.

## Conclusions

Our analysis of the first three year's operation of the CAC's procedure suggests that, within the terms of the Government's initial objectives, it is a qualified success. On the one hand, the procedure is providing a right for union recognition in the majority of cases where more than 50 per cent of the workforce wants it – 60 per cent of the completed cases passing through the CAC procedure have resulted in recognition or discussions on recognition. It is also seemingly encouraging the voluntary resolution of disputes and being used only as a last resort. The 1970's EPA procedure was bedevilled by unanticipated problems, and learning from this experience has been crucial for the design of the ERA procedure. There are signs that this learning has not been misplaced and that the procedure does seem more robust than the earlier one. Godard and Wood's third scenario, that the ERA would have some impact, perhaps comes closest to the experience so far. This impact is limited as the size of the bargaining units, at least in CAC cases, has tended to be small (of the 193 cases where we have information, the median unit proposed had 93 workers) and they have tended to be in a limited number of industrial sectors. The situation resembles the 1970s in that both applications and successful cases have been in manufacturing and other areas, such as in transport, print and newspapers, where trade unions traditionally have had a strong presence. Union membership has continued to decline – TUC membership by 0.05 per cent in 2001 and 0.07 per cent in 2002 – but we estimate that the decline would have been between 1.5 or 2.0 percentage points higher in the period 2000–2002 were it not for the new recognitions.

On the other hand, the experience of the first three years has highlighted problems with the procedure and its operation that may be constraining the right to recognition. The failure rate in ballots of 36 per cent reflect these problems and is not insignificant, especially given that the cases where ballots are held will have all have passed the CAC's majority support test. The procedure does little to constrain adversarial employer intervention or employer hostility in the workplace; consequently a number of CAC cases, and particularly ballots have been highly conflictual. The core problem remains: that the antagonism of some employers to unionism and more particularly to any state procedure designed to provide a legal right for trade union representation (providing certain conditions have been met) may reduce the procedure's effectiveness. If we are to continue the learning from experience in which the ERA procedure was rooted, our analysis suggests that the next stage in the evolution of union recognition policy is the designation of certain employers' practices as unfair labour practices. Learning from Canadian and US experience may well be vital for this.

## References

Adams, R. (1993) 'The North American model of employee representational participation: "a hollow mockery"', *Comparative Labor Law Journal*, 15 (4): 4–14.

Bronfenbrenner, K. and Juravich, T. (1998) 'It Takes More Than House Calls: Organizing to Win with a Comprehensive Union-building Strategy', in Bronfenbrenner, K., Friedman, S., Hurd, R., Oswald, R. and Seeber, R. (eds), *Organizing to Win: New Research on Union Strategies*, Ithaca: ILR Press, pp. 19–36.

Central Arbitration Committee (2002) *Annual Report 2001/2*, London: Central Arbitration Committee.

Department of Trade and Industry (1998) *Fairness at Work*, Cm. 3968, London: Stationery Office.

Department of Trade and Industry (2003) *Review of the Employment Relations Act 1999*, London: Department of Trade and Industry.

Employment Protection Act (1975) London: Stationery Office.

Employment Relations Act (2000) London: Stationery Office.

Ewing, K. D., Moore, S. and Wood, S. (2003) *Unfair Labour Practice: Trade Union Recognition and Employer Resistance*, London: Institute of Employment Rights.

Godard, J. and Wood, S. (2000) 'The British Experiment with Labour Law Reform: An Alternative to Wagnerism', in *Proceedings of the 52nd Annual Meeting of the Industrial Relation Research Association*, Madison (WI): IRRA, pp. 61–76.

Moore, S. (2004) 'Union Mobilization and Employer Counter-Mobilization in the Statutory Recognition Process', in Kelly, J. and Willman, P. (eds), *Union Organisation and Activity*, London: Routledge, pp. 7–31.

Trades Union Congress (2002) *TUC Trends: Focus on Recognition*, London: Trade Union Congress.

Wood, S. and Godard, J. (1999) 'The Statutory Union Recognition in the Employment Relations Bill: A Comparative Analysis', in *British Journal of Industrial Relations*, 37(2): 203–44.

Wood, S. (2000) 'Learning through ACAS: The case of Union Recognition', in Towers, B. and Brown, W. (eds), *Employment Relations in the UK: Britain's Advisory Conciliation and Arbitration Service 1974–2000*, Oxford: Basil Blackwell, pp. 123–52.

# 7
# Conservative Legislation and Trade Union Change

*Graeme Lockwood*

## Introduction

Conservative administrations from 1979 onwards challenged the traditional autonomous approach of trade union organisation by attempting to impose a prescriptive model for conducting the internal affairs of trade unions. The Conservative model sought to increase the influence of individual members in four specific areas: a) election of senior officials b) the creation and / or maintenance of political funds, c) industrial action d) the enforcement and regulation of internal trade union affairs. The expectation was that the empowerment of the individual member would result in more moderate decision-making. This chapter draws on empirical data gathered from an in depth analysis of seven trade unions: Transport and General Workers Union (TGWU), Electrical, Electronic Telecommunications and Plumbing Union (EETPU, now part of AMICUS), Civil and Public Services Union (CPSA, now part of the Public and Commercial Services Union (PCSA), Associated Society of Locomotive Engineers and Firemen (ASLEF), Rail and Maritime Trade Union (RMT), Bakers Food and Allied Trade Union (BFAWU) and National Association of Teachers in Further and Higher Education (NATFHE). The research also involved the execution of 101 interviews which included trade union officials, members, the Commissioner for the Rights of Trade Union Members (CROTUM), the Certification Officer (CO) and the Deputy General Secretary of the Trade Union Congress.

## Union elections

The legislative provisions relating to union elections were particularly significant since previously no external ground rules had ever existed as far as internal union elections were concerned (Deakin and Morris, 1998). Prior to the introduction of the legislation the election of senior officials varied substantially across the union movement. The legal provisions standardised the way in which the national executive committee (NEC) and general secretary were elected in all the case study unions' except for one. One union decided not to comply with the legislative requirements. To date the union has remained unchallenged. The majority of case study unions felt they had no alternative other than to jettison their traditional electoral practices and procedures however representative and democratic, in favour of the Conservative model.

The requirement to hold secret postal ballots for the election of senior officials has meant that in ASLEF, TGWU, RMT, NATFHE and the CPSA certain activists, groups and committees have been divested of the power, control and influence they traditionally held over such decisions. This right of decision making has now been transferred to the wider membership. However, whilst the legislation caused specific, substantive changes to union constitutions, it is evident that the legal provisions did not necessarily produce more moderate decision-making by the membership (Undy et al., 1996).

In respect to the results of union elections, it is evident that in ASLEF and the RMT there have been significant shifts to the left of the political spectrum. In the TGWU and BFAWU the status quo has been maintained with the left retaining control. In NATFHE and the CPSA moderate groupings emerged as the controlling group. There is evidence from ASLEF, the RMT and TGWU that the role of left wing activists and groups has changed in a complex manner. The requirement to hold secret ballots for the election of senior officials meant that although certain activists groups and committees have been divested of their power to determine the general secretary and the composition of the NEC they have been influential through other means (Undy et al., 1996).

### Political fund

The Trade Union Act, 1984 compelled trade unions with political funds to hold a 'review ballot' every ten years if they wish to retain them. In both 1985/8 and 1993/8, the union movement united and set up the Trade Union Co-ordinating Committee (TUCC). This duly orchestrated the highly successful campaigns that enabled unions (with the exception of the CPSA in 1997) to retain political funds (Grant, 1987; Grant and Lockwood, 1998; Leopold, 1986; Leopold, 1997 and 1999).

The political funds review ballots, procured some unexpected results for the Conservatives. It did not lead to moderate members voting against unions having political funds. In 1985/88, the case study unions mounted a well organised campaign on the political funds issue, with the result that they all held successful retention ballots. This was despite the fact that opinion polls published at the time of the initial round of political funds ballots held in 1985 indicated that in the majority of cases unions would fail to retain their funds. It was suggested that members would vote against retention because many of them were not trade union activists. Nor did it seem likely that they would vote to retain a fund that appeared to bankroll the Labour Party – a party that fewer than half (38.3%) of trade unionists in the UK had supported in the 1983 general election (Crewe, Fox and Day, 1995). In contrast to the political fund ballots held in 1985/8, case study unions approached the 1990s review ballots brimming with confidence. Indeed, the TUCC campaign guide made it clear that given the legislative requirement of postal ballots, the key objective was 'to achieve the largest yes vote on the highest possible turnout' (TUCC, 1995: 6). It was clear that unions felt they had learnt how best to approach the ballots as a result of the 1985/8 TUCC campaign. As the political officer at RMT put it:

The first time round nobody really knew how members would vote until the results started rolling in. This time we knew that we had a tried and tested formula and we knew that if we presented the issues the same way as before we would get the results we wanted.

The political funds legislation failed to produce any decline in the number of political funds. In fact it has had the reverse effect encouraging the union movement to promote the importance of the political fund and the importance of its link with the labour party. The TUCC campaign was an example of unprecedented collective solidarity and co-operation across the whole trade union movement in response to what was interpreted as anti-trade union legislation.

## Industrial action ballots

Prior to the introduction of Conservative legislation, each of the case study unions had its own method for calling industrial action. This had been part of their respective constitutions for many years and could be located in the rulebook. Since the introduction of Conservative legislation all but one of the case study unions has moved towards a system of strictly secret postal ballots. The Conservative legislation in this respect made a direct change to the practices and procedures of the case study unions.

An analysis of interviews, conference reports and national executive committee minutes revealed a significant shift in the attitude of ASLEF, the RMT and the TGWU towards the concept of balloting before industrial action. At the time legislation on industrial action ballots was introduced and for several years after, the stance taken by officials and members in these unions was confrontational. Activists argued for the retention of the status quo, disobedience and the refusal to pay fines levied against the union for breach. This fighting stance has gradually ebbed away, to the extent that the principle of holding a secret postal ballot before industrial action is now taken for granted in all cases. Industrial action ballots became viewed as a weapon that could be used against employers, as a barometer of membership opinion, and as an important way of legitimating their actions (Fredman, 1992; Kessler and Bayliss, 1995). John Monks (the then General Secretary of the Trade Union Congress) summed up the position as follows:

> It must be recognised that such laws have proved popular. No union leader would dare go anywhere near a group of workers, and say we are not having ballots before strikes. The fact is that prior to the introduction of the legislation many unions did not have them before no one can take that away from what the law achieved (ASLEF Conference Proceedings, 1999).

However, while the majority of trade unions have found it necessary to comply with the law surrounding balloting, it has not resulted in members of the case study unions voting in a necessarily more moderate direction. For example, the BFAWU, ASLEF and the RMT have never lost an industrial action ballot that they have called. Moreover, the experience of these unions is that whilst the balloting process isolated the individual member from the collective voice when casting their vote this could be countered by their union nurturing collectivism through other means of contact with the membership (such as pre meetings) in advance of the ballot. The comments of several national officials and shop stewards interviewed indicated an acceptance of the balloting process and recognition that there were some positive benefits to balloting:

> Prior to the introduction of secret ballots trade unions were vulnerable to the accusation that militant union leaders were forcing members to engage in industrial action. This argument no longer has credibility (Shop Steward EETPU).

> A vote in favour of industrial action can often act as a wake up call for the employer. It encourages the employer to come back to the negotiating table and reach a settlement without any industrial action being taken (National Official, ASLEF).

> In the rail industry where a ballot was in favour of industrial action it encouraged employers to the negotiating table to make a better offer (National Official RMT).

However, the legal provisions pertaining to industrial action have caused the case study unions some difficulties. The pre-industrial action ballot procedures were complex cumbersome and costly. The law on industrial action has been described as fragmented, complex, often unpredictable and sometimes unprincipled (Deakin and Morris, 1998). All the case study unions except for BFAWU have had injunctions granted wholly or partially against them for infringements of the balloting process. This resulted in strikes involving the case study unions being called off or delayed. The legalistic nature of the rules resulted in the EETPU, TGWU, NATFHE (higher education) and the CPSA introducing procedures, which increased centralisation of the bargaining process in an area of union operation that was previously far more decentralised. Senior officials of trade unions sent out the message to lower level officials and committees that if the advice was not followed it was impossible to comply with the law and organise an effective campaign of industrial action. The balloting process was a field in which shop stewards found they needed instruction and guidance from national officials and legal officers (Elgar, 1997). This in turn also increased the involvement and control from the centre over the balloting process.

However, despite the legalistic and complex nature of the law surrounding industrial action ballots the majority of case study unions found that industrial action ballots have not been as damaging as originally feared. It is apparent that ballots have assisted trade unions in both their negotiations with employers and their relations with the majority of their own members. Trade union officials and representatives across all levels asserted that balloting improved the negotiating position of trade unions. In situations where industrial action did take place, holding a ballot was seen to consolidate membership support – ballots bolstering collectivism and underpinning collective decision-making. Where industrial action did not take place union officials from both ASLEF and the RMT indicated that ballots provided a greater likelihood that a dispute would be settled via negotiation. Since the union had obtained a 'yes vote' in a ballot in favour of industrial action the ballot demonstrated the strength of feeling to the employer who became eager to settle the dispute (Brown and Wadhwani, 1990; Elgar and Simpson, 1993; Elgar, 1997).

However, in two unions NATFHE (further education sector) and the CPSA, officials reported that members had voted against industrial action on more occasions than they had voted in favour. In respect to NATFHE hostile action by employers resulted in the membership voting against industrial action, whilst in the CPSA the unpredictable voting behaviour of the membership meant the leadership found their call for industrial action rejected.

The majority of case study unions greeted industrial action ballots negatively on their inception. However, whilst there is no doubt from the evidence that the balloting requirements have caused substantive changes to the practices and procedures of trade unions, the fear of ballots, so deeply embedded in the rhetoric of union debate turned out to be somewhat misplaced. The notion that a moderate majority would automatically surface and that they would prevent the union embarking on industrial action has proved illusory and chimerical (Fatchett, 1992: 326).

## Enforcement of individual rights

Prior to the implementation of the *Trade Union Act, 1984* and the *Employment Act, 1988* there had been a rudimentary level of legal intervention in the internal procedures of trade unions (Deakin and Morris, 1998). This comprised of two strands. First, the CO had a specific administrative function pertaining to trade unions. Second, union members had recourse to the courts if trade unions failed to obey the rulebook or the rules of natural justice.

The Conservative legislation creating statutory rights that trade union members could enforce against trade unions in the courts via CROTUM and the expansion in the regulatory role of the CO constituted a significant alteration to the degree to which the law could intervene in trade union internal affairs. The statutory rights accorded to members did not result in significant numbers of cases being brought to the courts. In respect to the enforcement of statutory rights through CROTUM and the CO an analysis of the complaints made by individual union members to these Officials reveals that the majority were either out of scope or dropped by the applicant.

In respect to CROTUM the majority of complaints concerning the case study unions were related to specific breaches of statute, an analysis of the types of claims made to CROTUM overall, reveals that the majority concerned alleged breaches of a union's rulebook rather than alleged breaches of statutory rights.

The evidence collected from the fieldwork, also overwhelmingly suggests that many union members sought conciliation between themselves and their union or wished CROTUM to act as an arbitrator or ombudsman on some specific point. The experience of CROTUM was that in some cases trade unions did not have appropriate mechanisms for dealing with the grievances of individual members, and that quite often the member found himself or herself referred to the source of their complaint. Therefore, it appears that many people who contacted CROTUM assumed that it could investigate complaints on their behalf and referred to the Commissioner as the *Union Ombudsman*. Of course, CROTUM did not have such power. If CROTUM had been vested with such powers, the impact on internal union processes may have been more dramatic.

The moderate number of applications CROTUM assisted leads to the conclusion that the role had a negligible impact and was an irrelevance in terms of reforming union government. The traditional unpopularity of CROTUM amongst unions and unionists may have led to the suppression of a significant number of complaints.

Turning to the role of the CO, the COs annual reports for the period 1984–2000 reveal a steady increase in the volume of work arising from complaints by trade union members, compared to previous years. Some of the complaints to the CO are not of merit and therefore have not warranted any approach to the body concerned. However, where they did, generally these matters were resolved either through correspondence between the CO and the parties concerned or by means of informal meetings with the union or the individual or a combination of these methods. The evidence would suggest that most complaints could be dealt with in house with the operation of better grievance procedures. The CO has encouraged individual trade unions to improve their internal grievance procedures.

However, some of the complaints made via CROTUM and the CO against individual trade unions often resulted in time-consuming correspondence and activities. This restricted the action the unions could take and diverted resources from servicing their members in other respects. In this regard Conservative government's managed to add spoiling agencies to the anti-union legislative and policy agenda. That is to say, though 'independent' the presence and functions of the agencies maximised nuisance value by promoting individual against collective interests and freedoms (Lockwood, 2000).

Overall, the encouragement Conservative governments gave to trade union members to complain about the internal affairs of their trade unions fell upon 'deaf ears'. The legal regime did not result in large numbers of complaints and universal reform of union rulebooks.

## Trade unions and organisational change

An analysis of changes that have occurred over time in the respective case study unions reveals that substantial alterations to their internal affairs were caused by a variety of factors and not just the legal provisions introduced by the Conservatives during the 1980s and 1990s. This supports the view of McCarthy (1981) quoted in Steele (1990: 55):

Trade unions are not dinosaurs stuck in their ways unable to change nor, indeed, are union rules laid down in tablets of stone.

An analysis of developments in the internal affairs of trade unions enables a number of key reasons for change to be identified.

### Membership decline

Union membership grew steadily in the 1970s, as the then Labour Government encouraged union recognition and membership. However, during the 1980s and throughout the 1990s the EETPU, BFAWU, RMT, and TGWU all experienced increasing operational costs at a time of declining membership. The stark reality for the leaders of these unions was that the membership needed to be served more efficiently and cost effectively. Union leaders responded by streamlining structures in order to continue to exist. In the TGWU and EETPU the changes introduced resulted in the centralisation of power in both the administrative and bargaining channels of the union. In contrast, in the BFAWU and the RMT, whilst the respective leaderships set about tackling the financial problems raised by membership decline, changes to the organisation resulted in more decentralised union government.

## Internal union reviews

The BFAWU, RMT, TGWU, ASLEF and CPSA have all held formal internal reviews of their structure at some point since 1979. However, commonalities and differences can be exposed in respect of the motives behind these reviews. In the BFAWU membership unrest with the style of leadership between 1966 and 1979 led to a long and sustained process of democratic reform. The BFAWU mass membership and lay activists had a prominent role in the reform process. The changes introduced resulted in much greater autonomy for branches.

The RMT also embarked on union reform following an internal review, which was prompted for two main reasons. First, there was strong member dissatisfaction with the highly centralised administrative structure of the union (Hyman, Price and Terry, 1988). Second, the union faced significant financial difficulties arising from a decline in membership. Union structure was simplified and the membership given the right to directly elect members to the governing bodies of the union and senior officials.

The TGWU also launched an internal review due to membership decline and financial difficulties. However, whilst the union consulted members on their views, the direction of structural change was driven by a report from management consultants and the national leadership. The measures introduced were devised and implemented by the leadership. The changes were successful in reducing the TGWU £12 million deficit and producing much greater stability in the management of the union. Perhaps not surprisingly the changes that have occurred centralised power into the hands of senior officials and the executive.

ASLEF engaged in a review because of inefficiencies in its operation identified by the then moderate leadership during the late 1980s and 1990s. The moderate leadership attempted to centralise union government in order to take control of finances and improve communications between the branch and head office. Whilst there was extensive consultation with activists and the mass membership the changes ultimately made to resolve the perceived problems were determined by the leadership. However, the election of a recognised socialist leadership in 1997 resulted in a shift to a much more decentralised system of union government, particularly in the arena of collective bargaining.

The CPSA held an internal review on the initiative of the moderate group controlling the union in an attempt to make the union more democratic in advance of a merger. The leadership introduced change that gave members a greater direct voice in the determination of the policies of the union, but also designed to weaken the influence of the left. This acted to increase the power base of the moderate leadership.

## Industrial change

Privatisation of the railway industry resulted in substantial changes to the structure of both ASLEF and the RMT together with changes to the collective bargaining process of the respective unions. In the cases of both ASLEF and the RMT the changes have bolstered the position of local officials in respect of the bargaining process. A similar position is also detectable in the BFAWU where bargaining has also become more devolved. This contrasts with developments in the TGWU, EETPU, and the CPSA where changes that have taken place have tended to have the reverse effect, concentrating power into the hands of senior officials. Shop stewards have not become key actors in the bargaining process in these unions.

## Mergers

The EETPU, CPSA and RMT have all had their structures and procedures influenced by merger activity. In all three of these unions senior officials took the lead in the merger activity to which they were party, recommending and driving change. Whilst being prepared to make constitutional modifications to accommodate merger partners, they were also determined to protect their own political position once merger took place. In the case of the EETPU, merger with the Amalgamated Union of Engineering Workers resulted in the newly formed union adopting the EETPU structure. In the formation of the RMT, the then National Union of Railwaymen was the senior partner imposing change on the National Union of Seamen. In respect to the CPSA the prospect of an amalgamation provided the opportunity for the leadership to make alterations to structure and process that were perceived as necessary to the success of the amalgamation. However, at the same time the changes resulted in the leadership introducing measures, which centralised power within the union into the hands of the moderate leadership and out of the grasp of left wing activists.

## Equal opportunities

In the TGWU, BFAWU, EETPU and ASLEF, changes to rules relating to representation of particular groups have been made to ensure the advancement of equal opportunities. Traditionally it has been the case that female union members have been heavily under-represented at all levels within trade unions. This has been related both to the position of women in society generally, but also to the lack of encouragement given to female members to stand for elected positions within the union representative system. As a consequence, male interests have dominated union bargaining agendas – to the exclusion and detriment of women's' interests and have contributed to the subordination of women within work and society (Hartman, 1979; Cockburn, 1984). The above unions realised that unless this problem was addressed at section and branch level the under representation of women relative to men will be perpetuated at every level in the union. Of all the case study unions the TGWU is by far the most advanced union in terms of providing equal opportunity measures. Its diverse membership, the amount of resources the union allocates to equal opportunities and the importance the leadership attaches to inclusiveness of all groups are the key reasons for this.

### Mass Membership/factions/groups

Traditionally, the attitudes and policies of the mass membership, factions and union groups have influenced particular types of decision-making and union structure. Changes to union government caused by factional group activity have however been much less than in the past, most notably in the TGWU and EETPU. The challenges facing these unions brought about a realisation that it was not in the interests of individual unions to become distracted from the challenges that they faced by internal strife (Undy et al., 1996). In the cases of the TGWU and the EETPU the respective leaderships of each union built up a strong power base, taking the opportunity to draw decisions and financial control back to the centre.

In respect to the BFAWU, ASLEF and the RMT it was evident that at various junctures groups / factions had been successful in placing pressure on union leaders, forcing changes in union constitutions resulting in more devolved union government. This can be contrasted directly with the developments that have taken place in the TGWU, EETPU, CPSA and NATFHE all of which have become more centralised.

### Political complexion of the union

In ASLEF, RMT, NATFHE and the CPSA organisational changes occurred during the 1980s and 1990s due to shifts in the political control of the union. In ASLEF and the RMT, recent years have witnessed the growth and strength of recognised 'Militant' and Socialist Workers Party candidates in elections. This has resulted in the election of a recognised left wing national leadership and the election of socialist shop stewards. Developments in the privatised rail industry far from weakening union power have had the opposite effect enhancing the role of militant groups within the respective unions. These developments have both been influential factors in bargaining decentralisation and diffusion.

In contrast in NATFHE and the CPSA the emergence of a moderate or rightward leaning group contributed to a fall in militancy and alterations to democratic structure. In the CPSA, the membership contained its fair share of traditionally moderate and relatively inactive members. This was one reason why the moderate leadership did not face demands for a more militant stance against reforms to the civil service. It also helps explain how the leadership was able to implement constitutional change that it desired without significant opposition.

In the TGWU moderate national leadership has not come under pressure from any militant groups within. This enabled the leadership to pursue the policies it deemed necessary to rescue the union from its perilous financial situation, but as previously stated has centralised decision-making within the union.

Finally, in respect to the EETPU the moderate-right wing group remained in control of the union with an almost unchallenged ascendancy during the 1980s and 1990s.

## National leadership

An analysis of the respective unions reveals that changes to the processes of internal union government have been significantly influenced by the nature of its leadership. The general secretary is often the pivotal shaper and mover in constitutional reform (Undy et al., 1981). In this respect Marino BFAWU, Rix ASLEF, Morris, TGWU and the late Jimmy Knapp, RMT were all key figures in initiating and implementing change in their respective unions. Marino at the BFAWU and Rix at ASLEF are recognised left wing leaders who have always been strongly opposed to the Conservative legislation and the response of the union movement to it. During their periods as general secretary they have sought to retain their traditional union structures, and at the same time devolved decision-making power.

In the TGWU, the EETPU and ASLEF (during the tenure of the moderate leadership) the general secretaries introduced changes centralising power into the hands of senior officials. Such change substantially increased the authority of senior officials, reducing the influence of branches and lower level committees, thus subverting democracy within the unions, and perpetuating oligarchic tendencies. The respective leaders deployed language as an important strategic resource in facilitating a change of attitude amongst certain traditionalists and factions of the union, which enabled them to propel organisational change within the union. The rhetoric and key phrases utilised by union leaders focused the mind on the need for union restructuring and stressed that the approach advocated by the executive was the only sensible and logical option in a fast changing and hostile environment. The underlying message to opponents was that if they fought against change they were 'lost souls' who would be of no use in a modern and progressive union movement.

An analysis of the internal affairs of the case study unions over an extended period of time revealed that a combination of economic factors and financial factors, membership decline, changes in industry, merger activity, political change, the actions of union leaders and attitudes of members, and not just legal changes have contributed to changes in the institutions, processes and practices concerning union internal affairs. Many of these 'other' factors were occurring irrespective of the new legislation. Some changes they produced were in train before the legislation of the 1980s and 1990s. It didn't just need legislation to make unions change the way they were run.

## Conclusion

An analysis of internal trade union affairs from 1979 onwards enables conclusions to be drawn about the impact of Conservative legislation on trade union government and the reasons for changes to the internal affairs of trade unions.

Conservative legislation changed trade union government and decision-making processes. All the case study trade unions with the exception of one changed their rules to comply with Conservative legislation. However, whilst trade unions have complied with the Conservative model this has not transformed the political complexion of trade unions. It was erroneously assumed that individual union members would vote in union elections, political fund ballots and industrial action ballots in a moderate direction. In this respect the law acts as a blunt instrument, because whilst the law can make changes to particular rules relating to voting procedures it cannot influence the voting behaviour of the membership. This will be determined by members' beliefs, the political nature of the union and the economic and industrial environment. Secret ballots acted to provide credibility and legitimacy to trade union activities that the Conservatives clearly disliked. These were unintended and unwelcome consequences of the legal provisions from a Conservative perspective.

Whilst the majority of trade unions incorporated the individualistic elements of the Conservative model into trade union governance, they have also retained collective participation in many areas of union organisation. Membership involvement in trade unions is now through a mixture of individual and participative mechanisms.

The requirement to use only postal balloting caused a significant decline in participation across the trade union movement, and hence democracy. At the same time it has acted to perpetuate one of the main features of union government that the Conservatives claimed they wanted to eradicate, the influence of trade union activists. In this respect it is evident that the intervention of the law did not increase the participation of the assumed more moderate member in trade union affairs.

Furthermore, providing individual members with the right to complain to employment tribunals, the high court (with the aid of CROTUM), or directly to the CO did not result in significant numbers of legal claims being made against trade unions. This is not surprising given that trade unions generally act in the interests of their members and the fact that the majority of members expressed the view that they were disinclined to complain about their trade union to external agencies. The legislation relied too heavily on the notion of disaffected members launching actions against trade unions.

Finally, Conservative legislation was not the only influence on the internal affairs of trade unions. Changes in the nature of union government and behaviour were linked to a combination of 'other' non-legislative pressures. These 'other factors' included the economic environment, financial circumstances, the general industrial relations climate, employer tactics, the union leadership, membership attitudes, the political complexion of trade unions and industrial change. These factors caused trade unions to: improve their democratic processes, use the strike weapon more sparingly, and place more emphasis on developing social and industrial partnership with employers. As a result of their experiences, the case study unions are now better organised and more efficient. A key question for the trade unions is can they build on these internal strengths, together with a more favourable economic and political climate to increase union density?

## References

Brown, W. and Wadhwani, S. (1990) The Economic Effects of Industrial Relations Legislation Since 1979, *National Institute Economic Review* (Feb): 57–69.
Certification Officer (2000) *Annual Report 1999*, the Certification Office, London.
Cockburn, C. (1984) *In the Way of Women*, Macmillan: London.
Crewe, I., Fox, A. and Day, N. (1995) *The British Electorate 1963–1992*, Cambridge University Press: Cambridge.
Deakin, S. and Morris, G. (1998) *Labour Law*, Butterworths: London.
Elgar, J. (1997) *Industrial Action Ballots: an analysis of the development of law and practice*, PhD thesis, London School of Economics, University of London.
Elgar, J. and Simpson, R. (1993) *Union Negotiators, Industrial Action and the Law: Report of a Survey of Negotiators in 25 Unions 1991–1992*, Centre for Economic Performance Discussion Paper No. 171, London School of Economics: London.
Fatchett, D. (1992) 'Ballots, Picketing and Strikes, in Towers, B., *A Handbook of Industrial Relations Practice*, Kogan Page: London.
Fredman, S. (1992) The New Rights: Labour Law and Ideology in the Thatcher Years, *Oxford Journal of Legal Studies*, 12(1): 25–44.
Hartman, H. (1979) Capitalism, Patriachy, and Job Segregation by Sex, in Zillah Eisenstein (ed.) *Capitalist, Patriachy and the Case for Socialist Feminism*: Monthly Review Press.
Hyman, R., Price, P. and Terry, M. (1988) *Reshaping the National Union of Railwaymen*, NUR The Warwick Report.
Grant, D. (1987) 'Mrs Thatcher's Own Goal: Unions and the Political Funds Ballots', *Parliamentary Affairs*, 40(1): 73–79.
Grant, D. and Lockwood, G. (1999) 'Trade Unions, Political Fund Ballots and Party Political Funding', *Policy Studies*, 20(2): 77–94.
Leopold, J. (1986) 'Trade Union Political Funds: A Retrospective Analysis', *Industrial Relations Journal*, 17(4): 287–303.

Leopold, J. (1988) 'Moving the Status Quo: The Growth of Trade Union Political Funds' *Industrial Relations Journal*, 19(4): 287–95.

Leopold, J. (1997) 'Trade Unions, Political Fund Ballots and the Labour Party', *British Journal of Industrial Relations*, 35: 23–38.

Lockwood, G. (2000) 'An Epitaph to CROTUM and CPAUIA', *Journal of Industrial Relations*, 31(5): 471–481.

McCarthy, W. E. J. (1981), quoted in Steele, M. (1990) Changing the Rules: Pressures on Trade Union Constitutions, in Fosh, P. and Heery, E. (eds) *Trade Unions and Their Members*, Macmillan: Basingstoke.

TUCC (1995) *Political Fund Ballots 1994–95: Report of a Successful Campaign*, TUCC: London.

Undy, R., Ellis, V., McCarthy, Halmos, A. M. (1981) *Change in Trade Unions*, Hutchinson: London.

Undy, R., Fosh, P., Morris, H., Smith, P., Martin, R. (1996) *Managing the Unions: The Impact of Legislation on Trade Union Behaviour*, Oxford University Press: Oxford.

# 8

## Union-Based Pension Funds and Social Investment: A New Role For Unions in the Economy

*Isla Carmichael*

### Introduction

Trusteed pension funds in Canada are estimated at $543.8 billion as of the first quarter of 2002 and control 35 per cent of equity in the stock markets (Canada, 2003). Yet over $400 billion of these pension assets are under the control of fund managers in the financial industry. This paper argues that while unions have been relatively passive in the past about this massive capital pool, they are now viewing active ownership of pension capital as a strategy for union renewal.

This change in strategic direction over the last twenty years has been influenced by a number of factors such as restrictions on collective bargaining and the right to strike of public sector workers, high unemployment, the erosion of the manufacturing sector, stagnant wages, employer contribution holidays, pension plan wind-ups and conversions to defined contribution funds, the internationalisation of finance and the irrationality of the stock markets (Shiller, 2000).

Pension funds are tax exempt yet have been treated as private entities. However, there is a persuasive argument to be made that pension fund investment should be in the public interest and that pension funds should be publicly accountable for their investment decision-making. Furthermore, since under 50 per cent of the workforce is covered by workplace pensions and many of these workers are union members, unions run the risk of being marginalised for having as beneficiaries an increasingly narrow sector of the labour force.

First this paper will outline initial steps in active ownership of pension funds being taken by trade unions as well as the barriers they face. Evidence from an investigative study of levels of union control is considered. Second, socially responsible investment is examined as the most likely strategy to attain union investment goals. Third, the paper will examine a case study of Concert Properties, a real estate development company, established through the pooled capital of 26 pension funds and initiated by union pension trustees. Finally, the paper will discuss the potential for greater involvement by trade unions in pension capital strategies and how this may be achieved.

## Union control over pension fund investment

Historically, unions have had little control over pension benefits or investment. Workplace pension plans, in existence for about 150 years, were developed by employers as a means of quelling labour unrest, instituting control over the workplace, limiting the rise of unionism and containing demands from working people for a national social security pension for the elderly (Heron, 1996). Pension funds have primarily been a critical source of capital accumulation for employers (Greenough and King, 1976) and, more recently, the financial industry (Deaton, 1989).

In 1986, the Canadian Labour Congress passed a resolution that 'endorse[d] the goal of organised Canadian workers achieving greater control and direction of the investment of pension funds' (cited in Baldwin et al., 1991: 10). This resolution reflected a trend in British Columbia towards joint trusteeship in some private sector union-based funds and pension fund investment in economic development. Ken Georgetti, President of the B.C. Federation of Labour was reported as saying:

> It's just the old tired attitude that if you believe in labour or social democracy, you have to be against capital and profits. We can use pension income to create jobs, union jobs, that pay a fair rate and get a fair return. We can make a profit...but...without exploiting people (Casselton, D12).

Soon afterwards, a number of public sector unions in Ontario gained respective joint trusteeships of the Hospitals of Ontario Pension Plan, the Ontario Teachers' Pension Plan, the Ontario Public Service Employees Union Pension Trust and the Colleges of Applied Arts and Technology Pension Plan.

In 1998, an investigative study was conducted to assess the level of union control of the 24 largest pension funds in Canada (Carmichael, 1998). The study surveyed pension fund managers, union officials, union staff and members. Its findings identified eight models of pension fund governance of these plans, with differing relationships between government, employer, employees and union. These models range from a fully joint board of trustees, where union and employer representation is equal and the board has full control of plan administration and fund investment to what is commonly known as the company plan where the board of directors of the company is also the board of trustees of the pension plan is no union involvement. The trend to joint trusteeship among public sector unions has continued, as identified in the study.

Relatively few unions have control over investment of their pension funds; however, where there is control, the funds are often large and cover many unionised staff in public service workforces across the country. The National Union of Public and General Employees, whose component unions are the unions of provincial public service workers, has now identified control over investment as critical to joint trusteeship and is coordinating information on trusteeship models. Some private sector unions also have sole or joint trusteeship of their funds.

The Canadian Union of Public Employees has had little success in winning joint trusteeship over the Ontario Municipal Employees Retirement System, despite numerous campaigns. More recent campaigns have been driven by controversial investment projects which have been undertaken by OMERS, with the Canada Pension Board, through Borealis, its investment agency. Projects have been funded in schools, roads, hospitals and water systems. Two controversial projects are

- the commercial ownership of 16 schools in Nova Scotia, privatising public sector work and putting local schools under commercial control with no accountability to their communities and paying lower, non-union wages.
- an alliance with Extendicare to set up non-union, for-profit long term care homes in Ontario.

Both the Canadian Labour Congress (CLC) and the Canadian Labour and Business Centre (CLBC) have held conferences recently on union strategies for control over pension funds. The CLC has also established SHARE – an independent organisation in British Columbia – to promote shareholder activism, to monitor shareholder voting and to provide pension trustee education for union trustees. SHARE's board of directors are all union leaders with the exception of one who has spearheaded union-controlled businesses. The goals of SHARE are to build sound investment practices, protect the interest of beneficiaries and contribute to a just and healthy society.

Where unions have control, trustees may not exercise it through lack of training. Indeed, this has been noted as a reason against having union or 'lay' trustees (Canada, 1998). Union trustee education is critical to informed investment practice. Invariably, however, trustee education is delivered by financial industry representatives who perpetuate the mystification of investment processes (Carmichael, Thompson and Quarter, 2003; Rudd and Spalding, 1997).

Trustees may also lack confidence. While they have the responsibility for overseeing the policies and practices of a pension plan to ensure that it meets the long-term interests of the members and beneficiaries, the prudence requirements of the law are viewed as ambiguous enough that trustees are reluctant to engage in socially responsible investment for fear of lowering the rate of return (Yaron, 2001).

The *Cowan v. Scargill* case (1984) was the most damaging to union confidence in pension fund investment. Its legacy has ensured first, that some commentators persist in viewing a union agenda on investment as subjective, irrelevant and damaging to regular investment process (Romano, 1993); and secondly that there is often a distance between union trustees and their unions such that unions may provide no support to their trustees and trustees may rebuff any support or involvement of their union. Fortunately, since 1984, the effects of this case have been minimised through successive case law (Waitzer, 1990). However, the perception of legal barriers still discourage union trustees from engaging in socially responsible investment, the three-pronged investment strategy most likely to accommodate a broader socio-economic agenda leading to union renewal.

## Socially responsible investment

Socially responsible investment (SRI) is usually defined as the inclusion of various social and environmental criteria in the assessment of investment impacts (Bruyn, 1987). Theoretically, the concept falls within a body of knowledge challenging market autonomy and situating the economy in a social framework as an 'instituted process' (Polyani, 1957), in a relationship of 'embeddedness' (Granovetter, 1985), or more recently as 'social capital' (Putnam, 1995). Or SRI may be situated within an ethical or value framework, identifying a broader corporate accountability through stakeholder theory (Wheeler and Sillanpaa, 2000), and creating methods of accounting for corporate social responsibility (Carroll, 1999; Drucker, 1984) or corporate social performance (Asmundson and Foerster, 2002).

Socially responsible investment falls into three broad categories. First, is the investment in mutual funds promoting social ideals – environmental funds or funds reflecting best practices across a broad spectrum of industries; or, promoting the support of sanctions or disinvestment strategies in specific corporations, industrial sectors (e.g., tobacco or armaments) or in a nation (e.g., South Africa under Apartheid). Second, are various forms of corporate engagement (Clark and Hebb, 2002) including shareholder action strategies – for example, organised efforts to change the behaviour of specific corporations either by taking a seat on the board of directors or by putting pressure on management. Third, is the investment in community development practices – for example, housing for low-income citizens or investment in an underdeveloped region (Quarter, 1995). Taken together, these approaches are intended to promote 'high-road' practices among businesses (good wages, quality working conditions) and to create positive impacts in the community (environmental sustainability, greater regional equality) while contributing to the economic return of the investment.

## Socially responsible investment – the union debate

There is controversy over union involvement in SRI within the trade union movement. The first argument is that union involvement in the market through pension fund or labour-sponsored investment funds 'muddies' the 'traditional understanding' (Stanford, 1999, p. 372) between unions and employers, and undermines the role of unions in representing their members through collective bargaining. However, collective bargaining has been based on adversarial relationships that comparatively speaking may no longer be so effective in serving the interests of unions or employers (Adams, 1995), and also restricted agendas where residual rights – including control of capital – have remained with the employer (Drache and Glasbeek, 1992).

The second argument is that the workings of the market dictate losses in the rate of return of investments made in the benefit of a broader social good. Unions therefore would be obliged to make trade-offs between the interests of their members and the broader interests of a social investment.

## Social investment and rates of return

There is no evidence that the rates of return of any type of social invest-ment are lowered. The first, ethical investment, involves the application to an investment of social or ethical screens – either negative or positive. Research on ethically-screened mutual funds has been shown not to damage the rate of return either in the U.S. (Guerard, 1997) or in Canada (Asmundson and Foerster, 2002).

While there are few examples of pension funds with ethical screens to screen out or screen in investment, there are indications that Canadian union pension trustees view ethical screens as one of several strategies in social investment (Carmichael and Quarter, 2003). After a protracted strug-gle by union pension trustees, the California Public Employees' Retirement System (CalPERS), with assets of about (U.S.) \$170 billion, has recently instituted a comprehensive screen for international investment. The screen is based on the Global Sullivan Principles, using a broad range of environ-mental, labour and social justice criteria. There is considerable interest on the part of the international labour movement in this screen since it may provide a complimentary strategy to global activism to challenge corporate behaviour and set labour standards.

The second type of social investment are various forms of corporate engagement (Clark and Hebb, 2003), including shareholder action strategies for example, organised efforts to change the behaviour of specific corporations either by taking a seat on the board of directors or by putting pressure on management. Taken together, these approaches are intended to promote 'high-road' practices among businesses like good wages and quality working conditions and to create positive impacts in the community like environmental sustainability and greater regional equality while contributing to the economic return of the investment. CalPERS reports that corporate governance strategies improve share values dramatically. A study it commissioned (published by Wilshire and Associates of Santa Monica in 1994) examined the performance of companies targeted by CalPERS between 1987 and 1992. The stock price of these companies trailed the Standard and Poor 500 index by 66 per cent for the five years prior to the campaign, and out-performed the index by 41 per cent in the following five years.

Another study of CalPERS (Smith, 1996), finds that when shareholder action is successful in changing governance structure, it also results in added shareholder value. However, when the shareholder action is directed at improved operating performance, there is no statistically significant change in value. Overall, during the 1987–93 period, shareholder action resulted in a net increase of US$19 million. This finding is not corroborated by either Romano (1993) or Wahal (1996), who in a study of the activism of six funds (including CalPERS) for the same period (from 1987–1993) find that while pension funds are successful in changing the governance structure of targeted firms, their activism does not change the rate of return on investment. In summary, although the evidence is inconclusive as to whether shareholder activism actually increases the rate of return, there is no evidence of declining returns.

A third form of social investment is economically targeted investment (ETI), where a fund targets one or two per cent of its assets for specific social goals (for example, affordable housing for low-income earners). It is estimated that in the U.S., about $30 billion are currently placed in ETIs (Jackson, 1997), where pension fund investment is heavily regulated for ETI investment. In addition, government information requirements ensure regular reporting on rates of return. Many union programmes, like the AFL-CIO Housing Investment Trust, are reported to have 'solid track records' and competitive rates of return (Watson, 1995, p. 4).

Pension funds in Canada are beginning to invest in labour-sponsored investment funds, whose returns are published weekly in the Globe and Mail, Canada's national newspaper. Labour-sponsored investment funds have been created in most provinces under the umbrella of the provincial federations of labour. They provide capital to companies in the early stages of development, new technology and companies undergoing restructuring. Investments in labour-sponsored funds provide the investor tax credits of 30 per cent divided equally between the federal and the provincial governments. If shares are purchased as an RRSP, they qualify for further tax deductions. Since these funds are viewed as patient capital, investors are required to invest for a minimum of eight years.

These funds recruit union members who, after training and licensing, sell shares to co-workers. In 1995, the Canadian Labour and Business Centre reported that more than 379,000 Canadians were investors in funds across the country. More than half were union members (Canadian Labour and Business Centre, 1995). Educationals are often organised for employees in investee firms to encourage both transparency of the firm's books and employee understanding of accounts. In its first ten years, the Solidarity Fund in Quebec reported cumulative average returns of 5.88 per cent. With tax credits taken into account the returns jump to 18 per cent (Ellmen, 1997; Quarter, 1995).

## Pension funds and economically targeted investment (ETI)

An example of an ETI in Canada is Concert Properties, a real estate development company and its sister investment vehicle, Mortgage Fund One, both founded in the early 1990s. Both are funded by 26 pension funds shareholders, with small proportions – between 1 per cent and 5 per cent – of their total fund assets invested in each vehicle. Both use union labour only on construction sites. The boards of directors of each ETI consist of employer and union representatives of participating pension funds. The goals of both are to provide affordable and accessible rental and market housing, to generate adequate, long-term returns to the pension fund investors and, finally, to create union jobs.

The founders of both ETIs were longstanding union leaders in the British Columbia trade union movement and attested to the continuing loss in B.C. of unionised employment in the construction trades. The percentage of union work on construction sites had been decreasing for years as developers used more and more non-union labour. Also, the quality of housing was sinking, they argued, as 'leaky condo' civil suits proliferated in the industry. Ten years later, they estimated that the building trade unions were still only getting about 27 per cent of the commercial construction work in British Columbia, and even less of the residential construction. Construction workers, on average, are the lowest paid group of workers in the goods-producing industries, as reported by BCStats (Government of British Columbia, 2000), with gross weekly wages in 1998 of $723 or $20.67 per hour based on a 35-hour work week. By comparison, an average Concert construction wage is $33 per hour. Getting control of pension funds was strategic to stop the erosion of union membership, create union-wage jobs, build quality housing and community wealth.

A case study of Concert Properties and Mortgage Fund One was conducted from 1998–2000 [for a more detailed discussion, see Carmichael (2003)]. In its first ten years, Concert built approximately 1,400 units of affordable rental housing and was the leading real estate development company in the provision of affordable rental and market housing in the Vancouver region. Since it holds its buildings over the long term, Concert guarantees not to raise its rents beyond inflation plus 1 per cent. To date it has maintained this standard.

In January 2000, MFO had 14 investments with an approximate value of $91 million in term and interim construction loans, all in British Columbia. Since that time, it has diversified its portfolio by moving into the Ontario real estate market. MFO insists that any project funded, however partially, must be 100 per cent union built. The average maturity of loans is approximately five years. Mortgage Fund One has already established its track record of returns ranging from 8.26 per cent to 8.40 per cent from 1993–98. Further, MFO's management fees are less than two other Canadian mortgage benchmarks – Wyatt Pooled Mortgage funds and Scotia McLeod Mortgage Index. In addition, MFO's net annual yield exceeds those other benchmarks and therefore provides a higher return to the pension plan investors (MFO, April, 1999).

Both Mortgage Fund One and Concert Properties are remarkable examples of multi-sector collaboration across labour, employer and governments. Nor are they driven only by the involvement of construction unions. Unions from the retail food sector and the forestry industry are strongly represented. The anchor fund providing the largest amount of capital is the Telecommunication Workers' Union.

The Carpentry Workers' Pension Fund is just one of the partners in both Concert and Mortgage Fund One. The study estimates conservatively that, from Concert's construction activity between 1990 and 1999, 1.8 million hours of carpenters' work was created. The Carpentry Workers' Pension Fund received additional pension contributions of $4.25 million. This increase in contributions flows directly from the adherence to union labour on construction sites, since the pension plan is a creation of the Carpentry Workers' Union. It is unlikely that the pension plan would have received this increase in contributions had it not been for Concert projects and its ability, with other pension funds, to capitalise on a gap in the market by building and managing rental accommodation. The union also benefits directly through increased union dues (and membership) to the same extent (Carmichael, p. 182).

Has this work had spin-off benefits for the broader community? Concert's impact on indirect and induced employment created over 5.5 million hours of work and more than doubled its direct, attributable on-site employment. Furthermore, its value added or contribution to productivity (in the community) through its indirect and induced effects is just over $500 million, just over its total project cost for the ten years (ibid., p. 188).

Finally, the taxation revenues for the federal government generated through Concert's productivity total almost 74.7 million compared with foregone tax revenues from pension fund investments of both ETIs of $66 million. Therefore, in the first ten years, the federal government had a net gain of $8.7 million on its investment. For all levels of government, who gained $144.5 million in tax revenues, it is clear that the work of Concert and Mortgage Fund One yields opportunities for tax revenue that far outweigh government subsidisation of pension funds. Clearly, the benefits of Concert extend beyond the interests of construction workers and their pension funds.

## Discussion

Control over pension funds is a pre-requisite for control over investment. The trend towards joint trusteeship persists with public sector unions in British Columbia having recently signed trusteeship papers.

Previous efforts by some governments to establish investment funds with pension capital ignored the demands of unions to have joint control of pension funds. The initiatives failed. Joint control must be a first step to joint ventures in investment. The Manitoba government and pension funds are now discussing joint trusteeships as a pre-condition to joint investment ventures with the Crocus labour-sponsored investment fund.

The traditional arguments against more productive investment strategies on the part of pension funds – generating from within the trade union movement as well as from right-wing business – have not stood up to scrutiny. Minimally, research shows that ethical screens and shareholder action do not reduce rates of return, and in some cases actually increase rates of return. Economic development may provide good rates of return, and provides returns to governments in increased taxes as well as spin-off effects to the broader community.

Furthermore, models of social investment in existence in Canada are remarkably strong and may be more fruitful than present research suggests. More attention needs to be directed towards enabling legislation to support social investment initiatives and, in particular, economic development like affordable, long-term rental and market accommodation as well as social housing, small and emerging business, new technologies, and re-tooling older companies. This is just a beginning list of options for pension fund investment.

There is often scepticism about the possibility of legislation supporting trade union initiatives particularly by more conservative governments. Some key joint trusteeships across the country were negotiated with labour-sympathetic governments notably the OPSEU Pension Trust and the British Columbia General Employees' Union Pension Plan more recently. However, labour-sponsored investment funds were originally introduced under a conservative government. This suggests that there may be more opportunities for enabling legislation under a variety of political circumstances.

Governments are now looking at pension capital as a means of retooling older public sector infrastructure like water systems, schools and hospitals. Unions need to be at the table in these discussions representing the interests of their members and beneficiaries as well as the broader community. Union can forge a renewed role as protectors of the public interest in ensuring that high-road investment practices are followed.

The next step is for unions to be clear about the collateral benefits and/or damage of investment by having the tools to assess the social and economic value to beneficiaries and communities. For example, Borealis, a fund set up by the Ontario Municipal Employees Retirement System for infrastructure projects, was heavily criticised by the trade union movement for enabling school projects that were against the interests of their members and the community. The Concert Properties case study, for example, takes a broader view of collateral benefit to community and avoids the criticism that the trade union movement uses pension fund investment simply to create jobs for its members. However, this is only a beginning.

Finally, union pension trustee education is contested terrain. The trade union movement must develop its own body of knowledge on capital markets and investment as part of a larger critical discussion on making an economy that works in the interests of working people.

Traditionally, pension funds have regarded their beneficiary members as their only community. Similarly, unions in North America tend to have regard only for their members and becoming a member involves taking on a fairly onerous process of organising and certification (Adams, 1995). This paper has argued that union involvement in pension fund investment may serve to broaden the trade union movement's arena of influence in the economy. Such involvement will also extend the trade union movement's traditional constituency beyond the walls of its members. This new direction may lead to a renewed movement more representative of society's interests.

## References

Adams, Roy (1995) *Industrial Relations Under Liberal Democracy: North America in Comparative Perspective.* Columbia: South Carolina Press.

Asmundson, Paul, and Foerster, Stephen (2001) Socially responsible investing: Better for your soul or your bottom line [Electronic version]. *Canadian Investment Review*, Winter: 1–12.

Baldwin, Bob, Jackson, Ted, Decter, Michael, and Levi, David (1991, March) *Worker Investment Funds: Issues and Prospects.* Prepared for the Canadian Labour Congress. Ottawa.

Bruyn, Severyn (1987) *The Field of Social Investment.* Cambridge: Cambridge University Press.

Canada. Standing Senate Committee on Banking, Trade and Commerce (1998) *The governance practices of institutional investors: Report of the Standing Committee on Banking Trade and Commerce.* Retrieved July 2, 2003, from: http://www.parl.gc.ca/36/1/parlbus/commbus/senate/com-e/bank-e/rep-e/rep16nov98-e.htm

Isla Carmichael 115

Canada, Statistics Canada (2002) *Quarterly Estimates of Trusteed Pension Funds.* Ottawa: Queen's Printer. Third Quarter.

Canadian Labour Congress (1990) *A New Decade: Our Future.* Ottawa: CLC.

Carmichael, Isla (1998) *A Survey of Union Pension Trustees.* Results published in Canadian Labour and Business Centre. (1999, January). *Prudence, Patience and Jobs: Pension Investment in a Changing Economy.* CLBC: Ottawa.

Carmichael, Isla (2003) Its our jobs, its our money: A case study of Concert. In Carmichael, Isla and Quarter, Jack (eds), *Money on the line: Workers' capital in Canada.* Ottawa: Canadian Centre for Policy Alternatives.

Carmichael, Isla, Thompson, Shirley, and Quarter, Jack (2003) Transformative education for pension fund trustees. *Canadian Journal for the Study of Adult Education,* 17: 1.

Carmichael, Isla and Quarter, Jack (eds) (2003), *Money on the line: Workers' capital in Canada.* Ottawa: Canadian Centre for Policy Alternatives.

Carroll, Archie, B. (1999) Corporate social responsibility. *Business and Society,* 38: 3, 268–295.

Casselton, Valerie. The hard-hat capitalists. The Vancouver Sun. pp. D10–12.

Clark, Gordon L. and Tessa Hebb (2003) *Understanding pension fund corporate engagement in a global arena.* Oxford, Working Paper 03–01, School of Geography and the Environment, University of Oxford.

*Cowan v. Scargill* (1984) 2 All EAR., 750.

Deaton, Richard Lee (1989) *The Political Economy of Pensions: Power, Politics and Social Change in Canada, Britain, and the United States.* Vancouver: University of British Columbia Press.

Drache, D. and Glasbeek, H. (1992) *The Changing Workplace.* Toronto: James Lorimer.

Greenough, William Croan and King, Francis P. (1976) *Pension Plans and Public Policy.* New York: Columbia University Press.

Guerard, John B. Jr. (1997) Additional Evidence on the Cost of Being Social Responsible in Investing. *The Journal of Investing,* Winter, 31–35.

Heron, Craig (1989) *The Canadian Labour Movement: A Short History.* Toronto: James Lorimer.

Jackson, Edward T. (1997) ETIs: A Tool for Responsible Pension Fund Investment. *Making Waves,* 8: 2, 2–4.

Mortgage Fund One (1999) *Business Plan Summary 1999–2003: Investing in Today and Tomorrow.* Mortgage Fund One: ACM Advisors Ltd.

Polanyi, Karl (1957) The economy as instituted process. In Karl Polanyi, Conrad Arensberg, and Harry Pearson (eds), *Trade and market in the early empires,* pp. 243–270. New York: Free Press.

Putnam, Robert (1995) Bowling alone: America's declining social capital. *Journal of Democracy* 6: 1, 65–78.

Quarter, Jack (1995) *Crossing the Line: Unionized Employee Ownership and Investment Funds.* Toronto: James Lorimer and Company Ltd.

Romano, Roberta (1993) Public Pension Fund Activism in Corporate Governance Reconsidered. *Columbia Law Review,* 93: 795–853.

Rudd, Elizabeth C. and Spalding, Kirsten Snow (1997) Economically Targeted Investment in the Policies and Practices of Taft-Hartley Pension Funds: Two Case Studies. Prepared for the conference *High Performance Pensions: Multi-Employer Plans and the Challenges of Falling Pension Coverage and Retirement Insecurity.* Sponsored by the Institute of Industrial Relations at the University of California. September 4–5.

Shiller, Robert, J. (2000) *Irrational Exuberance.* Princeton: Princeton University Press.

Smith, Michael P. (1996) Shareholder activism by institutional investors: Evidence from CalPERS, *The Journal of Finance,* 51: 1, 227–252.

Stanford, Jim (1999) *Paper Boom*. Toronto: Lorimer and CCPA.

Wahal, Sunil (1996) Pension Fund Activism and Firm Performance. *Journal of Financial and Quantitative Analysis*, 31: 1–23.

Waitzer, Edward (1990) Legal Issues for Trustees and Managers. Proceedings of the Conference *Strategies for Responsible Share Ownership: Implications for Pension and Other Investment Funds*. Sponsored by the Centre for Corporate Social Performance and Ethics and the Task Force on the Churches and Corporate Responsibility, 67–70.

Watson, Ronald D. (1995, winter) The Controversy Over Targeted Investing. *Compensation and Benefits Management*, 1–9.

Wheeler, David, and Maria Sillanpää (2000) *The stakeholder corporation*. Southport, UK: Pitman.

Yaron, Gil (June 2001) The responsible pension trustee. *Estates, Trusts and Pensions Journal*, 20: 4, 305–388.

# 9
# Workers' Knowledge: Untapped Resource in the Labour Movement

*David W. Livingstone and Reuben Roth*

## Introduction

Behind the rhetoric about 'knowledge-based economies' and 'learning organisations', there is the reality of extraordinary increases in the incidence of adult learning activities in Western societies. In Canada, these increases include a doubling of post-secondary education completion over the past generation, a six-fold increase in adult education participation since the early 1960s, and even-larger increases in the amount of informal learning that adults do on their own (see Livingstone, 2001). In 1998, the first national survey of informal learning activities found that Canadians on average are spending about 15 hours per week in informal learning activities. This is significantly more time than the ten hours a week a prior U.S. national survey and a series of case studies found adults devoting to informal learning in the early 1970s. Many factors have encouraged these increases, including rapid economic and environmental changes, the availability of new information technologies and pressures to get more educational credentials.

Long established occupational class differences persist in both schooling and adult education course participation (see Livingstone, 1999a, 1999b). The majority of corporate executives, professionals and managers have university degrees, while less than ten per cent of service and industrial workers have obtained degrees. Over half of those in the employed labour force participate annually in some form of course or workshop, but corporate executives, professionals and managers are twice as likely to participate as industrial workers. However, there are no such class differences in the incidence of self-reported employment-related or general informal learning (Livingstone, 1999b). Industrial workers are almost as likely to devote time to employment-related informal learning activities as corporate executives and spend similar amounts of time engaged in informal learning projects. The vast majority of workers are actively involved in extensive employment-related learning activities. Indeed, industrial workers are found to spend more time in employment-related informal learning (an average of nine hours a week) than occupational classes with higher course participation rates, perhaps partly to compensate for limited access to organised courses. There is a massive, more egalitarian informal learning society hidden beneath the pyramidal class-structured forms of schooling and further education courses.

For the purposes of this paper, the most important point about the changes in profiles of adult learning since the 1960s is that they pervade all social classes, including the organised and unorganised working class of industrial and service workers (see Livingstone, 2001). While the majority of organised workers over 55 have not completed high school, nearly 90 per cent of those under 35 have done so and nearly half of those under 35 have completed a postsecondary degree or diploma programme. While the proportion of organised workers with university degrees remains much smaller than in the professional and managerial classes, it is about nine times greater among the 25–34 age group than in the over 55 age group. The increases for unorganised workers are similar. Most large workplaces in Canada now have a workforce that contains a substantial and growing number of hourly rated employees with advanced formal education, a majority of workers who are interested in pursuing further education and a vast majority of active informal learners.

In spite of impressive gains in formal educational participation and achievement by working class people, their collective skills and learning capacities continue to be underestimated or ignored by employers, government agencies and even many labour leaders. For one thing, the prevalence in schooling of forms of knowledge and language codes most familiar to the affluent classes continues to obscure the less visible forms of working class knowledge and competency. Contemporary social researchers have documented these discriminatory school practices in excruciating detail (e.g. Bourdieu and Passeron, 1977; Curtis, et al., 1992). But even such 'cultural capital' theorists have been preoccupied with delineating the cultural reproduction of inequality within fixed educational institutional forms; so they frequently fail to comprehend the creative cultural practices, independent education and learning activities or collective cultural agency of the organised working class (see Livingstone and Sawchuk, 2004).

Most empirical studies of learning and employment have also probably been conducted from standpoints too closely aligned with the current objectives of enterprise management to appreciate workers' repertoire of learning activities. From a conventional management perspective, virtually the only relevant learning for employees is job training that can enhance the productivity or profitability of the company. From this top-down vantage point, much of the learning that workers do both on and off the job is irrelevant and effectively non-existent. But recent survey studies have confirmed that most job-related training is done informally (see Betcherman et al., 1997; Center for Workforce Development, 1998). Through a combination of initial schooling, further adult education, and informal learning (including both informal training and 'non-taught' learning), the vast majority of workers manage to become at least adequately qualified for their current jobs. Yet the dominant discourse about a pressing need for creation of 'learning organisations' largely ignores or depreciates these realities of interaction between organised education, informal learning and job performance, and presumes that the central challenge for improved enterprise performance is for workers to become more active and motivated learners. Furthermore, many valuable transfers of knowledge and skill between these basic forms of learning and among the spheres of paid and unpaid work are similarly unrecognised or discouraged by the current organisation of paid workplaces (Livingstone, 1999b).

The few Canadian studies that have conducted comparative empirical assessments of the utilisation of knowledge by different occupational classes have found that they spend similar amounts of time in employment-related informal learning, but that corporate executives, managers and professional employees have been much more likely to be enabled to apply their general work-related learning in their jobs than were industrial and service workers (Livingstone, 1997). Since adult learning has increased rapidly while changes in skill and knowledge requirements of the job structure have been more gradual, many Canadians now find themselves *underemployed* in the sense that they are unable to use many of their employment-related skills in their current jobs. There are multiple dimensions to underemployment (see Livingstone, 1999b for discussion and documentation). For example, 'credential underemployment' which refers to the proportion who have attained at least one educational credential higher than is currently required for entry into their job is estimated at around 30 per cent for the current Canadian labour force (see Livingstone, 2001). But only around ten per cent of corporate executives, professionals and managers have educational credentials greater than their jobs require for entry, while about 40 per cent of service workers and industrial workers do. There appears to be a massive underutilisation of the achieved skills and knowledge of the Canadian working class in the current job structure.

Nevertheless, as Table 9.1 shows, the gap between current participation in organised education and desired engagement if there were significant recognition of prior relevant knowledge and skill development (via prior learning assessment and recognition mechanisms or PLAR) is very significant for working class people and non-existent for corporate executives, professionals and managers. Industrial workers and the unemployed would double their course participation if they could receive recognition for their prior informal learning experience. The pent up demand for further education that recognises already established learning competencies among the

*Table 9.1* Occupational class by further education, interest in PLAR credit and participation gap, Active Labour Force, 1998

| Occupational class | (1) Course last year (%) | (2) Interest in courses if PLAR* offered (%) | Participation gap (2)–(1) (%) |
|---|---|---|---|
| Corporate executives | 71 | 61 | –10 |
| Small employers | 52 | 58 | +6 |
| Self-employed | 52 | 69 | +17 |
| Managers | 72 | 62 | –10 |
| Professionals | 76 | 69 | –7 |
| Service workers | 54 | 73 | +19 |
| Industrial workers | 37 | 73 | +36 |
| Unemployed | 38 | 82 | +44 |
| Total | 50 | 70 | 20 |

*Source*: Livingstone (2001).
* Prior Learning Assessment and Recognition.

working class as legitimate and assists in developing them may have been almost as much ignored as extensive informal learning activities per se.

The national survey also found that unionised workers generally spend a greater average amount of time in employment-related informal learning than non-unionised workers (7 hours versus 4.5 hours per week) and that organised workers' underemployment rates are somewhat lower than unorganised workers (Livingstone, 1999b). This suggests the existence of previously unexplored links between knowledge and power in workers' learning practices. In general, the sites where subordinated groups have the greatest control over their social practices are the places where their own cultural knowledge reproduction and generation may be most frequent. Where workers have greater job control, they may more easily apply their prior knowledge. Much of workers' general knowledge may be irrelevant from employers' perspectives for the immediate objective of enhancing current job performance. But it is at least potentially applicable in the negotiation of redesigned jobs to more fully use workers' growing repertoire of skills – as well as in other socially useful and fulfilling household and community work where workers exercise more direct control. Furthermore, where worker-controlled education programmes are readily available, workers may be more likely in both material and motivational terms to integrate their further education and informal employment-related learning. Organised workers by definition have the greatest power to produce and apply their own knowledge.

Our case studies of workers' learning practices were conducted over the 1995–2000 period in southern Ontario in cooperation with a diverse array of five union locals (see Livingstone and Sawchuk, 2004). The research has included consultation with union leaders and key informants about general work and learning conditions in the workplace, in-depth semi-structured interviews with representative samples of workers (total N = 101) conducted near the worksite, and a giveback process in which we worked with each local to identify programme gaps and prospects. In general, we have found that there are both relatively closer links between workers' informal knowledge and their participation in further education programmes, and also lower levels of underemployment, in more economically powerful locals. These are large locals that have relatively extensive worker-run union education programmes as well as co-operative programmes with local educational institutions developed in response to worker demand, all of which are provided with sustainable resource support through negotiations with employers, national and district union offices, and government programmes. Conversely, small locals with very limited budgets and often spatially scattered memberships face much more difficult barriers to generating relevant worker education programmes.

But even the leading union education programmes appear to suffer from a failure to recognise many aspects of current workers' formal and informal knowledge and skills that could be used within the locals for mutual support, negotiations with employers, development of more responsive and creative worker education programmes, as well as to aid wider organising efforts in the labour movement. Advanced formal education may be seen as a disincentive to union engagement in some cases. Many assembly line workers in large manufacturing plants have developed informal learning networks to teach themselves how to use personal computers. Some of these workers have become competent computer programmers even though they have no employer encouragement and no immediate opportunities to use these skills in their jobs and, in some cases, no prior recognition of their skills by union leadership which could sorely use them (Sawchuk, 1996).

In the next section, we focus on the positive and negative experiences of some younger, well-educated autoworkers in trying to use their formal and informal knowledge within a well-endowed union local with relatively extensive education programmes. There are signs of underestimation of some workers' rich knowledge bases, the current underuse of their advanced skills in many jobs and in established union education programmes, and a lack of attention to legitimating and valorising such prior knowledge through union-led campaigns – with employers for better quality jobs to reduce underemployment and with educational institutions for PLAR. All this suggests that even in the most advanced unions there is still major untapped potential in workers' knowledge that can be mobilised both for internal strengthening and expansive growth of the labour movement. The potential in weaker unions must be even greater.

## Auto workers' case study

The Ontario manufacturing complex under study encompasses one of the largest groupings of industrial workers in Canada. Although still enormous by most standards, its employment base and membership size have dwindled greatly over the past 15 years. Few new employees have been hired since 1985 and the average age of this aging, mostly-male workforce is about 45. These employees are represented by the Canadian Auto Workers union (CAW), the largest private sector union in the country, with the most extensive collection of worker education programmes in the Canadian labour movement (see Yates, 1993; Friesen, 1994; Spencer, 1994; Taylor, 2001). Since the 1985 breakaway from the Detroit-based United Auto Workers union these programmes have deepened and widened substantially to include issues of politics and social and economic justice (Livingstone and Roth, 2004).

Workers here have relatively fertile educational opportunities. For example, while many industrial workplaces have a provision whereby employer funded training must be directly related to the workplace, this CAW local negotiated a broad-based programme that encompassed an extended range of subjects outside of the workplace. Although its original comprehensive mandate has been much narrowed in recent years, this programme has allowed workers to pursue postsecondary programmes in areas as diverse as golf club repair and computer animation. In our recent comparative case studies (Livingstone and Sawchuk, 2003), workers at this plant were found to spend much more time in organised courses than those in the other four union job sites.

### Informal learning among autoworkers

Organised courses are only the tip of the iceberg of adult learning (Tough, 1979). Like most adults, industrial workers do most of their learning informally in their everyday activities. It is the informal learning that workers do within their own workplace communities that provide the most basic knowledge ingredients. For production workers there is scant chance of advancement on the assembly line and therefore little advantage in demonstrating their job-related knowledge. But, among one's peers within the workplace or union, the multiple opportunities to deepen and display one's informal knowledge underline the social fact that this is a 'community of learners'.

Members of this CAW local have a significantly higher incidence of informal learning than those at the other sites we studied (Livingstone and Sawchuk, 2004). There is a vast array of informal learning practices, especially among the union activists. With zeal and a level of commitment some scholars suggest can be found only within the ranks of career professionals and executives (Senge, 1990; Reich, 1991), these workers' collective involvement can take them into intensive informal learning activities. Many CAW workers commented on how they use other members' lived experience as a source of informal, transferable knowledge.

> [we] can go sit down and have a beer, but we could be discussing union stuff and learning ... [we] were supposed...to watch a hockey game once, with some buddies ... [but] we never talked hockey [instead] we talked union issues and labour problems ... right from eight to one in the morning. I'm listening, I'm learning ... The whole time I did learn.

But much of the informally acquired knowledge of continues to be underestimated and neglected by both employers and their unions, even such a rich learning setting. A graphic illustration of an employer not only disavowing, but also filching a worker's knowledge, can be found in the experience of the following autoworker:

> ... they [management] found out that I had computer knowledge [and] my group leader [asked me to help].... During the [production] pilot I measured all these cars in a specific area. ... gathered all that information, put it on a spreadsheet, charts, and by the end of the pilot had it ready for the engineer to hand it in for presentation ... *the engineer, he took my name [off] and he put his name on it.*

After this bitter experience – and several like it – this worker has decided that he will no longer share his knowledge of computers with management. This learner reports that since this incident took place, his familiarity with computers has been exploited by his employer many times, with no recognition for his efforts other than time away from the drudgery of his usual assembly work. Since management has not recognised his skills in a concrete manner, he has refocused his learning efforts from employment-related areas to a community college certificate in computer graphics. In other words, this worker has surrendered the possibility that his employer might one day reward him for his learning, and extend employment commensurate with his knowledge. After several attempts at advancement within his workplace, he acknowledges that his education is 'wasted' there. The over-exploitation of this workers' knowledge and skill has not been addressed by the union, nor has he volunteered or been encouraged to apply his talents to aid union-based programme development.

## Two workers' learning profiles

The two assembly line workers highlighted here are examples of comparatively well-educated trade union activists. Both workers are under 45 and share progressive perspectives on trade unionism and working-class education. But they differ greatly with respect to their reliance on formal education and in their unions' responsiveness to their own knowledge.

'Pete Jones', is in his early thirties and has worked on the assembly line for most of his adult life. His parents were both union members in other industries. He is of European ancestry and his relatives have lived in Canada for many generations. 'Bob English', is in his early 40s. Bob and his family emigrated from the British Isles to Canada when he was a child. He has worked on the assembly line for about twenty years. Bob's parents have always been employed in blue-collar jobs.

The early school experiences of Pete and Bob provide illustrations of how working class childrens' creative abilities have been ignored or even denigrated by the established school system. Both recount how their creativity as young students was discouraged by some of their teachers (see Curtis et al., 1992). But, by different indirect paths, both managed to make it to advanced education programmes. Pete has some college experience while Bob now has completed a Bachelor's degree in Social Science, paid for courtesy of the negotiated programme.

Pete is an active rank-and-filer in his union local, has participated heavily in both union education programmes and informal training activities, and generally sees the union from an insider's perspective. In contrast, Bob has been unable to apply his formal knowledge in union activities. He feels shut out of his local and takes the view of an outsider who combines his own working class experience, street smarts and university-based critical analysis of class relations.

Overall, Pete's learning interests are directly linked to a clearly defined set of social and political principles. These he learned in part through the CAW's educational programmes. But for the most part he is a keen informal learner with a strong sense of curiosity and enthusiasm: 'If there's a piece of legislation coming, I'll look at a copy at the library, and I'll look up legal language on the Internet'. Pete pursues his learning passionately, through political projects:

> I'll spend time learning anything to be better, music, computers, but the *union* is the big passion for me, like I feel like that's the thing where I can have the most opportunity to do things. For me, it's like that's what I want to do, you know. I'd love to play music too, but realistically, if I had to choose, I'd have to take the union because you can always listen to music and you can always play it, and it doesn't matter whether people know who you are or not. But with the union, there's so much potential to change and to do things.

Pete feels that informal learning can be at least as relevant as formal education and should be even more highly valued within the labour movement:

> A grade eight education took Bob White [former president of the CAW] to the top of the labour movement and you'd be hard pressed to find

somebody that's more qualified to speak for workers and to negotiate their issues against a group of lawyers from Detroit or the captains of industry.... We have people that have succeeded in the labour movement, specifically in the Canadian Auto Workers, that have limited formal education. We have other ones that are highly educated. The bottom line is that intelligence can't be proven simply by a piece of paper.

In contrast, Bob has tried to rely on more formal methods of learning. He wanted to move from the line to a skilled trade. He used the joint programme to get relevant post-secondary qualifications. However, after several years of pursuing the necessary education, the apprenticeship programme was cancelled. Finding himself left with an array of college courses and nowhere to apply them, Bob went back to his employer with his dilemma:

I went down to Personnel ... I said 'well I'm frustrated, help me out with this. What am I going to do? Do I continue at ... college with my practical work and getting as much practical experience with my tools and trade or do I go to university?' He says: 'go to university'. I thought fine. Then it clicked. *I'm never going to let [my employer] control my future again. Never.* So I thought university's the way to go.

Bob found his continually frustrated attempts to pursue a tradesperson's career were an instructive life experience. Although he conformed to the requirements of his employer's apprenticeship programme at every turn, he was still left out in the cold. He resolved that he would continue his education independently, taking advantage of the employer's training allowance:

I started with one [university] course, just to see if I was going to be successful, if I was cut out for it, and I liked it. I got a lot of stimulation from it and.. I did relatively well at it, and I decided to continue. .... I took a Soc[iology] course and I fell in love with 'Soc'. It just showed me where I fit into the big picture.

So Bob's passion for learning became centred within the formal school system, in a discipline that helped him to interpret his own life experiences.

Bob is emphatic as to why more working-class people, and especially trade union activists, should get a university education. He feels that the understanding of larger societal forces is information hoarded by the upper classes, and shared only within the confines of a university classroom:

I mean, if you want to fight the beast you have to think like the beast.... You have to know ... where they're going to come at you from. And if they're gonna use one set mode of thinking, we're as predictable as they are. And I think predictability is ... fatal.

Bob acknowledges that many of his co-workers on the assembly line are equipped with real talents, although few recognised credentials. But when asked whether the union was putting these people to use he replied:

> Absolutely not ... I think it's politics, it's pure [factional] politics. ... You've got people in the union they're in there for different reasons. ... Myself [I come] from an attitude of working-class advancement – and there's guys that may feel that, but they also want to get off the line.

Bob advocates that his union blends members, like him, who have credentials, with workers who possess experiential knowledge.

> You know ... I felt that, my education [was not] being used in a positive way towards real working class advancement. ... And it's like your own people kicking you in the teeth and saying 'you're not one of us'. You know, 'you're not playing by the old rules'. Well, it's a new world. The rules have changed. So we have to change. And we have to ... attract the best that we have within our own working-class people, to compete with management, with the so-called upper class. We have to adapt. ... I don't have aspirations of leaving the CAW. I mean, my aspirations are advancing the working-class cause.... I think we should use everything available to us to advance the working-class cause. That's where formally educated workers come in. I'm a worker. I'll never forget my roots.

Bob also keenly feels his contradictory position. He is caught between his credentialed status, paid for via a contract clause which was negotiated by his own union local, and the rejection of his formal knowledge by the same local:

> [I]f formal education is so terrible and to be feared, why are all these guys I work with putting their kids through university? ... Why did this union negotiate formal education and a rebate for their kids? Why? If it's to be feared – there's part of my frustration right there, it's a contradiction. Why have they negotiated formal training for me and for my kids if they're not going to respect it [once you get the degree]?

In some respects, Pete's sentiments with reference to the underutilisation of workers' capacities and the future direction their union should support are similar to Bob's. As Pete says:

> There should be greater worker control in the workplace in order to allow employees to make fuller use of their knowledge ....You know, anybody will say utilising people is the most important part of the success of a corporation, of a union, of any kind of organisation, fully utilising people, you know. We can argue about the tools that fully

utilise, whether they're adding more work or not, but to fully allow people to participate using their skills is I think a dream for most people, to be able to do what you do best or want to do and to be able to do it and function and perform in society.

The full extent of workers' formal credentials and employment-related informal learning activities and knowledge generally remain unrecognised by both employers and union leaders. Even in the most advanced unions, with the most extensive and wide-ranging education programmes, there is still much untapped potential for critical education. There should be room as union educators for both the growing numbers, like Bob, who have critically appropriated university education without committing the equivalent of 'class suicide', as well as for many more like Pete who rely heavily on their experiential informal knowledge base.

As acknowledged by both Pete and Bob, there are many untapped resources in the unrecognised informal knowledge and tacit skills of the general membership of this union local. Our research confirms the pivotal role of informal skills training among workers. Older, more experienced workers are often found training their younger peers in many things. These unionists and workers should be recognised for these activities and encouraged to share their knowledge more fully with others by both their union and management. This recognition should not imply that workers give up control of this knowledge. Many workers have the capability to teach others many interesting and valuable things, from political analysis to their work-related duties. Promotion by union leaders of the collective combination of this wealth of informal knowledge with increasing critical knowledge from formal studies could empower and expand the organised labour movement and enrich more workers' quality of life.

## Concluding remarks

The Canadian working class is increasingly highly educated in terms of formal schooling and in course-based adult education, and also engaged in much more widespread informal learning activities. The CAW local that is the focus of this paper has among the most extensive organised education programmes in Canada. The gap between workers' actually existing knowledge and skills and the provision of worker-centred education programmes is probably much greater at most other paid workplaces in the country.

Our studies have found a very sizable pent-up demand among working people to link their extensive informal knowledge both with more equitable access to further formal education, and with more control of their jobs commensurate with this existing knowledge ( Livingstone and Sawchuk, 2004). As long as the extent of working peoples' useful knowledge continues to be underestimated by leaders in the labour movement, it will continue to be depreciated by educational institutions and over-exploited by employers. Unions could easily document the levels of formal and informal knowledge of their existing members, through participatory research which could be conducted quickly and at low cost (see Lior and Martin, 1998). This information could then be used as a pivotal strategic resource in campaigns with employers to negotiate better working conditions for workers to apply their skills, and with educational institutions to provide more accessible prior learning assessment and recognition (PLAR) processes.

The fuller documentation and recognition of union members' actually existing knowledge can provide a sound basis for building more extensive education programmes; recruiting uninvolved, but highly knowledgeable union members to lead in-house education programmes; making concerted demands for workplace democratisation and the design of better quality jobs; and demonstrating the capacity of unions to enhance learning and work conditions. This is probably the most strategically effective way to recruit other currently unorganised workers of all levels of formal education. As Bob English says:

> We don't have to hire the best [union lawyers, negotiators, educators, etc.], we've got the best within our own ranks, *we do*, and I firmly believe that. There's more of us than ... them. ...We've got the talent, no doubt in my mind. *I know, I work with them.* I know we've got the talent. I see it.

### References

Betcherman, G., Leckie, N. and McMullen, K. (1997) *Developing Skills in the Canadian Workplace: The Results of the Ekos Workplace Training Survey.* Ottawa: Canadian Policy Research Networks.

Bourdieu, P. and J. -C. Passeron (1977 [1970]) *Reproduction in Education, Society and Culture.* London: Sage.

Center for Workforce Development (1998) *The Teaching Firm: Where Productive Work and Learning Converge.* Newton, Mass.: Education Development Center.

Curtis, B., Livingstone, D. W. and Smaller, H. (1992) *Stacking the Deck: The Streaming of Working Class Kids in Ontario Schools.* Toronto: Our Schools/Our Selves Educational Foundation.

Friesen, G. (1994) 'Adult Education and Union Education'. *Labour/le travail.* 34 (Fall): 163–88.

Lior, K. and Martin, D. (eds) (1998) *The Skills and Knowledge Profile.* Toronto: ACTEW (Advocates for Community-Based Training and Education for Women).

Livingstone, D. W. (1997) 'The Limits of Human Capital Theory: Expanding Knowledge, Informal Learning and Underemployment'. *Policy Options* 18, 6: 9–13.

Livingstone, D. W. (1999a) *The Education-Jobs Gap: Underemployment or Economic Democracy.* Toronto: Garamond Press.

Livingstone, D. W. (1999b) 'Exploring the Icebergs of Adult Learning: Findings of the First Canadian Survey of Informal Learning Practices', *Canadian Journal for the Study of Adult Education* 13, 2: 49–72.

Livingstone, D. W. (2001) *Working and Learning in the Information Age: A Profile of Canadians.* Ottawa: Canadian Policy Research Networks.

Livingstone, D. W., Hart, D. and Davie, L. (1999) *Public Attitudes Toward Education in Ontario 1998: Twelfth OISE/UT Survey.* Toronto: University of Toronto Press.

Livingstone, D. W. and Reuben Roth (1998) 'Workplace Communities and Transformative Learning: Oshawa Autoworkers and the CAW'. *Convergence* 31, 3, pp. 12–23.

Livingstone, D. W. and Roth, R. (2004) 'Autoworkers: Lean Manufacturing and Rich Learning' in Livingstone and Sawchuk. *Hidden Knowledge.* Toronto: Garamond Press.

Livingstone, D. W. and Sawchuk, P. (2000) 'Beyond Cultural Capital Theory'. *Review of Education, Pedagogy and Cultural Studies*, 22, 2: 203–224.

Livingstone, D. W. and Sawchuk, P. (2004) *Hidden Knowledge: Organized Labour in the Information Age.* Toronto: Garamond Press.

Reich, R. (1991) *The Work of Nations.* NY: Vintage Press.

Roth, R. (1997) *'Kitchen-Economics for the Family': Paid-Education Leave in the Canadian Region of the United Auto Workers.* Unpublished M. A. Thesis, University of Toronto.

Sawchuk, P. H. (1996) *Working-Class Informal Learning and Computer Literacy.* M. A. Thesis, University of Toronto.

Senge, P. (1990) *The Fifth Discipline: The Art and Practice of the Learning Organization.* NY: Doubleday.

Spencer, B. (1994) 'Educating Union Canada'. *Canadian Journal for the Study of Adult Education* 8, 2 (November); 45–64.

Taylor, J. (2001) *Union Learning: Canadian Labour Education in the Twentieth Century.* Toronto: Thompson Educational Publishing.

Tough, A. (1979) *The Adult's Learning Projects.* Toronto: OISE Press.

Yates, C. (1993) *From Plant to Politics: The Autoworkers Union in Postwar Canada.* Philadelphia: Temple.

# 10

# Unions and Procedural Justice: An Alternative to the 'Common Rule'

*David Marsden*

## New work systems and 'procedural justice'

New management thinking on work organisation and pay brings it into direct conflict with long-established methods trade unions have used to defend their members' interests and their ideas of fairness. No doubt, this has contributed to the declining management interest in 'joint regulation' with unions in recent decades, and not just in Britain and the U.S. As employers have striven to make their organisations more responsive to more competitive and faster changing markets, they have sought to devolve decision-making in their organisations, and to rely more upon employees thinking for themselves and using their initiative. To break away from bureaucratic patterns of organisation, they have needed to adopt more performance-oriented reward systems so that they can reward initiative and flexible working, and reinforce the message about the need for 'performance' (Cappelli et al., 1997, Ch. 1).

Historically, the 'common rule' has been a key principle of trade union regulation of workers' pay and conditions, and has given substance to notions of fairness (Webb, S. and Webb, B., 1898). One of its most important manifestations has been the 'standard rate', the idea that unions should seek to establish a minimum rate of pay for particular types of work: a minimum rate per unit of time, or per piece or job realised. Today, in continental Europe and still in large parts of the British public services, there are sectoral agreements establishing such standard rates of pay, usually linking these to complex systems of job classification.

In the workplace too, the idea of a common rule fitted with traditional payment-by-results (PBR) systems that applied common rates of pay to particular jobs, or applied common rules for the number of pieces produced. William Brown's famous study of piecework bargaining (1973) illustrates just how the logic of a common rule could apply even in at the workgroup level. Management acts, of commission or omission, establish precedents, and the workplace representatives use these to lever up the pay of all, establishing a new common rule.

For many decades, such rules also fitted with management's approach to work organisation and performance, often referred to as the 'bureaucratic' model of work organisation (Jacoby, 1985). For unions and their members, such rules are simple to enforce as it is relatively easy to detect backsliding by management. For management, having a standard set of rates of pay greatly eases day-to-day work assignments by removing the incentive to use each change as a pretext for renewed negotiation over pay. In a word, one might characterise the 'common rule' as focusing on the *job* or the *skill* as the bearer of rewards, with adjustments being made for workloads and working conditions. Fairness meant giving the same rewards for comparable jobs. Employee performance was assumed to be determined by the job. This was always a fiction. Any line-manager or experienced trade unionist would tell you there are 'good' and 'bad' workers. But as bureaucratic work systems set rather narrow limits within which individual employees could vary their performance, it was a reasonable approximation.

Rewarding individual performance rather than the job makes the old-style 'common rule' inapplicable, and has boosted management's preference for non-union arrangements. I should like to argue that by maintaining the fairness with which modern incentive systems operate, their 'procedural justice', unions have a very important role to play. The early Christian missionaries understood that they had to win over the local chief as well as the people to establish their churches. In the same way, unions' success in representing their members depends upon gaining recognition from employers. In turn, this depends on convincing them that jointly managed reward systems work better than those they manage unilaterally.

## The advantages for management

Across the UK public sector, performance management and performance pay have been introduced over the past 15 years, mostly being based on line management appraisals of individual employee performance. This follows a similar movement in the private sector (Richardson, 1999). There increasing numbers of employees are on some kind of performance related pay, with line-manager appraisal playing a key role. At the same time, traditional methods of payment-by-results have greatly declined.

The heart of the problem for management is to induce their employees to use their work discretion to the benefit of the organisation. This has also been at the core of theories of Personnel Economics and of Work Psychology. In both cases, the dominant theories teach that monetary incentives will only achieve this if employees believe their efforts will be rewarded, or at least, there is a good chance they will be.

The economic theory of incentives, broadly covered by the 'principal-agent' problem, alerts us to three kinds of problems with performance incentive schemes. First, it assumes that employers and employees are self-interested maximisers. This leads to the conclusion that if employee rewards are the same whatever the level of their effort, then they will be better off if they slack than if they work hard, especially if they can avoid detection. Performance incentives are designed to make employees better off if they work harder, and to punish them if they slack.

By making pay at least partly contingent on performance, employee rewards become variable, which introduces a degree of uncertainty. This leads to the second observation: that employees themselves differ in their preferences about the stability of their income, and differ as to what they regard as a reasonable trade-off between pay levels and pay variability. Some may be very risk averse, whereas others enjoy a challenge. It is quite likely that most employees are rather risk averse, and there is some rather fragmentary evidence that public sector employees may be more so than those in the private sector as risk averse people seek more secure jobs (Mayntz, 1985). Performance-linked pay systems introduce a third element, that is how accurately and honestly management measure performance. Employees may fear that their managers will cheat when assessing employee performance in order to save money or engage in favouritism.

In a perfect market, such problems may not matter too much. Workers can choose between similar jobs offering different kinds of incentives: one can work as an accountant in local government or for a performance-oriented private firm. Similarly, if a firm gets a bad reputation for manipulating its performance schemes, it will find it harder to attract good employees, and so will have to pay more. Either way, fairness issues are dealt with at the moment of hiring: people won't accept job offers they consider unfair. However, most employees continue to be engaged in long-term jobs, and so a rather different set of issues arises (Auer and Cazes, 2000).

With incumbent employees, market sanctions are greatly diminished by the costs to either party of breaking the employment relationship. Employees have acquired organisation-specific skills and knowledge they cannot easily use elsewhere, and from which their employers also benefit. This creates scope for either party to exploit the other by trying to appropriate all the gains, and pushing the other almost to the point at which they would quit. Within these limits, then, one side can impose its preferences on the other, and each side knows this. This is sometimes called the 'hold-up' problem and it becomes an obstacle to free cooperation (Teulings and Hartog, 1998).

Management bad faith can take two forms, both of which are relevant for the understanding of performance pay systems. Management may simply not be competent to measure performance accurately, and as a result, make employees' pay more of a lottery than they would like. Although management's intentions may not be devious, they choose to ignore employee feelings about the appropriate level of uncertainty in their pay. Cheap performance appraisal systems, in which management invests few resources, but which it uses to determine pay, can also be a form of cost-saving for management. More seriously, management may be seen as devious rather than incompetent. The latter is probably the more common of the two, but its consequences are often similar. Employees are likely to regard both kinds of behaviour as 'unfair' because they believe management is going back on what was agreed, and is trying to get away with it because it knows that quitting is an expensive option.

Employee perceptions of the risk of bad faith by management greatly complicate the operation of incentive schemes that seek to mobilise employee discretion. If employees don't believe the rewards for extra effort will be forthcoming, they are less likely to respond to the incentive scheme. If they suspect management is being devious, they may resort to the minimum prescribed performance standards for their jobs as a sanction against management. In practice, as job descriptions are seldom complete or up-to-date, this may mean sticking to conventionally accepted performance standards. Often it is precisely these that management is seeking to change. The general prediction then is that performance pay systems will not work unless employees regard them as fair in their design and operation, and corresponding to their own preferences for incentives and variability.

The psychological theory of expectancy (Lawler, 1971) makes rather similar predictions (sketched in Figure 10.1). According to this view, employees will respond to performance incentives if they value the reward, if they believe their extra effort will generate additional performance, and that management will reward it. If they believe that management cannot measure performance accurately, or that it will renege on promised rewards, then again they will not respond to them. The expectancy framework highlights an additional source of potential unfairness, namely that employees may not be in a position to improve their performance because of inadequate skills, or poor goal setting and coordination by management.

The argument has been taken a step further by Cropanzano and Fulger (1974). They argue that 'procedural justice' is as important for motivating employees as 'distributive justice'. The former relates to procedures that operate fairly, and give employees a fair chance of gaining a particular reward, in this context, a performance increment. The latter relates to the structure of rewards provided. These authors show that employees are more likely to accept adverse performance ratings if they believe management's procedures are fair, and hence they argue that 'procedural justice' is a key element in the motivational aspects of incentive pay systems.

The Centre for Economic Performance (CEP) work on performance pay systems and their effects on employee motivation underline the relevance

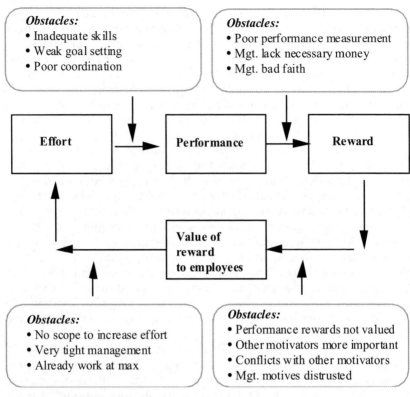

*Figure 10.1*   Outline of the 'expectancy' framework

of these considerations (Marsden and Richardson, 1994; Marsden and French, 1998). Table 10.1 summarises employee responses to the CEP surveys concerning employee confidence in management's operation of performance pay systems.

All of these PRP schemes depended on performance appraisal by line-managers except for the group-PRP scheme in one of the trust hospitals, which separated performance appraisal from pay. There was a widespread belief that management could not be trusted. Line-managers were often thought to act through favouritism, and senior management was believed to operate a quota on good ratings however well people actually performed. The perceived motivation for the quota was exactly that predicted by the principal-agent model, to save on pay costs: three quarters of Inland Revenue respondents in the 1996 survey believed the purpose of PRP was to save money. Another sign of employee cynicism was the belief that those getting performance pay were cleverer at negotiating their performance agreements. In other words, it was felt that those who had learned how to

Table 10.1  Do public servants trust their management over PRP?

| Question: % replying 'agree' | Civil service | | | NHS trust hospitals | | Schools (head teachers) | |
|---|---|---|---|---|---|---|---|
| | Inland revenue 1991 | Inland revenue 1996 | Employment service | Individual PRP trust | Group PRP trust | Primary | Secondary |
| **Relations with management** | | | | | | | |
| My last appraisal was NOT a fair reflection of my performance* | 27 | 28 | 31 | 33 | 19 | 33 | 29 |
| Management use PRP to reward their favourites | 35 | 57 | 41 | 41 | 27 | na | na |
| There is a quota on good assessments | 74 | 78 | 74 | 57 | na | 48 | 45 |
| *Line manager views:* | | | | | | | |
| PRP has reduced staff willingness to cooperate with management | 20 | 45 | 39 | 30 | 27 | na | na |

* reverse scored.

*Note:* Civil service: middle-ranking and junior administrative staff; hospitals: all staff except doctors who were outside the scheme; Schools: head teachers – classroom teachers had no performance pay scheme at the time.

*Source:* Marsden and French (1998), and Marsden and Richardson (1994).

work the system were the ones who got the rewards, and not necessarily those who put in the increased effort the schemes were designed to promote.

These expressions of employee distrust of management are not peculiar to Britain, and so not just a reflection of British 'them and us' social attitudes. Milkovitch and Wigdor (1991) report similar suspicions of favouritism and quotas in the U.S. Federal Service performance management systems. And indeed, Koike (1994) provides evidence on how Japanese workers seek to control favouritism by line managers in their performance management systems.

Although our studies have only very limited performance data, it is possible to trace the impact of such beliefs on aspects of employee motivation. Using a more synthetic analysis, we ran logit regressions on the same CEP data sets to assess the likelihood that employees would be motivated or de-motivated by different aspects of PRP schemes (Marsden, French and Kubo, 2000). These highlight the debilitating effects of perceived management bad faith, and when it was felt that management could not evaluate performance properly. When employees did not believe management knew enough to evaluate their performance, they were more likely to find the PRP schemes de-motivating. Conversely, if they believed appraisals were conducted properly and fairly, they were more likely to find it motivating. Summarising these and other research findings on the main public service performance pay schemes, the government's Makinson report (2000: p. 3) concluded that current arrangements were 'ineffective and discredited' and contrasted 'approval of the principle and disenchantment with the practice of performance pay'.

Both theory and this evidence indicate that management has much to gain from measures that can build employee confidence in the design and operation of their performance management systems. The problem is that it is hard for them to demonstrate the credibility of their promises to employees who are already cynical about them. They are caught in the trap of 'they would say that wouldn't they'.

## A role for unions?

In the course of the CEP's research on performance management, discussions with public service unions, and the survey results, show that unions have a potentially important part to play in improving the procedural justice of these new types of pay and performance management systems. This role can be of benefit both to their members and to management. Management can benefit for the reasons just outlined. Employees can benefit because they may gain some protection against unfair treatment by their managers, and perhaps more important, it is not pleasant to work in an environment in which colleagues are demoralised and relations with management soured.

Let us consider three key areas in which unions can intervene:

- the operation of PRP schemes and performance management;
- the choice of incentives that employees feel are appropriate for their work;
- conveying employees' views on measurement difficulties.

Our surveys provide some useful indicators on all of these counts.

## Operation of performance management

A recurrent theme across the public services covered by our studies has been the need for some kind of control over the way management operates performance management systems. The fear of favouritism and the belief that management operated a quota on good assessments are both areas in which independent review of management's actions would seem relevant. In the organisations in which we asked about appeals procedures (civil service departments/agencies, hospitals and classroom teachers) there was a clear concern among a substantial minority, and a majority in the case of teachers, that appeal procedures needed to be more effective.

In fact, in the civil service and the hospitals, management went to considerable lengths to communicate with staff and their representative organisations. Our survey results were discussed jointly. More importantly, a certain amount of information about the operation of performance management systems is shared. Management have usually given the unions information on the distribution of appraisal scores at a fairly aggregated level. Under the March 2000 'Partnership Agreement' between the Cabinet Office and the Civil Service unions, union involvement in the operation of pay reform was accorded an official place, although relations became more strained subsequently.

## The design of performance management systems

A recurrent theme in our survey returns has been that while most public servants in the civil service and hospitals (but not schools) approve of the principle of linking pay to performance, they are much less happy about the way in which this is done. While some of this no doubt reflects concerns about the operation of performance management systems, some may also reflect deeper unease about the type of incentives offered. Three examples arise from our work: whether professional employees respond differently to performance incentives compared with those in bureaucratic occupations; how effective pay incentives are for organisationally committed employees; and divergent views about the purposes of the organisation and consequently about the relevance of different kinds of performance.

*Professional versus bureaucratic occupations*

Our logit regressions showed that public servants in professional occupations were less happy about performance pay than those in what might be called 'bureaucratic' ones (Marsden, French and Kubo, 2000). Teachers were far less happy than civil servants. Within the hospitals we have a broader mix of professional and bureaucratic occupations, and there we find a clear sign that professionals are less happy than their bureaucratic colleagues. Professionals were also more likely to respond that performance pay had no effect on their performance because they already worked to a professional standard. Such standards are inculcated during the training process, and sustained by peer group activities and professional organisations. Employees in bureaucratic functions are more likely to be used to more direct management control of their work so that performance appraisal and performance pay appear as less of an intrusion into their professional activities.

*Incentive pay and organisational commitment*

If one follows the 'principal-agent' analysis of performance incentives, it is easy to overlook the importance of the initial behavioural assumptions: that employees will opt for low levels of effort unless they have financial incentives to put in more effort. This may not be an appropriate assumption for certain categories of workers, particularly those with a strong professional or public service orientation. The CEP PRP surveys all showed quite high levels of organisational commitment, using standard measures, compared with studies of other employees, and the regression analysis mentioned earlier also found that commitment played an important part as a stabiliser of employee motivation. Although the public servants found many aspects of their PRP schemes de-motivating, organisational commitment seemed to counteract these feelings to some extent. If commitment is strong enough to do this, it may also counteract the key danger predicted by principal-agent analysis, namely that of moral hazard. Committed employees with a strong professional ethic may work to what they consider appropriate standards rather than seeking to minimise effort for a given reward, thus rendering short-term performance incentives inappropriate, and possibly counter-productive.

One other piece of evidence on this score comes from teachers' explanations of why they work long hours during term time (and possibly also into school holidays). These hours are worked on top of a weekly 'directed time' of about 33 hours. Directed hours are those for which teachers' work is directed by the school's management. 'Non-directed' hours are discretionary, during which teachers would work to fulfil their professional duties. The dispersion of non-directed hours worked reveals the discretion teachers have, but at the same time, the number of such hours they work each week, and the reasons they give for this are largely at odds with the assumptions of the principal-agent model. This appears to be driven by their strong concern for their pupils, a high level of commitment to their schools, and strong professional values (Table 10.2).

The teachers' unions have worked hard both to oppose the introduction of a form of performance pay for classroom teachers, and to ensure that the final version implemented fits the conditions and aspirations of teachers. There are some aspects of their scheme, introduced in 2000, which differ from the forms of PRP applied elsewhere in the public services, and which make it almost more akin to acquiring an additional qualification than to appraisal-based pay. It would be tempting to see this as a manifestation of the influence of the teachers' unions, but this has to be confirmed by more careful research.

### Different views concerning organisational objectives and legitimate incentives

There may also be divergent views on the objectives of public services. In health services, the relative weights attached to aspects of performance that

*Table 10.2* 'Non-directed' hours worked by teachers and their reasons

| Type of out of hours activity | Mean weekly hours devoted to each activity | STRB mean * | First reason | Second reason |
|---|---|---|---|---|
| Lesson preparation and marking | 14.3 | 15.0 | Quality of education | To get the work done |
| Seeing parents and pupils outside class time | 2.3 | 5.8 | Quality of education | Activities occur after hours & don't let down pupils & colleagues |
| Involvement in school clubs, sports, orchestras, etc. | 1.9 | na | Activities after hours | Enjoy the work |
| School/staff management: meetings | 3.3 | 3.1 | Management pressure | To benefit school |
| General administrative tasks | 4.2 | 2.0 | To get the work done | Quality of education |
| Individual & professional development activities | 2.0 | 3.1 | Quality of education | Activities occur after hours |

* As a rough check on our results, the distribution of hours between these activities is compared with that found by the STRB survey of teachers' working time in the spring of 1996. The figures relate to secondary schools, but they are very similar to those for primary schools. STRB (1996, Table B 2.5).
*Source*: Marsden (2000).

relate to patient care and budgetary management are very controversial. How long should a ward cleaner or a nurse chat to a sick patient? No doubt it improves the quality of a stay in hospital, and perhaps assists recovery, but it also consumes scarce resources. In the Employment Service, public employees saw their main purpose as helping job seekers find suitable work, but it was often hard to do this within the time limits for interviews set by management to control costs. Teachers, it seems, are prepared to contribute large amounts of their own time towards supporting their pupils because budgetary pressures leave them little alternative if they are to give the quality of education they think right.

Top management, which decides on whether to adopt certain types of incentive schemes, is often far removed from such information. Yet inappropriately designed incentives often lead to a great deal of needless conflict.

### Practical difficulties of performance measurement and improvement

Whatever the philosophical and moral problems of determining performance objectives, there are also much more down-to-earth problems of measuring performance and determining whether people can actually improve their performance even if they want to.

There was widespread concern about management's ability to measure different aspects of performance, and to cover what might be called performance in the whole job. Our civil service respondents thought there was too much emphasis on quantity, which is more easily measured than quality, despite management information campaigns stressing the importance of quality. The latter may have been their agenda, but it was not successfully communicated to their staff.

Performance assessment in team working raises particular measurement problems, especially when management focus on individual performance. In schools for example, both heads and classroom teachers strongly believed that it was hard to relate pupil performance to the work of individual teachers. Thus a scheme that purports to link pay to the performance of individual teachers' pupils is felt to be measuring the wrong thing.

From the civil service and hospital studies, we find that a substantial number of line managers who carry out appraisals believe PRP is problematic because staff have insufficient control over their jobs to increase their performance. Around 60 per cent thought this in the civil service, and around 40 per cent in the two hospitals. Our more recent study of classroom teachers sheds further light on this issue as we asked teachers whether they thought there were significant variations in teaching effectiveness among experienced teachers in their school, to which about 55 per cent replied 'yes'. Even more interesting are the reasons teachers gave for these individual variations (Table 10.3). Of these, only differ-

*Table 10.3* Reasons teachers gave for differences in teaching effectiveness

| If you believe there is such variation in teaching effectiveness, could you please say what you think is the most important cause: | *(Please circle one only)* (%) |
|---|---|
| a) different levels of teaching skills | 25.4 |
| b) differences in motivation or morale | 33.4 |
| c) differences in age | 1.6 |
| d) ability to motivate their pupils | 19.7 |
| e) some teachers have a very difficult workload | 11.3 |
| f) several of the above | 3.1 |
| g) other, please specify: | 5.4 |
| Total | 100.0 |

*Source*: Marsden (2000).

ences in motivation or morale would seem to fit well with the principal-agent model, and this is probably an upper limit as some morale may be the result of school-wide factors, or of management. Many of the others probably cannot be addressed without management support: more time for training, better organisation of workloads by management, and so on.

It is often difficult for individual employees to communicate such information to their line managers. There is a fine line between failing to perform because one is incompetent, and failing because one lacks necessary resources. Line managers may also think their staff are bargaining for easier targets. If the problem is poor line management, it becomes even harder to transmit the information to higher management. For these, and other reasons, higher management may well be cut off from the information it needs to design and operate its incentive schemes effectively: hence the potential role for collective voice.

## Do public employees believe the unions are the bodies to represent them?

Whether or not unions are the best-placed bodies to take up these issues must depend on the confidence of their members. If they do not believe their unions can help redress unfair action by their managers, then there is little unions can do to boost procedural justice and its beneficial effects on the operation of performance management.

Our study of classroom teachers provides some evidence on this issue (Marsden, 2000). We asked which groups teachers identified as being on their side in connection with performance management (Table 10.4). 'Other teachers' came out unsurprisingly as the group most likely to share the same interests. However, the teachers' unions and professional associations came out strongly, much more so than the DfEE or LEA and the school's governors.

We also asked who might provide a legitimate voice for teachers' views about the goal of performance standards: who should determine standards of excellence in teaching? The teaching profession emerged as the leading candidate (Table 10.5). As the unions play an important part in maintaining the overall coherence of the teaching profession, this suggests that they can have a clear role.

*Table 10.4*   Which groups do you identify as sharing the same interests as you in connection with Performance Management?

| When considering the implementation of PM, which groups do you feel share broadly the same interests as yourself? *(Please circle)* | Broadly the same % | Mostly different % | It's hard to say % |
|---|---|---|---|
| a) Your school's governors | 23.3 | 14.3 | 62.4 |
| b) The leadership group/management team in your school | 53.7 | 17.0 | 29.4 |
| c) Other teachers in your school | 79.8 | 5.2 | 15.0 |
| d) Other teachers in your union or professional association | 63.5 | 4.8 | 31.6 |
| e) Your union or professional association | 60.4 | 7.5 | 32.0 |
| f) The DfEE or your LEA | 10.7 | 35.4 | 53.9 |

*Note*: DfEE: Dept for Education and Employment; LEA: Local Education Authority.
*Source*: Marsden (2000).

*Table 10.5*   Who should determine standards of teaching excellence?

| Who do you think should have most say in determining standards of excellence in teaching? *(Please select the top two)* | *Please circle* % |
|---|---|
| a) The government and its agencies (eg. DfEE, Ofsted, QCA) | 10.5 |
| b) Practising teachers as a whole (the teaching profession) | 36.5 |
| c) Practising teachers in one's own discipline | 23.4 |
| d) The management team in individual schools | 21.8 |
| e) The school's governors | 1.5 |
| f) Parents | 1.7 |
| g) Local and national employers | 1.6 |
| h) Other (please specify) | 1.9 |
| i) Several of the above | 1.1 |
| All items | 100.0 |

*Source*: Marsden (2000).

In view of the union involvement with management in the operation of all of the schemes studied, one might object that this demonstrates the counter argument. The first Inland Revenue performance pay scheme was introduced as part of the 1988 pay agreement in which it was enshrined. The Employment Service scheme had the unions negotiating the pot of money to be distributed as performance pay. The two hospitals involved the unions in the operation of their schemes, and the schemes for school heads and classroom teachers have gone through a lengthy process of public debate. These are hardly schemes that were just dropped on the staff from out of the blue, and on which employee organisations have had no voice.

Nevertheless, all of these schemes could have enlisted greater involvement from unions and professional organisations. In the 1988 Inland Revenue agreement the then Inland Revenue Staff Federation (IRSF) was more or less told if it did not accept PRP there would be no agreement. Similarly, the scheme examined in 1996 kept the unions at arm's length. Given its emphasis on team working, the Employment Service would have benefited from a group incentive scheme had not Treasury policy insisted on individual schemes. In the two NHS trust hospitals, the schemes were designed and introduced by management, and only then did the staff organisations become involved. The classroom teachers' new pay system has involved rather more consultation, but still less than was legally required judging by the successful National Union of Teachers (NUT) action in July 2000 (The Guardian Newspaper, 15.7.02).[2]

### Tensions within the 'procedural justice' role for unions

In the past, the 'common rule' was an effective basis for worker mobilisation in defence of common interests. Dealing with procedural justice issues implicates the unions more closely with management because of the nature of the issues to be handled. One cannot take an arm's length approach while at the same time giving an employee input into the design and running of performance management systems. There is then a risk of 'incorporation', that is to say, of becoming so involved in joint management of a scheme that one ends up by giving too much weight to managerial considerations, and too little to the concerns of ordinary employees.

This is a real risk, but it is not a new one. Although the 'common rule' has been a long-standing trade union method of regulation, it has never been possible to rely solely upon it. Piecework is never as simple in reality as it is in theory because 'pieces' are never quite the same, and more important, working conditions are variable. What seemed a fair rate of earnings when people could produce a target number of pieces a week becomes inadequate if conditions change and it is possible to produce only a fraction of these. Older piecework systems built up complex sets of rules for managing this. Adjustments would be made if the quality of components, or the working environment, deteriorated. Someone had to decide whether the change was sufficiently great for the special adjustment to be applied. Management cannot do this alone for the very reasons discussed earlier. Workplace union representatives became heavily involved in such issues, and had to manage the tensions involved in this role.

The ability of workplace representatives to manage this role depends heavily on the amount of back-up provided to them by their unions and professional organisations. With rising levels of general and higher education, management may have less of an educational advantage over union representatives than in the past, but they still have greater organisational resources at their command. Whether management should subsidise this function, given the benefits it derives from effective procedural justice, is a moot point. On balance, it would probably leave the unions too much in management's debt, and vulnerable to threats to reduce the expenditure. Management might also feel it wanted to have a say in the content of training of local representatives, and that might undermine their independence in the eyes of the membership.

This argument may seem like asking unions to help management. However, promoting procedural justice is also protecting their members against unfair treatment by their managers, and perhaps more important, it is not pleasant to work in an environment in which colleagues are demoralised and relations with management soured.

### References

Auer, Peter and Cazes, Sandrine (2000) The Resilience of the Long-Term Employment Relationship: Evidence from the Industrialised Countries. *International Labour Review*, 139: 4, pp. 379–408.

Brown, W. E. (1973) *Piecework bargaining*. Heinemann, London.

Cappelli, P., Bassi, L., Katz, H., Knoke, D., Osterman, P., and Useem, M. (1997) *Change and work*. Oxford University Press, New York.

Cropanzano, R. and Folger, R. (1991) Procedural Justice and Worker Motivation. In Steers, R. and Porter, L. (eds) *Motivation and Work Behavior*, 5th edn. McGraw-Hill, New York, pp. 131–143.

Jacoby, S. M. (1985) *Employing bureaucracy: managers, unions, and the transformation of work in American industry, 1900–1945*. Columbia University Press, New York.

Koike, K. (1994) Learning and incentive systems in Japanese industry. In Aoki, M. and Dore, R. (eds) *The Japanese Firm: the Sources of Competitive Strength*. Oxford University Press, Oxford.

Lawler, E. E. III. (1971) *Pay and organisational effectiveness: a psychological view*. McGraw-Hill, New York.

Makinson, J. (Chair) (2000) *Incentives for change: rewarding performance in national government networks*. Public Services Productivity Panel, HM Treasury, London.

Marsden, D. W. and Richardson, R. (1994) Performing for Pay? The Effects of 'Merit Pay' on Motivation in a Public Service. *British Journal of Industrial Relations*, 32: 2, pp. 243–262, June.,

Marsden, D. W., French, S. and Kubo, K. (2000) *Why does Performance pay de-motivate? Financial incentives versus performance appraisal.* Centre for Economic Performance Discussion Paper No. 476, November 2000, London School of Economics, London.

Marsden, D. W. (2000) *Teachers before the 'Threshold'.* Centre for Economic Performance, Discussion Paper 454, London School of Economics.

Marsden, D. W. and French, S. (1998) *What a performance: performance related pay in the public services.* Centre for Economic Performance Special Report, London School of Economics, London.

Mayntz, R. (1985) *Soziologie der öffentlichen Verwaltung.* Müller Juristischer Verlag, Heidelberg. (dritte überarbeitete Auflage).

Milkovich, G. T. and Wigdor, A. K. (eds) (1991) *Pay for performance: evaluating performance appraisal and merit pay.* National Academy Press, Washington D.C.

Richardson, R. (1999) *Performance pay trends in the UK.* Institute of Personnel and Development Survey Report No. 9, IPD, London, September 1999.

School Teachers' Review Body (1996) *First Report on 1996 Teachers' Workloads Study.* School Teachers' Review Body, July, London.

Teulings, C. and Hartog, J. (1998) *Corporatism or competition? Labour contracts, institutions and wage structures in international comparison.* Cambridge University Press, Cambridge.

Webb, S. and Webb, B. (1920) *Industrial democracy.* Longman, London.

# 11
# Changing Patterns of Unionisation: The North American Experience, 1984–1998*

*Chris Riddell and W. Craig Riddell*

## Introduction

Unionisation has declined substantially in several Anglo-Saxon countries, especially the U.S. and UK. In contrast, Canadian unionisation has been relatively stable. Nonetheless, during the 1980s and 1990s Canada experienced a gradual but steady decline in union density. The principal objective of this paper is to analyse the causes of the decline in union coverage observed in Canada during the past two decades. For comparative perspective we also examine changes in U.S. unionisation during the same period.

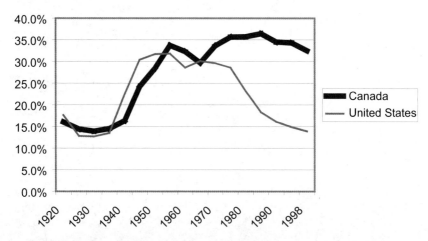

*Figure 11.1*   Union density in Canada and the U.S.

* An earlier version of this paper was presented at the International Conference on Union Growth, University of Toronto, May 2001. We thank Harry Katz for helpful comments and the SSHRC for research support.

Figure 11.1 shows union density (union membership as a per cent of non-agricultural paid workers) over the 1920–1998 period. Beginning in the late 1960s, union density rose in Canada from about 30 per cent to over 35 per cent by 1975, but declined in the U.S., especially after 1980. By the mid-1980s a typical Canadian worker was twice as likely to be represented by a union as his or her American counterpart. This gap in the likelihood of union coverage existed in both the public and private sectors and across a wide range of demographic and labour force characteristics (Riddell, 1993). However, beginning in the early to mid-1980s union density began a gradual but steady decline in Canada. In fact, by 1998, union density had fallen to 32.5 per cent, a level not seen in Canada since the late 1960s.

Canadian research on unionisation and its impacts has long been hampered by the lack of household data in which the union status of individual workers is observed, a situation that has recently improved substantially. This study uses micro-data on individual workers to estimate models of the extent of union coverage in the early 1980s and late 1990s. We then use these estimates to investigate the sources of the change in union density observed over this period.

The causes of the decline in unionisation in the U.S. and UK have been the subject of considerable research and debate. One explanation holds that a major contributing factor is structural change in the economy and labour force that results in employment growing relatively rapidly in sectors that traditionally have had a low propensity to unionise, and declining – in relative, if not absolute terms – in sectors that traditionally have had a high proportion of workers represented by unions (Farber, 1985; Dickens and Leonard, 1985; Troy, 1990, 1993). Examples of these sorts of structural shifts in employment include the growth of female, part-time, white collar and service sector employment and the relative decline of primary, manufacturing, male, full time, and blue collar employment. The experience in some countries of relatively rapid growth in self-employment and employment in small and medium sized enterprises is another example of this type of structural change. We refer to this as the 'structural' hypothesis. According to this perspective, the extent of union organisation in the economy could decline even if there is no change in the likelihood of union coverage of a worker with a given set of demographic and individual characteristics.

Other explanations for changes in union density emphasise reasons why the propensity for union representation may decline for a worker with given characteristics. Several such forces have been suggested, especially in the context of declining unionisation in the U.S. One factor, emphasised by Weiler (1983) and Freeman (1985, 1988), is the rise in management opposition to unions in the U.S. Changes in the legal regime – the laws and their interpretation and administration – relating to union formation and collective bargaining have also been put forward as factors contributing to declining success in union organising as well as to increased management opposition to unions (Weiler, 1983; Freeman, 1985, 1988; Riddell, 2001; Johnson, 2002). Increased trade and openness and a generally more competitive global economic environment are also argued to have reduced the attractiveness of unions to employees and to have increased the desire of employers to operate in a 'union free environment'.

Another hypothesis is that there has been a reduction in the demand for collective representation because of the growth of substitute services. For example, Neumann and Rissman (1984) argue that governments have gradually provided more of the employment protection and non-wage benefits that were originally factors contributing to workers' desire for collective representation. Similarly, employers have increasingly become more sophisticated in their human resources practices and now provide services such as grievance procedures that previously only existed in unionised firms (Kochan, Katz and McKersie, 1986).

An additional explanation advanced by Lipset (1986) is that there has been in the U.S. a reduction in public support for unions and collective bargaining. This shift in attitudes has reduced workers' desire for collective forms of representation. Lipset (1990) also attributes much of the Canada–U.S. differential in union density to fundamental value differences in the two societies – with Canadians placing more reliance on government, state intervention in the economy, and collective forms of organisation and Americans being more oriented towards free enterprise and individual rather than collective rights.

The common feature of these various non-structural explanations is that they predict a decline in the likelihood that a worker with a given set of characteristics will be represented by a union. This change in the propensity to be unionised may occur because of changes in the demand for union representation (for example, because of changes in preferences for collective forms of representation) or changes in the supply (for example, if unions reduce the number of certification attempts because of increased management opposition). We refer to this group of explanations as the 'propensity to unionise' hypothesis.

In this paper we assess the extent to which the decline in union density that took place in Canada – and the similar fall in the U.S. – during the 1980s and 1990s was due to changes in the structure of the economy and labour force or due to changes in the propensity of an individual worker to be unionised.[1] Our principal finding is that, for both countries, most of the drop in union density in the 1984–1998 period can be attributed to changes in the likelihood of an individual worker being unionised. For Canada in particular, none of the decline in union coverage can be attributed to changes in the structure of the economy and workforce.

## Empirical framework

The growth and incidence of unionisation can be analysed using a demand and supply framework (Farber, 1983). The demand for union representation emanates from employees and depends on the expected benefits and costs of collective representation. The supply of unionisation emanates from the organising and contract administration activities of union leaders and their staff. Employers can affect the demand for union representation by altering the costs and/or benefits as perceived by unorganised employees. Employers may also influence the supply of unionisation by changing the costs and/or benefits to union leaders of representing existing members and organising new members.

Thus union status is determined by the decisions made by individual workers, employers and union leaders and their staff. Let

$$US_{it} = 1 \qquad \text{if } y_{it} > 0 \qquad \qquad (1)$$
$$= 0 \qquad \text{otherwise}$$

where i refers to individual worker i and t refers to year t, and

$$y_{it} = X_{it} \, B_t + e_{it} \qquad \qquad (2)$$

Equation (1) is a reduced-form equation that reflects the combined outcome of demand and supply factors on union status. $y_{it}$ is an unobserved variable that incorporates the net benefits of union coverage to worker i and the influences of the behavior of employers and union leaders and organisers. $e_{it}$ is a random error term. $X_{it}$ is a set of demographic and individual characteristics of workers and $B_t$ is a vector of parameters, which we allow to change over time.

In terms of the hypotheses discussed previously, the structure of the labour force and economy is captured by the set of control variables $X_{it}$ and the propensity to unionise is captured by the vector of parameters $B_t$. That is, each element of the parameter vector $B_t$ represents the marginal effect of the associated characteristic (the associated element of the set of controls $X_{it}$) on the likelihood of worker i being covered by a collective agreement.

We estimate this model of union coverage with individual data from 1984 and 1998, allowing the parameter vectors to differ between the two periods. Two specifications are estimated: a linear probability model and a probit model. The latter has the advantage that the parameter estimates are consistent if the model is correctly specified and the error term is normally distributed. The linear probability model does not yield consistent estimates but has the advantage that the results are more straightforward to decompose into 'structural' and 'propensity to unionise' components.

Given that the marginal effects estimated with the probit model are very similar to the linear probability results, to simplify exposition we present only the linear probability results and the associated decomposition.[2]

Let $U_{84}$ and $U_{98}$ denote the mean values of union coverage in 1984 and 1998 respectively and $X_{84}$ and $X_{98}$ denote the mean values of the control variables $X_{it}$ in these two years. Using the standard Oaxaca method, we can decompose the change in collective agreement coverage as follows:

$$U_{98} - U_{84} = X_{98}\, b_{98} - X_{84}\, b_{84}$$
$$= (X_{98} - X_{84})\, b_{98} - (b_{98} - b_{84})\, X_{84} \qquad (3)$$

where $b_{84}$ and $b_{98}$ are the estimated parameter vectors from the linear probability model.

The first term on the right hand side of equation (3) is the portion due to structural change in the economy and labour force. The magnitude of this term depends on the change between 1984 and 1998 in the portion of the labour force that is female, works part-time, is employed in the public sector, and similarly for other characteristics such as age, education, industry, occupation, province, and job tenure. The second term on the right hand side is the portion of the total change in coverage that is associated with changes in the propensity to unionise of a worker with a given set of characteristics. The magnitude of this term depends on the changes between 1984 and 1998 in the parameters $b_t$, or the marginal effects of a given characteristic on the likelihood of unionisation.

## Data

For the Canadian analysis, we use the Survey of Union Membership (SUM), a supplement to the Labour Force Survey carried out in December 1984, and the December 1998 Labour Force Survey (LFS). For the United States, we use the December 1984 and December 1998 Current Population Survey (CPS). All of the above surveys provide micro-data on representative samples of individual workers, including questions on union membership and coverage by a collective agreement. These data also provide information on a number of worker characteristics, including gender, age, education, province, part-time or full-time work, public or private sector employment, job tenure (duration of employment with the current employer) and industry and occupation. One difference between the Canadian surveys and the U.S. surveys is that job tenure is not available in the CPS. The Canadian surveys use the same industry and occupation coding (the 1980 SIC and 1980 SOC respectively) and – with the exception of educational attainment – ask identical questions on other characteristics.[3]

The years 1984 and 1998 were chosen for several reasons. The SUM was the first Canadian household survey to include questions on union membership and collective agreement coverage. Since coverage is our preferred measure of union status, this is an important consideration.[4] Another reason is that the overall state of the Canadian economy was similar in 1984 and 1998. In order to not confound changes in unionisation that are due to long term trends with those due to short term cyclical movements in economic activity, we wish to compare periods in which the economy was at a similar stage of the business cycle. Canada experienced sharp recessions in the early 1980s (1981–82) and the early 1990s (1990–92). The slump in the early 1990s was especially severe (Fortin, 1996) and the recovery from that downturn was extremely slow and uneven. Only after 1995 did a gradual recovery begin to take hold, in contrast to the situation in the 1980s when the economy bounced back relatively quickly from the 1981–82 recession. In both 1984 and 1998 the economy had returned to a normal level of economic activity but had not yet reached a cyclical peak. Unfortunately 1984 and 1998 were not as comparable for the United States since the American economy was close to a cyclical peak in 1998, but still approaching a peak in 1984. However, all things considered including data constraints, these two years are the best available options.

Both surveys include (identical) questions on union membership and collective agreement coverage. Because we wish to distinguish between the 'unionised sector' and the 'nonunion sector' we prefer to use coverage as a measure of union status. All Canadian jurisdictions adhere to the principal of exclusive jurisdiction whereby a union, once certified as the representative of a bargaining unit, represents all workers in the bargaining unit whether or not they choose to join the union. Covered non-members are thus in the 'union sector' in the sense that their wages and working conditions are determined by collective bargaining between the employer and union. Nonetheless, in both Canada and the United States the difference between union membership and collective agreement coverage is not large (as it is in Australia and many European countries) and use of union membership rather than coverage would not change our results in a substantial way.[5]

## Empirical results

Tables 11.1 and 11.2 show the mean coverage rates in 1984 and 1998 for the labour force as a whole and broken down by demographic and individual characteristics, for Canada and the U.S. respectively. Overall, union coverage fell by almost seven percentage points in Canada, a drop of about 17 per cent, while in the U.S. union coverage fell by about eight percentage points, a decline of around 34 per cent. In both countries, the decline in coverage was much larger in the private sector than in the public sector and larger among males than females. While coverage among part-time

*Table 11.1*   Coverage rates for Canada

| Variable | Per cent of individuals covered by collective agreement | | | |
|---|---|---|---|---|
| | 1984 (1) | 1998 (2) | (2) – (1) | [(2) – (1)/(1)] * 100 |
| Total | 0.403 | 0.335 | –6.860 | –17.020 |
| **Sector:** | | | | |
| Private | 0.300 | 0.220 | 0.080 | –26.670 |
| Public | 0.787 | 0.759 | –0.028 | –3.558 |
| **Hours worked:** | | | | |
| Full time | 0.435 | 0.359 | –0.076 | –17.471 |
| Part time | 0.234 | 0.237 | 0.003 | 1.282 |
| **Gender:** | | | | |
| Male | 0.434 | 0.354 | –0.080 | –18.430 |
| Female | 0.363 | 0.314 | –0.049 | –13.498 |
| **Tenure:** | | | | |
| 1–6 months | 0.226 | 0.159 | –0.067 | –29.646 |
| 7–12 months | 0.245 | 0.183 | –0.062 | –25.306 |
| 1 to 5 years | 0.328 | 0.232 | –0.096 | –29.268 |
| 6 to 10 years | 0.490 | 0.396 | –0.094 | –19.183 |
| 11 to 20 years | 0.599 | 0.524 | –0.075 | –12.520 |
| Over 20 years | 0.564 | 0.632 | 0.068 | 12.056 |
| **Province:** | | | | |
| Newfoundland | 0.452 | 0.402 | –0.05 | –11.061 |
| PEI | 0.348 | 0.327 | –0.021 | –6.034 |
| Nova Scotia | 0.415 | 0.315 | –0.1 | –24.096 |
| New Brunswick | 0.395 | 0.295 | –0.1 | –25.316 |
| Quebec | 0.480 | 0.403 | –0.077 | –16.041 |
| Ontario | 0.364 | 0.298 | –0.066 | –18.131 |
| Manitoba | 0.414 | 0.368 | –0.046 | –11.111 |
| Saskatchewan | 0.409 | 0.370 | –0.039 | –9.535 |
| Alberta | 0.317 | 0.270 | –0.047 | –14.826 |
| British Columbia | 0.436 | 0.361 | –0.075 | –17.201 |
| **Age:** | | | | |
| 15 to 19 | 0.110 | 0.085 | –0.025 | –22.727 |
| 20 to 24 | 0.290 | 0.159 | –0.131 | –45.172 |
| 25 to 34 | 0.434 | 0.289 | –0.145 | –33.410 |
| 35 to 44 | 0.476 | 0.387 | –0.089 | –18.697 |
| 45 to 54 | 0.456 | 0.459 | 0.003 | 0.657 |
| 55 to 64 | 0.457 | 0.408 | –0.049 | –10.722 |
| Over 64 | 0.323 | 0.146 | –0.177 | –54.798 |
| **Education:** | | | | |
| Elementary | 0.473 | 0.330 | –0.143 | –30.232 |
| High school | 0.369 | 0.292 | –0.077 | –20.867 |
| Some post–secondary | 0.340 | 0.250 | –0.09 | –26.470 |
| College diploma | 0.454 | 0.368 | –0.086 | –18.942 |
| University degree | 0.462 | 0.396 | –0.066 | –14.285 |

*Table 11.1*   Coverage rates for Canada – *continued*

| Variable | Per cent of individuals covered by collective agreement | | | |
|---|---|---|---|---|
| | 1984 (1) | 1998 (2) | (2) – (1) | [(2) – (1)/(1)] * 100 |
| **Industries:** | | | | |
| Primary | 0.364 | 0.270 | –0.094 | –25.824 |
| Non-durable manufacturing | 0.500 | 0.325 | –0.175 | –35.000 |
| Durable manufacturing | 0.450 | 0.391 | –0.059 | –13.111 |
| Construction | 0.355 | 0.321 | –0.034 | –9.577 |
| Transportation, storage | 0.630 | 0.504 | –0.126 | –20.000 |
| Wholesale trade | 0.147 | 0.112 | –0.035 | –23.809 |
| Retail trade | 0.147 | 0.140 | –0.007 | –4.761 |
| Finance | 0.123 | 0.113 | –0.01 | –8.130 |
| Community services | 0.668 | 0.605 | –0.063 | –9.431 |
| Personal services | 0.110 | 0.089 | –0.021 | –19.090 |
| Business and misc. | 0.105 | 0.093 | –0.012 | –11.428 |
| Public administration | 0.746 | 0.731 | –0.015 | –2.010 |
| **Occupation:** | | | | |
| Managerial and admin. | 0.214 | 0.183 | –0.031 | –14.486 |
| Engineering | 0.369 | 0.260 | –0.109 | –29.539 |
| Social sciences | 0.499 | 0.461 | –0.038 | –7.6152 |
| Religion | 0.053 | 0.042 | –0.011 | –20.754 |
| Teaching | 0.694 | 0.764 | 0.07 | 10.086 |
| Medicine and health | 0.813 | 0.672 | –0.141 | –17.343 |
| Artistic and recreational | 0.243 | 0.207 | –0.036 | –14.814 |
| Clerical | 0.352 | 0.282 | –0.07 | –19.886 |
| Sales | 0.105 | 0.095 | –0.01 | –9.523 |
| Service | 0.312 | 0.262 | –0.05 | –16.025 |
| Agricultural related | 0.366 | 0.310 | –0.056 | –15.300 |
| Fishing | 0.392 | 0.148 | –0.244 | –62.244 |
| Forestry | 0.430 | 0.257 | –0.173 | –40.232 |
| Mining | 0.427 | 0.308 | –0.119 | –27.868 |
| Processing | 0.613 | 0.494 | –0.119 | –19.412 |
| Machining | 0.610 | 0.426 | –0.184 | –30.163 |
| Fabricating | 0.456 | 0.379 | –0.077 | –16.886 |
| Construction related | 0.547 | 0.499 | –0.048 | –8.775 |
| Equipment operating | 0.482 | 0.394 | –0.088 | –18.257 |
| Material handling | 0.521 | 0.345 | –0.176 | –33.781 |
| Other crafts | 0.582 | 0.491 | –0.091 | –15.635 |

workers actually increased slightly in Canada, the decline was concentrated among full-time workers in both countries as well.

There was some variation by province in the decline in Canadian coverage, with the largest drops (in percentage terms) occurring in Nova Scotia and New Brunswick, followed by Ontario and British Columbia, and the smallest declines taking place in Manitoba, Saskatchewan and P.E.I. For the most part

*Table 11.2*   Coverage rates for the United States

| Variable | Per cent of individuals covered by collective agreement | | | |
| --- | --- | --- | --- | --- |
| | 1984 (1) | 1998 (2) | (2) – (1) | [(2) – (1)/(1)] * 100 |
| Total | 0.231 | 0.152 | –0.079 | –34.199 |
| **Sector:** | | | | |
| Private | 0.180 | 0.100 | –0.080 | –44.444 |
| Public | 0.461 | 0.424 | –0.037 | –8.026 |
| **Hours worked:** | | | | |
| Full time | 0.248 | 0.171 | –0.077 | –31.048 |
| Part time | 0.118 | 0.064 | –0.054 | –45.763 |
| **Gender:** | | | | |
| Male | 0.273 | 0.171 | –0.102 | –37.362 |
| Female | 0.180 | 0.131 | –0.049 | –27.222 |
| **Race:** | | | | |
| White | 0.217 | 0.147 | –0.070 | –32.258 |
| Non-white | 0.319 | 0.174 | –0.145 | –45.454 |
| **Region:** | | | | |
| New England | 0.246 | 0.152 | –0.094 | –38.211 |
| Middle Atlantic | 0.326 | 0.232 | –0.094 | –28.834 |
| East North Central | 0.297 | 0.218 | –0.079 | –26.599 |
| West North Central | 0.240 | 0.157 | –0.083 | –34.583 |
| South Atlantic | 0.139 | 0.084 | –0.055 | –39.568 |
| East South Central | 0.192 | 0.125 | –0.067 | –34.895 |
| West South Central | 0.117 | 0.079 | –0.038 | –32.478 |
| Mountain | 0.186 | 0.081 | –0.105 | –56.451 |
| Pacific | 0.257 | 0.177 | –0.080 | –31.128 |
| **Age:** | | | | |
| 15 to 19 | 0.074 | 0.046 | –0.028 | –37.837 |
| 20 to 24 | 0.131 | 0.078 | –0.053 | –40.458 |
| 25 to 34 | 0.209 | 0.119 | –0.090 | –43.062 |
| 35 to 44 | 0.293 | 0.161 | –0.132 | –45.051 |
| 45 to 54 | 0.297 | 0.226 | –0.071 | –23.905 |
| 55 to 64 | 0.267 | 0.216 | –0.051 | –19.101 |
| Over 64 | 0.108 | 0.081 | –0.027 | –25.000 |
| **Education:** | | | | |
| Elementary | 0.224 | 0.112 | –0.112 | –50.00 |
| High school | 0.245 | 0.153 | –0.092 | –37.551 |
| Some post–secondary | 0.226 | 0.147 | –0.079 | –34.955 |
| College diploma | 0.209 | 0.141 | –0.068 | –32.535 |
| University degree | 0.219 | 0.166 | –0.053 | –24.200 |

Table 11.2    Coverage Rates for the United States – *continued*

| Variable | Per cent of individuals covered by collective agreement | | | |
|---|---|---|---|---|
| | 1984 (1) | 1998 (2) | (2) – (1) | [(2) – (1)/(1)] * 100 |
| **Industries:** | | | | |
| Primary | 0.192 | 0.179 | –0.013 | –6.770 |
| Non-durable | 0.252 | 0.155 | –0.097 | –38.492 |
| manufacturing | | | | |
| Durable manufacturing | 0.299 | 0.173 | –0.126 | –42.140 |
| Construction | 0.263 | 0.186 | –0.077 | –29.277 |
| Transportation, storage | 0.490 | 0.308 | –0.182 | –37.142 |
| Wholesale trade | 0.068 | 0.081 | 0.013 | 19.115 |
| Retail trade | 0.085 | 0.049 | –0.036 | –42.352 |
| Finance | 0.059 | 0.039 | –0.020 | –33.898 |
| Community services | 0.304 | 0.237 | –0.067 | –22.039 |
| Personal services | 0.118 | 0.049 | –0.069 | –58.474 |
| Business and misc. | 0.084 | 0.035 | –0.049 | –58.333 |
| Public administration | 0.384 | 0.350 | –0.034 | –8.854 |
| **Occupation:** | | | | |
| Managerial | 0.095 | 0.069 | –0.026 | –27.368 |
| Other professionals | 0.319 | 0.216 | –0.103 | –32.288 |
| Technicians and related | 0.135 | 0.098 | –0.037 | –27.407 |
| Sales | 0.073 | 0.041 | –0.032 | –43.835 |
| Clerical | 0.195 | 0.140 | –0.055 | –28.205 |
| Service | 0.203 | 0.135 | –0.068 | –33.497 |
| Precision production | 0.326 | 0.239 | –0.087 | –26.687 |
| Fabricating | 0.360 | 0.233 | –0.127 | –35.277 |
| Equipment operating | 0.361 | 0.242 | –0.119 | –32.964 |
| Material handling | 0.349 | 0.195 | –0.154 | –44.126 |
| Primary | 0.239 | 0.188 | –0.051 | –21.338 |

in the United States, all regions experienced similar declines with the exception of the Mountain region where the fall in coverage was considerably higher. By industry, the steepest declines in Canada occurred in non-durable manufacturing and primary industries, followed by transportation, communication and utilities, wholesale trade, and personal services. The smallest declines occurred in public administration, retail trade, and finance, insurance and real estate. The industrial decline in the United States was quite different from Canada with business services and personal services experiencing the largest declines while union coverage fell only slightly in the primary sector. Coverage actually increased in wholesale trade in the United States. There is also some variation in the decline in union coverage by age, education, job tenure, and occupation. Nonetheless, the main point that is evident in Tables 11.1 and 11.2 is that the drop in unionisation was quite widespread, and took place in a wide range of industries, occupations and regions.

The SUM and LFS provide information on industry and occupation at the three digit level (approximately 50 industries and 50 occupations) and at a more aggregate level similar to the two digit level (13 industries and 21 occupations).[6] We have carried out the analysis with both the finer industry and occupation breakdowns and the more aggregate breakdowns. The results from the coverage regressions that use the smaller set of industry and occupation controls are presented in Table 11.3. Using the more detailed set of industry and occupation controls added little to the overall analysis and so, to simplify the reader's task, we will only refer to the above-noted results.[7]

Similar changes occurred in the two countries' labour forces between 1984 and 1998. The proportion of the labour force that works part time and the participation rate increased by similar amounts in both countries. As would be expected, the proportion of workers in older age categories increased while the proportion of workers in the younger age categories fell. Also as expected, there were large increases in the educational attainment of the work force. In both countries there were some minor changes in the industrial composition, with the size of the public administration, primary and non-durable manufacturing sectors falling and services – especially business services and community services – increasing. Conversely, there were essentially no changes in the provincial/regional composition of the two work forces and, interestingly, there was also little change in the public-private composition. On the whole, the change – or lack of change – in the Canadian and American labour forces was very similar over the 1984 to 1998 period.

For both countries, many of the estimated parameters are also quite similar across the 1984 and 1998 surveys. However, several noteworthy changes have also occurred. For instance, in both countries public sector workers were even more likely to be unionised relative to private sector workers in 1998 than in 1984. The estimated coefficient for part-time workers increased by almost twofold for Canada, but this substantial increase was not experienced in the U.S. In addition, for Canada, there was a large increase – about seven percentage points – in the propensity to unionise for the highest tenure category.

The absence of significant change in the propensity to unionise across provinces is also noteworthy. One of the important developments in Canada during the 1980s and 1990s was the change from card-signing or 'automatic certification' procedures to mandatory voting for union certification in several provinces (Riddell, 2001; Johnson, 2002). The province of Ontario – the omitted category – introduced mandatory voting for union certification in 1996 whereas this change was introduced earlier in British Columbia, Newfoundland and Alberta (although the B.C. mandatory voting requirement was subsequently reversed). Given that there is a lag between changes in certification procedures and changes in

Table 11.3  Means and estimated coefficients from coverage regressions

| Variable | Canada | | | | United States | | | |
|---|---|---|---|---|---|---|---|---|
| | 1984 | | 1998 | | 1984 | | 1998 | |
| | Mean | Coefficient | Mean | Coefficient | Mean | Coefficient | Mean | Coefficient |
| Public | 0.211 | 0.313 (.008) | 0.218 | 0.373 (.007) | 0.181 | 0.296 (.012) | 0.160 | 0.330 (.011) |
| Part-time | 0.159 | -0.056 (.007) | 0.198 | -0.028 (.005) | 0.132 | -0.082 (.010) | 0.182 | -0.079 (.009) |
| Age: 15 to 19 | 0.070 | -0.061 (.010) | 0.058 | -0.042 (.009) | 0.036 | -0.127 (.019) | 0.059 | -0.013 (.014) |
| Age: 20 to 24 | 0.149 | 0.002 (.008) | 0.106 | -0.04 (.007) | 0.136 | -0.115 (.011) | 0.105 | -0.046 (.011) |
| Age: 25 to 34 | 0.301 | 0.028 (.006) | 0.258 | -0.003 (.005) | 0.312 | -0.061 (.009) | 0.248 | -0.024 (.008) |
| Age: 35 to 44 | 0.234 | Reference | 0.288 | Reference | 0.238 | Reference | 0.271 | Reference |
| Age: 45 to 54 | 0.152 | -0.026 (.007) | 0.208 | -0.011 (.005) | 0.152 | -0.001 (.011) | 0.205 | 0.045 (.008) |
| Age: 55 to 64 | 0.086 | -0.044 (.009) | 0.073 | -0.039 (.007) | 0.106 | -0.023 (.012) | 0.090 | 0.039 (.011) |
| Age: Over 64 | 0.008 | -0.183 (.024) | 0.007 | -0.191 (.021) | 0.020 | -0.115 (.024) | 0.024 | -0.033 (.020) |
| Female | 0.437 | -0.026 (.005) | 0.485 | -0.026 (.004) | 0.452 | -0.040 (.008) | 0.484 | -0.009 (.007) |
| Elementary | 0.101 | 0.028 (.008) | 0.035 | -0.053 (.010) | 0.049 | -0.069 (.010) | 0.047 | -0.043 (.014) |
| High School | 0.499 | Reference | 0.340 | Reference | 0.490 | Reference | 0.388 | Reference |
| Some Post-secondary | 0.103 | -0.004 (.007) | 0.097 | 0.005 (.006) | 0.083 | 0.010 (.012) | 0.087 | 0.007 (.011) |

*Table 11.3* Means and estimated coefficients from coverage regressions – *continued*

| Variable | Canada | | | | United States | | | |
|---|---|---|---|---|---|---|---|---|
| | 1984 | | 1998 | | 1984 | | 1998 | |
| | Mean | Coefficient | Mean | Coefficient | Mean | Coefficient | Mean | Coefficient |
| College diploma | 0.152 | 0.001 (.007) | 0.338 | 0.001 (.004) | 0.148 | −0.016 (.010) | 0.210 | 0.013 (.008) |
| University degree | 0.145 | −0.047 (.008) | 0.188 | −0.017 (.006) | 0.230 | −0.039 (.010) | 0.269 | −0.003 (.009) |
| Primary | 0.026 | 0.085 (.018) | 0.018 | 0.031 (.017) | 0.011 | 0.064 (.033) | 0.006 | 0.061 (.038) |
| Non-durable manufacturing | 0.109 | 0.163 (.010) | 0.087 | 0.039 (.009) | 0.089 | 0.063 (.015) | 0.064 | 0.030 (.015) |
| Durable manufacturing | 0.093 | 0.126 (.010) | 0.092 | 0.099 (.009) | 0.143 | 0.089 (.013) | 0.103 | 0.020 (.013) |
| Construction | 0.046 | 0.023 (.014) | 0.039 | 0.026 (.013) | 0.057 | 0.056 (.021) | 0.057 | 0.019 (.015) |
| Transportation | 0.081 | 0.209 (.011) | 0.080 | 0.157 (0.161) | 0.081 | 0.267 (.015) | 0.082 | 0.157 (.014) |
| Wholesale trade | 0.044 | −0.048 (.012) | 0.048 | −0.067 (.009) | 0.045 | −0.057 (.018) | 0.040 | 0.002 (.016) |
| Retail trade | 0.137 | Reference | 0.129 | Reference | 0.154 | Reference | 0.174 | Reference |
| Finance | 0.056 | −0.050 (.011) | 0.058 | −0.057 (.009) | 0.065 | −0.006 (.016) | 0.068 | −0.009 (.014) |
| Community services | 0.181 | 0.269 (.011) | 0.196 | 0.076 (.009) | 0.186 | 0.057 (.015) | 0.208 | 0.045 (.012) |
| Personal services | 0.086 | −0.010 (.011) | 0.098 | −0.057 (.009) | 0.041 | 0.021 (.019) | 0.050 | −0.011 (.015) |
| Business and misc. | 0.061 | −0.027 (.011) | 0.089 | −0.035 (.008) | 0.072 | −0.022 (.015) | 0.100 | −0.029 (.012) |

Table 11.3  Means and estimated coefficients from coverage regressions – *continued*

| Variable | Canada 1984 Mean | Canada 1984 Coefficient | Canada 1998 Mean | Canada 1998 Coefficient | United States 1984 Mean | United States 1984 Coefficient | United States 1998 Mean | United States 1998 Coefficient |
|---|---|---|---|---|---|---|---|---|
| Public administration | 0.080 | 0.232 (.013) | 0.063 | 0.137 (.011) | 0.057 | -0.009 (.021) | 0.049 | -0.045 (.019) |
| Constant | 1.000 | 0.088 (.011) | 1.000 | 0.099 (.009) | 1.000 | 0.191 (.022) | 1.000 | 0.075 (.018) |
| **Other controls** | | | | | | | | |
| Occupation | | 24 occupation dummies | | | | 11 occupation dummies | | |
| Race | | No | | | | Yes | | |
| Regions | | Province dummies | | | | 8 region dummies | | |
| Job tenure | | Yes | | | | No | | |
| Adjusted R² | | 0.36 | | 0.37 | | 0.22 | | 0.21 |
| Sample size | | 35523 | | 47904 | | 13275 | | 12852 |
| F-stat | | 338.50 | | 479.21 | | 87.34 | | 80.34 |

*Notes:* Standard errors are in parentheses. Estimation is by OLS. To simplify the table only means and coefficients for variables consistently available across countries are shown. Further results (probit models; finer industry/occupation controls) are available from the authors.

union coverage, the Ontario provisions introduced in 1996 would probably not have much influence on union density by December 1998. However, among the provinces that introduced mandatory voting prior to Ontario, only Alberta experienced a decline in the associated coefficient, and this drop was modest in size.

One of the few notable differences between the two countries was in the impacts of age. For Canada, little changed over the period while dramatic changes in the propensity to unionise by age were experienced in the U.S. In particular, younger workers were much more likely to be unionised in 1998. For instance, in 1984 individuals of age 15–19 were 13 per cent less likely to be unionised relative to 35–44 year olds. In 1998, however, there was no statistical difference between these age categories. As well, 20–24 year olds went from being about 12 per cent less likely to be unionised to only 5 per cent less likely.[8]

Clearly the most striking results for Canada, and to some extent the United States, are the large declines in the estimates for many industry categories. For Canada, relative to retail trade, there were large declines in the estimated parameters for every industry group. As well, there were huge declines in the propensity to unionise in community services and public administration. In fact, the coefficient for community services fell by 72 per cent! For the U.S., the more dramatic declines were in the same industries as Canada with the exception of community services. Specifically, the propensity to unionise fell substantially in manufacturing, construction, transportation, and public administration.

With respect to occupations – where the omitted category is sales – the decline in the propensity to unionise was less striking with most categories showing no large decline. Three interesting exceptions for Canada were primary occupations (fishing and forestry), machining and material handling. For instance, the estimated coefficient on machining fell by 13 percentage points while that of material handling fell by ten percentage points. Both occupations are normally associated with high unionisation rates.

Table 11.4 presents the decomposition of the 1984–98 change in union density for Canada and the U.S. into 'structural' and 'propensity to unionise' components, as discussed previously. The major finding is that structural changes in the economy and labour force played essentially no role in Canada and only a minor role in the U.S. Specifically, for the U.S., only 1.84 percentage points out of a total decline in coverage of about eight percentage points – or approximately 20 per cent – was due to structural factors. Interestingly, for Canada, structural change in the labour force actually worked to increase unionisation, albeit only slightly. In fact, the decline in the propensity to unionise in Canada was a full percentage point greater than in the U.S. It is worthwhile noting that our finding for the U.S. is very similar to that of Farber (1990) who concluded that structural factors can account for about 20 per cent of the decline in unionisation

*Table 11.4*  Decomposition of decline in union density, 1984 to 1998

|  | Canada | | United States | |
|---|---|---|---|---|
|  | **Structural** | **Propensity** | **Structural** | **Propensity** |
| Public | 0.277% | – | –0.689% | – |
| Part time | –0.112% | – | –0.389% | – |
| Tenure | 0.819% | – | – | – |
| Race | – | – | 0.057% | – |
| Regional | –0.032% | – | –0.439% | – |
| Age | 0.274% | – | 0.428% | – |
| Gender | –0.133% | – | –0.030% | – |
| Education | 0.290% | – | 0.079% | – |
| Industrial | –0.488% | – | –0.127% | – |
| Occupational | –0.801% | – | –0.725% | – |
| Constant | 0.000% | – | 0.000% | – |
| **Total** | **0.105%** | **–6.964%** | **–1.835%** | **–6.134%** |

over the 1977–1984 period. For the U.S., the key structural factors were the recent decline of the public sector, the increase in part-time work and the decline of certain blue-collar occupations.

Given that the changes that have occurred in the Canadian and American labour forces are roughly similar, why were structural factors unimportant in Canada? The explanation is threefold. First, the decline in the U.S. public sector, while modest, was not experienced in Canada. Second, while part-time work increased by a similar amount in Canada, the 1998 estimated coefficient – which is the weight on the propensity term from equation (3) – was very small due to an increase in the likelihood of part-time workers being unionised. Such an increase was not experienced in the U.S. where part-time workers in 1998 were just as likely to be unionised as those in 1984. Lastly, the decline in blue-collar occupations in the U.S. was not observed to the same extent in Canada. For instance, while the prevalence of some blue-collar occupations fell slightly in Canada, workers involved in fabricating actually increased by nearly a percentage point.

Unfortunately, there is no unique way to sub-decompose the 'propensity to unionise' contribution because the coefficients will change with a change in the omitted category (Jones, 1983). However, with appropriate caveats in place, a thorough analysis (i.e., working through all reference groups) of a given categorical variable can yield useful conclusions. For Canada, in particular, Tables 11.1 and 11.3 indicate that community services appears to be playing a key role given the huge decline in the estimated coefficient, and the fact that community services is a large sector (and thus receives relatively more weight). Analysis indicates that the decline in the estimated coefficient on community services alone constitutes close to half of the total decline in 'propensity' – regardless of what reference group is used.[9] This intriguing result requires further analysis. An examination of the full set of industry controls shows that most of the decline in community services coverage was in the health sector although there was a non-trivial decline in educational services as well. Some further analysis indicates that virtually all of the decline of coverage in the health sector was in private sector health services, where average coverage fell from 57 per cent to 31 per cent over the period. Although beyond this paper's scope, the reason for the decline in union coverage in private sector health services is worthy of future research.

## Conclusion

We have investigated the determinants of union coverage in Canada and the U.S. over the 1984 to 1998 period using micro-data on individual workers. These data provide a large set of explanatory variables for analysing the factors that influence union density. During this period, collective agreement coverage declined by almost seven percentage points for non-agricultural paid workers in Canada and eight percentage points in the U.S.

   Our analysis allows the decline in unionisation to be decomposed into two major factors that we refer to as the 'structural' and 'propensity' components. The former corresponds to changes in the composition of the labour force and the structure of the economy that shift employment from sectors with a high degree of unionisation to sectors with a low degree of union coverage. Previous analyses of this nature have been done in the U.S. over the 1960 to 1984 period, but to our knowledge there has been no analysis of the continuing decline of unionisation in the United States through the 1990s. Early work by Farber (1985) and Dickens and Leonard (1985) suggested that structural factors were important, contributing to around 40–50 per cent of the fall in unionisation. However, Farber (1990) found that structural factors only accounted for about 20 per cent of the decline during the 1977–1984 period and Farber and Krueger (1993) found that structural factors were decreasing in importance when the 1984–1991 period is examined. There appears to be no empirical literature investigating the fall in union coverage in Canada during the 1980s and 1990s.

   We find that structural changes accounted for a minor amount of the American decline in union coverage during the sample period – about 20 per cent of the total decline. Thus, our findings coupled with Farber (1990) suggest that while structural change in the economy and labour force may have been an important factor in the decline of unions through the late 1960s and 1970s, it no longer plays an important role. The main reason for the drop in unionisation during the 1980s and 1990s was a decline in the likelihood that a worker with a given set of characteristics is represented by a union. This finding is consistent with the views of Weiler

(1983) and Freeman (1988) and who believe that management opposition and the lengthy nature of organising drives are responsible for the dramatic decline in organising bids. Farber and Krueger (1993) also conclude that a decline in the demand for union representation is the primary reason for the fall in union density.

The Canadian results suggest that structural change accounts for none of the decline in union coverage over the 1984 to 1998 period. The lack of any impact from structural change in Canada is primarily due to the stability of public sector employment (versus the decline in the U.S.) and a large increase in the propensity of part-time workers to be unionised in Canada (relative to no change in the parameter estimate in the U.S.).

The decline of union coverage in Canada can be entirely attributed to a fall in the probability of a worker with a given set of characteristics being unionised. This finding is consistent with recent work that suggests that a shift in the political environment – away from 'pro-union' legislation and towards 'anti-union' legislation – may underlie the fall in union organising success rates and the number of organising drives (Riddell, 2001; Johnson, 2002). Interestingly, it appears that nearly half of the decline in union coverage in Canada is due to a decline in union coverage in private sector health services. Understanding this latter phenomenon is a worthwhile subject for future research.

## References

Akyeampong, Ernest 'Non-unionised but covered by collective agreement'. *Perspectives on Labour and Income* 12 (Autumn 2000) 33–38.
Budd, John, W. and In-Gang Na 'The Union Membership Wage Premium for Employees Covered by Collective Bargaining Agreements'. *Journal of Labor Economics* 18 (October 2000) 783–807.
Dickens, William, T. and Jonathan, S. Leonard 'Accounting for the Decline in Union Membership, 1950–1980'. *Industrial and Labor Relations Review* 38 (April 1985) 323–334.
Farber, Henry, S. 'The Determination of the Union Status of Workers'. *Econometrica* 51 (September 1983) 1417–37.
Farber, Henry, S. 'The Extent of Unionism in the United States'. In Thomas Kochan (ed.) *Challenges and Choices Facing American Labor*. Cambridge, Mass.: MIT Press, 1985, 15–43.
Farber, Henry, S. 'The Decline of Unionization in the United States: What Can be Learned from Recent Experience?' *Journal of Labor Economics* 8 (January 1990) 57–105.
Farber, Henry, S. and Alan, B., Krueger 'Union Membership in the United States: The Decline Continues'. In Bruce, E. Kaufman and Morris, M. Kleiner (eds). *Employee Representation: Alternatives and Future Directions*. Madison, Wisc.: Industrial Relations Research Association, 1993, 105–134.
Fortin, Pierre 'The Great Canadian Slump'. *Canadian Journal of Economics* 29 (November 1996) 761–87.
Freeman, Richard, B. 'Why Are Unions Faring Poorly in NLRB Representation Elections?' in Thomas Kochan (ed.) *Challenges and Choices Facing American Labor*. Cambridge, Mass.: MIT Press, 1985, pp. 45–64.

Freeman, Richard, B. 'Contraction and Expansion: The Divergence of Private Sector and Public Sector Unionism in the United States'. *Journal of Economic Perspectives* 2 (Spring 1988) 63–88.

Johnson, Susan. 'Card Check or Mandatory Representation Vote? How the type of union recognition procedure affects certification success'. *Economic Journal* 112 (2002) 344–362.

Jones, F. L. 'On decomposing the wage gap: A critical comment on Blinder's Method'. *Journal of Human Resources*, 18 (1983), pp. 126–30.

Kochan, Thomas, A., Harry Katz, and Robert, B. McKersie. *The Transformation of American Industrial Relations*. New York: Basic Books, 1986.

Lipset, Seymour, M. 'North American Labor Movements: A Comparative Perspective' in Seymour, M. Lipset (ed.). *Unions in Transition*. San Francisco: ICS Press, 1986, pp. 421–452.

Lipset, Seymour, M. *Continental Divide: The Values and Institutions of the United States and Canada*. New York: Routledge, 1990.

Neumann, George and Ellen Rissman 'Where Have All the Union Members Gone?'. *Journal of Labor Economics* 2 (April 1984) 175–192.

Riddell, Chris 'Union Suppression and Certification Success'. *Canadian Journal of Economics*, 34 (May 2001) 396–410.

Riddell, W. Craig 'Unionization in Canada and the United States: A Tale of Two Countries', in *Small Differences That Matter: Labor Markets and Income Maintenance in Canada and the United States*, edited by David Card and Richard Freeman. Chicago: University of Chicago Press, 1993, pp. 109–148.

Tory, L. 'Is the U.S. Unique in the Decline of Private Sector Unionism?'. *Journal of Labor Research* 11 (Spring 1990) 111–43.

Troy, L. 'Convergence in International Unionism: The Case of Canada and the U.S.A'. *British Journal of Industrial Relations* 30 (March 1993) 1–43.

Weiler, Paul 'Promises to Keep: Securing Workers Rights to Self-organization under the NLRA'. *Harvard Law Review* 96 (1983) 1769–1827.

# 12
# Trade Union Survival and Women Workers in Australia

*Glenda Strachan and John Burgess*

## Declining trade union density in Australia

In the past decade there has been concern over the declining rates of unionisation in Australia and this has focussed attention on women workers who historically had a lower rate of union membership than men. This paper examines the evidence in relation to union membership, and demonstrates that the difference in male and female union density has narrowed significantly in recent years. Attention has been drawn to the fact that women were less likely to become union activists and union officials (for example Donaldson, 1991; Manning, 1994; Pocock, 1995, 1997; Rodan, 1990; Thornthwaite, 1992; Yates, 1996). Over the past two decades Australian trade unions have taken on board the reality that recruiting, retaining and addressing the aspirations of women members will be one of the most important factors in reversing the decline in union membership and the union density.

As with many other OECD economies, trade union density has systematically been eroded in Australia over the past quarter of a century (Griffin, 1996). Australia's union density reached its peak at 61 per cent in 1961 and since then has declined steadily to rest at around one quarter of the workforce. A dramatic decline in the trade union density is observed not only because trade union membership has not matched jobs growth, but also because membership itself has declined (see Table 12.1). Throughout the 1990s there was a major reduction in union density and also an absolute decline in members in the face of strong jobs growth over the period 1993–2000 of 1.3m. (Burgess and Mitchell, 2001). The Australian record of falling trade union density has been dramatic but not as extreme as that observed in other countries such as New Zealand, the United Kingdom, France and the USA (Griffin, 1996: 502).

The convention is that the trade union density is the percentage of employees who are trade union members (Griffin and Svenson, 1996: 505). This results in the density estimate being susceptible to the business cycle.

*Table 12.1*   Australian Trade Union Membership and Density, 1976–2002

| Year | Trade union members (m.) | Trade union density % |
|------|--------------------------|-----------------------|
| 1976 | 2.51 | 51.0 |
| 1982 | 2.57 | 49.5 |
| 1986 | 2.59 | 45.6 |
| 1988 | 2.54 | 41.6 |
| 1990 | 2.66 | 40.5 |
| 1992 | 2.51 | 39.6 |
| 1993 | 2.38 | 37.6 |
| 1994 | 2.28 | 35.0 |
| 1995 | 2.25 | 32.7 |
| 1996 | 2.19 | 31.1 |
| 1997 | 2.11 | 30.3 |
| 1998 | 2.03 | 28.1 |
| 1999 | 1.87 | 25.7 |
| 2000 | 1.90 | 24.7 |
| 2001 | 1.91 | 24.5 |
| 2002 | 1.83 | 23.1 |

*Source*: Peetz (1998: 6). ABS Catalogue 6310.0 Earnings, Benefits and Union Members (2003).

We can trace membership pattern changes leading into and out of the last recession in Australia (1991/93) when net job losses of 237,000 were matched by a loss of 283,000 trade union members. In the recovery phase 1993–1995, 580,000 net jobs were generated yet trade union membership declined by 125,000. In general, male full-time and unionised jobs were lost in the recession while coming out of the recession many service, part-time, female and partly unionised jobs were being generated. In Australia many of these additional jobs were contingent, especially temporary work, and filled by women (Campbell and Burgess, 2001).

In Australia, trade union density is not an accurate representation of trade union coverage across the workforce. Under awards and collective agreements negotiated by trade unions, minimum employment conditions and standards apply to both union and to non-union members. For example, in 1998 the trade union density was 28 per cent while between 65 and 80 per cent of the workforce were estimated to be covered by awards and certified collective agreements that are negotiated by trade unions on behalf of members and non-members (ACIRRT, 1999: 43). Since then there has been an expansion in individual contracts and non-union workplace agreements, nevertheless the reach of trade unions vastly exceeds their membership base. This is an important issue to consider with respect to women workers who, on average, have a lower trade union density than men. Under the post 1990s decentralised bargaining arrangements many women workers find it difficult to organise, give voice to preferences and have effective input into the collective bargaining agenda (Sullivan, Strachan and Burgess, 2003).

## The role of gender in declining trade union density

Men have always had a higher trade union density than women. This reflects a mixture of historical, institutional and structural features of Australian industrial relations. The development of trade unions and the arbitration system was largely a response to male based employment in the pastoral, manufacturing, mining and transport sectors. The Australian system formally gave legal recognition to trade unions and unions were parties to the system of award determination and to national wage decisions. While women were collectivised and active in some pockets of industry (see Frances, 1993), in the main women's work was outside of the domain of trade unions and the industrial relations system (Ryan and Conlon, 1989; Thomson and Pocock, 1997). Indeed, the system formally sanctioned a subordinate and disadvantaged status for women workers through lower wage rates and reduced benefits and protection (Ryan and Conlon, 1989). In addition, the segregation of women into service work and into part-time jobs also tended to shift them outside of the traditional focus of trade union activity in Australia.

Structural shifts in the composition of the Australian workforce have seen declining shares of employment in the traditionally highly unionised and male sectors (manufacturing, mining and utilities), decline in the full-time job share (male dominated) and decline in the permanent job share (male dominated) (Burgess, 1994; Burgess and Mitchell, 2001). At the same time the male job share has systematically declined as a result of structural shift, periodic recessions and male early age exits from the workforce. Overall, the Australian workforce is becoming systematically feminised. Accompanying this growth in the female workforce share is a growth in the female share of trade union members (see Table 12.2).

How important have compositional shifts in the workforce, including gender composition, been in explaining the decline in the trade union density in Australia? In a shift share analysis of the change in the density between 1986 and 1992 the ABS (1994) suggested that around one third of the decline was due to compositional changes. Within the possible compositional changes the three most important effects were the change in job status (the shift towards part-time and casual employment arrangements), the changing industry composition of employment and the shift towards private sector employment. In this analysis the gender shift in the workforce was a relatively minor contributor to the declining trade union density.

The systematic decline in the gender union density gap over the past decade is illustrated in Table 12.3. If account is taken of the higher full-time and permanent employment share of males together with their different industry distribution, then the gender union density difference considerably narrows. Peetz (1998: 78) suggests that the gender gap is declining not

*Table 12.2*  The Systematic feminisation of the Australian workforce and unions, 1990–2002

| Year | Workforce '000 | | Union members '000 | | Union density % | | Female share % | |
|---|---|---|---|---|---|---|---|---|
| | Male | Fem. | Male | Fem. | Male | Fem. | Workf. | Unions |
| 1990 | 4562 | 3246 | 1683 | 975 | 45.0 | 34.6 | 41.6 | 36.7 |
| 1992 | 4385 | 3232 | 1536 | 972 | 43.4 | 34.8 | 42.4 | 38.8 |
| 1994 | 4536 | 3350 | 1375 | 907 | 37.9 | 31.4 | 42.5 | 39.7 |
| 1996 | 4730 | 3589 | 1307 | 886 | 33.5 | 28.1 | 43.1 | 40.4 |
| 1998 | 4846 | 3765 | 1189 | 848 | 30.0 | 25.8 | 43.7 | 41.6 |
| 2000 | 5109 | 4032 | 1095 | 806 | 26.3 | 22.8 | 44.1 | 42.4 |
| 2002 | 5180 | 4129 | 1045 | 788 | 24.5 | 21.5 | 44.3 | 43.0 |
| 2002 less 1990 | 618 | 883 | –638 | –187 | –20.5 | –13.1 | 2.7 | 6.3 |

*Source*: ABS Catalogues 6325.0 (1996), 6310.0 (2000, 2002), 6203.0 (various).

*Table 12.3*  The gender trade union density gap 1990–2002
(Trade union density males less trade union density females)

| 1990 | 1992 | 1994 | 1996 | 1998 | 2000 | 2002 |
|---|---|---|---|---|---|---|
| 10.4 | 8.6 | 6.5 | 5.4 | 4.2 | 3.5 | 3.0 |

*Source*: Calculations derived from ABS Catalogue 6203.0 (Aug. 1994) and Catalogue 6310.0 (Aug. 2000, 2002).

only because of structural shifts in the composition of the workforce but because women are more likely to either stay in or join a union than men. The main attributable factors are the decline in compulsory unionism and the shift in unions towards providing voice to the issues that impact on women workers (Peetz, 1998: 78).

In general, it is not so much compositional effects that are hampering trade union membership growth, but a falling propensity to belong to trade unions across all sectors (Peetz, 1998). This may reflect indifference or hostility towards unions, legislative and other difficulties facing trade unions in recruitment, the failings of trade unions in representing membership, the growth in difficult to organise contingent employment or an environment that discourages or excludes trade unions from the workplace.

Women account for more than half the workforce in retail trade, accommodation/cafes, finance/insurance, education and health/community services. They account for more than half of union members in the same sectors. The union membership share of women is well below their workforce share in mining, construction, transport, business/property services, agriculture, wholesale trade, culture/recreation, personal/other services and communications. The sectors where women are clearly over-represented in union membership relative to workforce shares are retail trade and finance/insurance (see Table 12.4). The sectors most contributing to employment growth over the past decade have been property/business services, retail trade, health/community services and construction (Burgess and Mitchell, 2001). Occupational segregation and other employment characteristics result in divergence in major workforce characteristics between unionists on the basis of gender (see Table 12.5).

## Women's participation in trade unions

It is well documented that women have been underrepresented in Australian trade union structures and their interests were not always well served by the previous centralised industrial relations system (O'Donnell and Hall, 1988; Ryan and Conlon, 1989). The sexual division of labour is manifest in both structures and practices that remain entrenched within industrial relations institutional life in Australia and employers, unions, the courts, the arbitration system and governments have made their unique contributions to the entrenchment of male privilege in the Australian

*Table 12.4*   Sector union densities by gender 2002

| Sector | Female workforce share (%) | Female union density (%) | Male union density (%) | Female union share (%) |
|---|---|---|---|---|
| Mining | 11.5 | 0.0 | 31.0 | 0.0 |
| Manufacturing | 26.1 | 18.5 | 30.5 | 16.7 |
| Utilities | 20.5 | 22.5 | 56.0 | 9.5 |
| Construction | 12.0 | 2.0 | 31.2 | 0.8 |
| Retail trade | 50.7 | 18.9 | 14.0 | 59.4 |
| Accommodation cafes | 56.6 | 12.2 | 11.2 | 59.6 |
| Transport | 23.2 | 24.4 | 40.4 | 15.6 |
| Finance | 53.8 | 22.3 | 11.9 | 70.2 |
| Business services | 44.7 | 5.6 | 7.3 | 42.4 |
| Government administration | 46.5 | 29.9 | 44.8 | 36.9 |
| Agriculture | 29.4 | 5.0 | 5.1 | 25.0 |
| Wholesale trade | 30.9 | 5.6 | 7.8 | 25.0 |
| Culture, recreation | 47.4 | 12.0 | 13.3 | 46.2 |
| Personal services | 48.3 | 13.1 | 39.9 | 23.3 |
| Communications | 29.6 | 23.3 | 37.1 | 21.7 |
| Education | 68.6 | 41.2 | 44.0 | 66.8 |
| Health community services | 77.4 | 30.4 | 31.9 | 78.1 |

*Source*: ABS Catalogue 6310.0 (2002), 6203.0 (2002).

*Table 12.5*   Union members by gender: broad characteristics

| Characteristic | Males | Females |
|---|---|---|
| Industry | 3 largest sectors for members: manufacturing, construction, transport | 3 largest sectors for members: health/community services, education, retail trade |
| Hours | 7.7% are in PT employment | 36.8% are in PT employment |
| Status | 9.6% are casuals | 12.4% are casuals |
| Earnings | 27% of FT members earn more than $1,000 pw | 11% of FT members earn more than $1,000 pw |
| Occupation | 3 largest groups for members: tradespersons, intermediate production/transport, professionals | 3 largest groups for members; professional, intermediate clerical/sales, elementary clerical/sales |

*Source*: ABS Catalogue 6310.0 (2001).

labour market and wage fixing (Thomson and Pocock, 1997: 67). Recent feminist scholarship has illuminated the patriarchal structures in Australian unions that have excluded women and obscured industrial issues of particular relevance to women.

In recent decades the goals of the union movement have broadened to encompass notions of equality framed by gender. In Australia, changes have occurred within the union movement as a result of the activities of women trade union members. Trade unions respond to wider social movements and there is often an overlap of membership between unions and other social movements such as women's lobby groups. The practical experience in the realisation of these policies must be characterised as one of continual struggle, a struggle that has made great gains and continues to do so.

Women in unions were in a very different place in 1990 to that of 1970. Indeed, women in the workplace had obtained rights that were not there in 1970 and for which the trade union movement has been the major instigator. In 2003 there is an expectation within the union movement that women will be active and policies are designed to encourage this. From the 1970s, women in unions fought to achieve space for women's representation and faced many battles in the struggles to achieve this. There are still concerns that major changes are needed. For instance, Pocock asserts that 'a genuine transformation' of the Australian union movement is needed if women's needs are to be taken seriously. This would require 'a shift in perception and examination of union methods, organising habits, and support structures for activism' (Pocock, 1995: 399).

## Trade unions and equity policies

The history of women's participation in trade unions, and unions' role in the achievement of equality in employment is complex. Historically, trade unions pursued unequal wages for women and, in some instances, their removal from the workplace. Yet trade unions have been a major force in the moves for equal pay and equal treatment in Australian society since the 1970s. Major changes have occurred which have resulted in successful equal pay cases, legislation designed to promote equal employment opportunity (EEO) and related policies. Trade unions have been an important force in promoting these changes along with women's groups and the Australian Labour Party (ALP), a political party that grew out of the trade union movement in the late 19th century and has retained (at times tenuous) links with the union movement.

In terms of policy initiatives, the Australian Council of Trade Unions (ACTU) (the major peak trade union organisation) initiated the equal pay cases in 1969 and 1972. The impact of the December 1972 judgement was widespread as potential wage increases covered an estimated one and a half million female workers (out of 1,795,000 women in the workforce) (Ryan and Conlon, 1989: 162). In 1986 the ACTU, supported by the women's movement, submitted a claim in relation to nurses' salaries along comparable worth lines because such cases had been successful in the USA. The industrial commission refused to accept the general nature of the claim (Australian Conciliation and Arbitration Commission, 1986) and the nurses' claim was processed as an individual case to ensure that it had no ramifications for women's wages generally (Rafferty, 1994: 467). The union movement continues to bring some cases for equal pay before the commission, even under the decentralised industrial relations system of the 1990s (Strachan and Jamieson, 1999). The ACTU has lobbied for the introduction of anti-discrimination legislation, first enacted in 1975 and introduced in most states in the 1980s (Ronalds, 1991). Women have been able to pursue remedies after an alleged case of discrimination and a number of major cases have been conducted by trade unions. The ACTU has also been the major instigator of other rights for women workers, including major test cases on maternity and parental leave (ACTU, 1999a).

The other significant piece of legislation is the *Affirmative Action (Equal Opportunity for Women) Act, 1986*, replaced by the *Equal Opportunity in the Workplace Act, 1999*. While using the American term, 'affirmative action' in Australia it was defined as 'the pursuit of equal employment opportunity by means of legislative reform and management programmes' (Ziller, 1983: 23) which requires that the barriers that restricted employment and promotion opportunities for women in the workplace are systematically eliminated (Affirmative Action Agency, 1990: 1). The 1986 Act compelled organisations with more than 100 employees to implement an affirmative action programme that was based on an analysis of women's position in the organisation. Organisations were required to devise strategies that addressed some of the problems identified and set targets against which future progress could be judged (Strachan and Burgess, 2000). The ACTU and many women's groups lobbied the ALP for the introduction of this legislation and the ACTU produced an extensive manual for unions on how an affirmative action programme should be negotiated (ACTU, c.1980s). Following the election of a conservative federal government in 1996 the legislation changed in 2000 and the demands on employers were reduced substantially (Strachan and Burgess, 2002) and consultation with trade unions, which was a feature of the 1986 Act, has been removed.

## ACTU women's policies

The Working Women's Charter (WWC), formulated by women unionists, was accepted by the ACTU Congress in 1977. By 1980 it was printed in newspaper format in 11 languages for widespread distribution to workplaces (ACTU, c.1980). This document outlined the position of women in the workforce and union movement. Priorities for action were the establishment of comprehensive maternity protection; provision of adequate childcare facilities; achievement of equal remuneration for work of equal value and increased recruitment and involvement of women trade union members. It asserted that women workers should be actively encouraged by trade unions to attend trade union education and to stand for office and 'where necessary, positive provisions should be considered to provide specific representation of women to ensure that union executives are fully representative of all its members' (ACTU, c.1980).

The expansion of women's union membership in white-collar public sector employment in the 1970s and 1980s saw the initial expansion of women into leadership positions in individual unions (Elton, 1997: 112). By the beginning of the 1980s EEO and AA were on the trade union agenda and the first woman was elected to the national executive of the ACTU in 1982. This was Jenny George who became president of the ACTU in 1996. By 1987 five women had been elected to the ACTU executive and by 1989 ACTU policy advocated a long list of priorities which included childcare, increased involvement of women in trade unions, equal pay, EEO and AA programmes and policies, policies against sexual harassment, superannuation and the importance of trade union training for women (Lynch, Strachan and Burgess, 2000). These changes at the peak level of the ACTU were in themselves important policy shifts indicating a growing consciousness within the movement of a need to focus on equity.

Evidence of the changes in attitude can be seen in the speeches of one senior ACTU official. In 1978 the ACTU called a special federal unions' conference to discuss ways of implementing the WWC (*Courier Mail*, 1978).

The women unionists 'demanded' a special section in the ACTU to promote more participation by women and to research women's issues. This proposal was 'vigorously and at times bitterly opposed' by ACTU officers. Bill Kelty, ACTU assistant secretary, said 'there was no way the ACTU could afford the extra staff....He was hissed and booed when he accused the conference of trying to create women's societies rather than work through a unified trade-union movement'. Indeed, 'there was obvious hostility toward the ACTU – attributed by some observers to the frustration of women activists dissatisfied with the ACTU's past record on working for the advancement of women' (*Australian*, 16 Mar. 1978). A decade later at the 1989 ACTU Congress, Secretary Kelty declared that

the Australian trade union movement cannot pretend to be representative of women if we have within the ranks of congress and union leadership far fewer women than is warranted. It is simply not good enough for us year after year, congress after congress, resolution after resolution to discuss it. It's about time we started to do it. That is, we have to ensure that women are seen and involved in unions as equal partners. Anything else is a failure (quoted in Yates, 1996: 629).

In 1997 the ACTU Congress resolution dealing with women and unions stated that

the union movement has been presented with a unique opportunity to put forward a platform of action for women as part of the core of it's [sic] activities....the ACTU...should act as a coordinator linking unions, community organisations, churches and other relevant parties to promote socially progressive policies (ACTU, 1997a).

The ACTU Women and Unions Policy from the 2000 Congress is extensive and includes a continued 'commitment to affirmative action in its decision making processes' and calls on affiliated unions to 'continue efforts to ensure that women are proportionally represented as workplace representatives, organising and industrial staff and elected officers'. The ACTU undertakes to ensure that its governing bodies and structures include at least 50 per cent women. Policies for the improvement of conditions for casual and part-time workers are included as well as policies relating to parental leave and carers' leave (ACTU, 2000a).

The resolutions concerning union membership campaigns present a different picture. The 1997 Membership and Services Resolution contains only one passing reference to women: one of the components of enhancing membership and community involvement is 'understanding the aspirations of young people, women and the precariously employed' (ACTU, 1997b). There is no mention in the 2000 21st Century Organising and

Campaigning Policy (ACTU, 2000b). Likewise, the 1999 Report of the ACTU overseas delegation titled 'Unions @ Work – The challenge for unions to create a just and fair society', contains very few references to women. Where this occurs it is in the context of groups which have been marginalised from the union movement, usually young people and women (for example, ACTU, 1999b: 28). In a section of the report titled 'The key issues from overseas', women rate one mention: 'Union structures and methods are being overhauled in response to falling membership in traditional industries and occupations, and the necessity to attract and involve young people, women, shift workers, and casuals' (ACTU, 1999b: 32).

The unions have recently been active in three areas that affect women members. First, there has been a concerted attempt to regularise the employment arrangements and conditions for casual workers, largely through state jurisdiction (Whitehouse and Rooney, 2003). Second, the ACTU has mounted a test case over long and unreasonable hours as well as promoting recognition of women's caring responsibilities in workplace policies (Cooper, 2003). Third, in the face of Federal government intransigence and indifference to paid maternity leave, the ACTU has developed a policy aimed at extending paid maternity rights across the workforce (Baird, 2003; Cooper, 2003).

While the ACTU has developed and pursued specific policies relating to women members, little consideration has been given to this group of workers as union members and whether or not specific union policies and structures would encourage more women to join. It could be an example of what Forrest calls 'post-feminist' industrial relations thinking about women which presents a model of gender similarity. She asserts that this continues a tradition that finds

> The possibility that women workers might have distinct reasons for joining (or avoiding) a union...has never been fully considered (Forrest, 2000: 48).

## Women and trade unions in 1990s

While there has been an increase in female employment in trade unions over the last two decades (McManus, 1997: 27), this has not always translated into women holding positions of power. It is now commonplace for a trade union to have positions such as women's officers and extensive policies designed to overcome problems of inequality. In the Australian Service Union (ASU) for example, between 42 and 45 per cent of the national membership of 136,000 are women. This union established a policy of proportional representation in 1995. However, implementation of these policies has proved problematic with inadequate nominations received to fill the elected rank and file positions with women members (Lynch, Strachan and Burgess, 2000). Evidence of the continuing struggle within unions over questions of equity suggests that while these policy developments at the peak level are necessary and welcome, putting these into practice is less straightforward. Male dominance of society and unions makes it difficult for women to participate in union life at any level. A woman's chances of participating in union life as a shop steward or local union officer depend for the most part on many aspects of her family life and activism flouts the sexual contract that reserves public life for men, with evening meetings or weekend conferences alienating a woman's husband/partner (Cockburn, 1991: 87; Cook, Lorwin and Daniels, 1992: 49).

The literature on women union officials in Australia has identified other barriers. Women's advance into union leadership positions slowed in the mid 1990s due to the long incumbency of male union leaders. Union amalgamations reduced leadership opportunities for women because of the need to absorb existing senior officials and staff. (The number of federal unions was reduced from 143 in 1989 to 47 in 1995). Gender solidarity is another factor that has contributed to the downward trend in women in leadership positions, with male leaders resistant to change that might threaten patriarchal power. The processes and criteria for selection or encouragement to stand for election often work to maintain male dominance while purporting to be about merit. The segregation of the workplace by gender, and the concentration of women's employment in a narrow range of occupations and industries is replicated within the union movement thereby limiting women's avenues for union participation (Elton, 1997: 112–118).

Features of trade union jobs such as the long hours of work, unusual hours and distances organisers have to travel to cover a vast geographical area and which can necessitate long periods of time away from home, remain (Lynch, Strachan and Burgess, 2000). The union membership may work varied hours or shifts work and the role of many women as primary childcare provider clashes with the needs of union members. In contrast to this, men's role in the family, even when there are small children, is not an obstacle to their involvement in trade union activities (Pocock, 1995: 381). Issues recognised by women in the 1970s still remain. Workplace activism, which is an essential part of the progression to a position of union official, often consists of regular after-hours meetings. This is an important part of the traditional training model (Callus, 1986).

In common with women working in 'non-traditional' jobs, women may not be recognised as legitimate union officials. Women union officials feel that the masculine culture within unions places demands on them that for the most part men do not experience (Lynch, Strachan and Burgess, 2000). In the research conducted by Lynch, all interviewees were at pains to point out that it was not all men in the unions or employers that behaved in a sexist or patronising way towards them. Indeed, it was the minority of men who did. However, their consistent observation was that 'there always seems to be at least one in every group in either the employer ranks and the union ranks'. Moreover, as the women explained, that is all it often takes to construct barriers. As one interviewee noted 'you cannot be one of the rest because you are a female'. Sexist or inappropriate behaviour, though more visible, was only one form of behaviour that these women said created barriers to equal participation. For example, there were some male, mostly older, leaders, who treat women officials in a respectful yet patronising way. The benchmark of social behaviour is a male benchmark and men do not see themselves as acting contrary to social norms and thus do not see the implication of this behaviour (Lynch, Strachan and Burgess, 2000).

## Conclusion

The examination of issues surrounding women's employment and the involvement of trade unions has shown that unions are responsive to attitudes in the wider community and also the particular interests and lobbying activities of their own members. Trade unions have reflected social changes and the dominant societal beliefs – but they have also shaped changes, not least because some people who are active in organisations working for change such as women's organisations have also worked within trade unions to shape their policies and actions. Issues related to employment equity are accorded a higher priority than 20 years ago and the union movement is at the forefront of taking cases that promote equity in employment. In his study of declining union membership, Peetz surmised that the narrowing of the gender gap in union density was likely to be the result of two major factors: the decline in compulsory unionism (as men were more likely to be employed in closed shops than women) and relative improvement in the way unions offer services to women members (Peetz, 1998: 78). There has certainly been a change in this in recent decades.

Yet discussions of women and unions have been relegated frequently to the realm of special issues and excluded from the mainstream discussions of union activities. As many feminist writers have mentioned, women are seen as the 'other'. As Pocock (1997: 3) pointed out, 'in the discourses of unionism..."member" has stood for "male member", and identities like "shop steward" have become saturated with masculinity'. Indeed, these terms 'deny women' (Pocock, 1997: 3). While, on the one hand, the ACTU has developed policies judged to promote women's membership and activism, this may not have expanded into 'mainstream' policies such as those on union membership. If women are painted as the 'other', they are usually depicted as the problem. A different way of viewing the situation is to see it as one with issues relating to gender, that is both masculine and feminine cultures within workplace and unions. There is no doubt that the masculine culture has dominated historically, to the point of exclusion of women as union members in some cases. There is also no doubt that extreme efforts have been made in recent decades to remove discriminatory policies and to increase the involvement of women members.

## References

Affirmative Action Agency (1990) *Taking Steps: Employers' Progress in Affirmative Action*. Canberra: Australian Government Publishing Service.

Australian Bureau of Statistics (ABS) (1996) *Trade Union Members*. Catalogue, 6325.0.

ABS (1998) *Earnings, Benefits and Union Members*. Catalogue 6310.0.

ABS (1994) *The Labour Force*. Catalogue 6203.0. Supplement – Trade Union Members.

Australian Centre for Industrial Relations Research and Teaching (ACIRRT) (1999) *Australia at Work*. Sydney: Prentice Hall.

Australian Conciliation and Arbitration Commission (1986). Private Hospitals' and Doctors' Nurses (ACT) Award variation (Comparable Worth), Decision, 18 Feb., print G2250.

ACTU (c. 1980) *A.C.T.U. Working Women's Charter*. Melbourne: ACTU.

ACTU (c. 1980s) *Affirmative Action Manual: Part 1: In the Workplace*. Melbourne: ACTU.

ACTU (1997a) Women and Unions Resolution. ACTU Congress. Internet address: http://www.actu.asn.au/national/about/policy/97women.htm.

ACTU (1997b) Membership and services resolution. ACTU Congress. Internet address: http://www.actu.asn.au/national/about/policy/97mbrshp.htm.

ACTU (1999a) History of parental and family leave provisions in Australia. ACTU Research and Information. Internet address: http://www.actu.asn.au/workers/fact/updates/parham.htm.

ACTU (1999b) *Unions @ Work*. Melbourne: ACTU.

ACTU (2000a) Women and unions policy. ACTU Congress. Internet address: http://www.vtown.com....ED6E588-5244-11D4-A72C00062950E46C.

ACTU (2000b) 21st Century organising and campaigning policy. ACTU Congress. Internet address: http://www.vtown.com....ED6E588-5244-11D4-A72C00062950E46C.

Baird, M. (2003) Paid maternity leave: The good, the bad and the ugly. *Australian Bulletin of Labour*, 29(1): 97–109.

Burgess, J. (1994) Restructuring the Australian labour force: From full employment to where? *Journal of Australian Political Economy*, 34: 103–127.

Burgess, J. and Mitchell, W. (2001) The Australian labour market. *Journal of Industrial Relations*, 43(2): 124–147.

Campbell, I. and Burgess, J. (2001) Casual employment in Australia and temporary employment in Europe: Developing a cross country comparison. *Work, Employment and Society*, 15(1): 171–184.

Cook, Alice H., Lorwin, Val R. and Daniels, Arlene K. (1992) *The Most Difficult Revolution: Women and Trade Unions*. Ithaca, N.Y.: Cornell University Press.

Cooper, R. (2003) Trade Unionism in 2002. *Journal of Industrial Relations*, 45(2): 205–223.

Donaldson, Mike (1991) Women in the union movement: Organisation, representation and segmentation. *Journal of Australian Political Economy*, 28: 131–147.

Elton, Jude (1997) Making democratic unions: From policy to practice. In Barbara Pocock (ed.) *Strife Sex and Politics in Labour Unions*. Sydney: Allen and Unwin: 109–127.

Forrest, Anne (2000). What do women want from union representation? *Hecate*, 26(2): 47–61.

Foster, R. (1996) *Australian Economic Statistics*. Reserve Bank of Australia Occasional Paper no. 8. Sydney.

Frances, Raelene (1993) *The Politics of Work: Gender and Labour in Victoria, 1880–1939*. Melbourne: Cambridge University Press.

Griffin, G. (1996) Introduction. *Journal of Industrial Relations*, 38(4): 501–504.

Griffin, G. and Svenson, S. (1996) A decline in trade union density: A survey of the literature. *Journal of Industrial Relations*, 38(4): 505–547.

Lynch, C., Strachan, G. and Burgess, J. (2000) Australian unions and equality. Paper presented at IIRA 12th World Congress Japan, 29 May–2 June.

Manning, Haydon (1994) Women and union politics in Australia. *Policy Organisation and Society*, 9: 38–52.

McManus, S. (1997) Gender and union organising in Australia. In Barbara Pocock (ed.) *Strife Sex and Politics in Labour Unions*. Sydney: Allen and Unwin: 26–44.

O'Donnell, C. and Hall, P. (1988) *Getting Equal: Labour Market Regulation and Women's Work*. Sydney: Allen and Unwin.

Peetz, D. (1998) *Unions in a Contrary World*. Melbourne: Cambridge University Press.

Pocock, Barbara (1995) Gender and activism in Australian unions. *Journal of Industrial Relations*, 37(3): 377–400.

Pocock, Barbara (ed.) (1997) *Strife Sex and Politics in Labour Unions*. Sydney: Allen and Unwin.

Rafferty, F. (1994) Equal Pay: The evolutionary process, 1984–1994. *Journal of Industrial Relations*, 36(4): 451–467.

Rodan, Paul (1990) Women and unionism: The case of the Victorian colleges staff association. *Journal of Industrial Relations*, 32(3): 386–402.

Ronalds, C. (1991) *Affirmative Action and Sex Discrimination*. Sydney: Pluto Press.

Ryan, E. and Conlon, A. (1989) *Gentle Invaders: Australian Women at Work*. Melbourne: Penguin.

Strachan, Glenda and Burgess, John (2000) The incompatibility of decentralised bargaining and equal employment opportunity in Australia. *British Journal of Industrial Relations*, 38(3): 361–382.

Strachan, Glenda and Burgess, John (2001) Unfinished business: Employment equality in Australia. In Agocs, C. (ed.) *Workplace Equality: An International Perspective on Legislation, Policy and Practice*. Amsterdam: Kluwer International: 47–64.

Strachan, G. and Jamieson, S. (1999) Equal opportunity in Australia in the 1990s. *New Zealand Journal of Industrial Relations*, 24(3): 319–341.

Sullivan, A., Strachan, G. and Burgess, J. (2003) Women workers and enterprise bargaining. In J. Burgess and D. Macdonald (eds), *Developments in Enterprise Bargaining*. Melbourne: Tertiary Press: 158–175.

Thomson, C. and Pocock, B. (1997) Moving on from masculinity? Australian unions industrial agenda. In Barbara Pocock (ed.) *Strife Sex and Politics in Labour Unions*. Sydney: Allen and Unwin: 67–91.

Thornthwaite, Louise (1992) A half-hearted courtship: Unions, female members and discrimination complaints. *Journal of Industrial Relations*, 34(4): 509–529.

Whitehouse, G. and Rooney, T. (2003) Employment entitlements and casual status: Lessons from two Queensland cases. *Australian Bulletin of Labour*, 29(1): 62–75.

'Union talks on women's rights' (1978) *Courier Mail*, 8 Feb.

'Women fight for rights in ACTU' (1978) *The Australian*, 16 Mar.

Yates, Charlotte A. B. (1996) Neo-Liberalism and the working girl: The dilemmas of women and the Australian union movement. *Economic and Industrial Democracy*, 17: 627–665.

Ziller, A. (1983) *Affirmative Action Handbook*. 2nd edn, Sydney: Pot Still Press.

# 13
## The ICFTU and Trade Unions in the Developing Countries: Solidarity or Dependence?[1]

*Rebecca Gumbrell-McCormick*

## Introduction

The relationship between international trade union confederations and trade unions in the developing countries[2] is complex , and has provoked considerable debate both within and outside the labour movement. From the earliest period of international trade union organisation – going back to the formation of the first ITSs in the last decades of the 19th century, then of the International Federation of Trade Unions (IFTU) at the beginning of the 20th – the labour movement has faced the immense difficulty of constructing international unity of action out of a maze of conflicting interests, beliefs, political and economic systems, and languages. Over the past century, the task has not become any easier, indeed it could be said that today's extremes of wealth and poverty, of power and powerlessness, make it even more difficult. Yet if the labour movement is to move forward in the 21st century it must learn to act more effectively than ever at the international level. In presenting here some of the lessons of the recent past of international trade unionism, I hope to clarify the tasks now facing the movement and give some indication of its future.

'International' trade unionism was initially, and remained for many years, a largely European affair. Both the international trade secretariats (ITSs), representing workers in particular branches of industry, and the confederations of national trade union centres (like the IFTU), were based almost entirely on unions in Europe, with a few exceptions in North and Latin America and Oceania, until well after the first world war. However, some early leaders of the movement, in particular Edo Fimmen, general secretary first of the IFTU and later of the International Transportworkers' Federation (ITF), saw that capital was beginning to extend global power and control, and that the labour movement would have to become truly global in response (Fimmen, 1924). This task became all the more important in the years immediately after the second world war, when the pre-war empires began to break up in response to anti-colonialist movements, often led by trade unionists, and when the colonies became the focus of competing political forces. The divisions of the inter-war period were briefly overcome with the creation of the World Federation of Trade Unions (WFTU), uniting for a few brief years communist, social democratic and other trade unions. But the labour movement soon succumbed to cold war divisions, and the ICFTU was founded in 1949 as an anti-communist breakaway from WFTU. Subsequently both international organisations, and the third, much smaller International Federation of Christian Trade Unions (IFCTU, later World Confederation of Labour, WCL) all sought to establish their global representativeness and legitimacy by extending their membership to all regions of the world. All three confederations faced the same difficult task, not only of finding new affiliates in the rest of the world but of developing appropriate regional structures in order to represent them and to build unity at the world level.

The attention paid to internationalism within the labour movement in recent years has tended either to brush this issue under the carpet, or to engage in polemics without close attention to the facts. On the basis of my own work on the strategies of the international trade union movement around world economic issues, I will examine the relationship between the international and regional levels, and between the international organisations and unions in the developing countries. While this chapter concentrates on the ICFTU and its work in the Third World during the last quarter century, many of the points raised are of general interest in the analysis of the relation between unions in the developing and industrialised countries, and the nature of regionalism within the framework of international trade unionism itself.[3]

## Union organisation and regional structures in the developing countries

From the beginning of the international labour movement, union organisation has been strongest in the industrialised countries, for a variety of reasons. Agricultural workers and those in the informal sector, in developed and developing societies, have been much harder to organise; colonial and dictatorial governments have impeded union growth; traditional societies marked by strong ethnic and religious cleavages have made workers' solidarity more difficult to achieve. Within this general picture, the regions outside Europe demonstrated highly varying levels of economic and social development, levels of trade union membership and financial and organisational resources. Within the ICFTU, Asia was at first the strongest developing region in terms of union organisation and economic resources, while Africa was clearly the weakest and the one least able to mount an effective regional organisation on its own. The ICFTU's organisation in the

Americas, ORIT, brought together two completely distinct regions, North and South America, and was heavily subsidised by the former. All three regions made significant progress in the following decades, through their own efforts, changes in the political and economic setting, and greater attention from the Confederation, but still had less influence on the politics of the Confederation as a whole than Europe, North America and Oceania.

The ICFTU established its regional organisations for the Americas, Asia and Africa shortly after its foundation in 1949, the first post-war labour international to do so. But it did not intend that the regional organisations should set policy for their own regions; rather, they should concentrate on union organisation and act as a 'conduit' to feed information and policy proposals from the regions to the secretariat and back to the regions.[4] This form of regionalism was very different from the vision developed by Edo Fimmen in the 1920s, when he had proposed the creation of regional structures in the ITF not only to encourage union organisation but also to promote autonomy of action (Reinalda, 1997). His plans did not materialise, because of the low level of union organisation and the lack of resources. After the second world war, conditions for labour organisation were more promising; but the ICFTU was determined to maintain a common policy for all five continents, and was keen to avoid the formation of competing regional blocs. It went so far as to state that members of the Executive Board (EB) did not represent their own regions but the Confederation as a whole. Like the founders of the earliest international labour organisations, the leaders of the ICFTU championed the unity of the world's workers against the divisions of nation and region, expressing dismay when national or regional conflicts arose. The only division that was openly expressed was that of the 'free' trade unions in battle against Communists, fascists, and other movements that did not adopt a strategy of 'free collective bargaining' by politically independent unions. Neither nationalism nor regionalism had any place in this scheme of things, making it more difficult for the organisation to face the problems posed by conflicting national and regional interests.

## Representation in the structures of international trade unionism

Representation within the international trade union movement has always been based on national organisations: central confederations in the case of the ICFTU and its forerunners, or industrial unions in the case of the ITSs. While the different organisational base of the confederal and industrial organisations has had many long-reaching consequences (Gumbrell-McCormick, 2000c), the effect has been rather similar from the point of view of unions in the developing countries: both types of international organisation have tended to be dominated by the unions of the major industrialised countries (Reinalda, 1997). In the early years, this was in part because very few unions from outside Europe were even affiliated, but the pattern has persisted to varying degrees even though membership in the developing countries has expanded and now represents the majority of the affiliates of the ICFTU and of several of the ITSs. The problem is often not so much one of formal representation, but of power and influence.

The governing bodies of the ICFTU are based on regional constituencies. At the beginning of the 1970s the EB consisted of three members from Africa, five from Asia, two from the Middle East, three from Latin America, one from the Caribbean, eight from Europe, six from North America[5] and one from Australia and New Zealand, in addition to the president and general secretary. The ITSs (almost all headed by Europeans) nominated two representatives, while the chair of the consultative committee on women workers' questions attended as an observer. Membership was expanded in the 1980s and 1990s; from 1992 there were five members from Africa, eight from Asia, two from the Middle East, five from Latin America, one from the Caribbean, 14 from Europe (including new affiliates from eastern Europe), six from North America, two from Oceania (including one Fijian) and one from West Asia (a seat created to allow Turkey a representative), in addition to the president and general secretary. Following changes in the constitution, all ITSs were now entitled to send representatives, and the Women's Committee had five members by right. The number of meetings of the Board was reduced from two to one per year.

The formal representation of affiliates from the developing countries in the ICFTU's governing bodies, presented in Table 13.1, suggests the predominance of the unions of Latin America, Asia and Africa, which were indeed over-represented in relation to their total membership (at least from the 1970s until the early 1990s, when their membership caught up with their representation). Yet the policy-making capacity of the EB was reduced when it started to meet only once a year. Furthermore, the real locus of decision-making in the ICFTU, as in many large organisations, has long been in smaller official committees and unofficial networks that have met more frequently. Most important of these has been the Finance and General Purposes Committee (FGPC), which throughout the history of the ICFTU has played a key role, making recommendations regarding personnel and policy which have normally been endorsed by the EB. The membership of these committees has always been drawn from the largest affiliates in the industrialised countries, in particular those that make the highest financial contributions to the work of the Confederation. In 1972, the FGPC had seven members (including the general secretary), of whom only one came from outside Europe and North America; in 1982, the figure was three out of ten; in 1992, it was three out of 11.[6]

A perusal of the minutes of the EB, the FGPC and the Steering Committee over the past 30 years reveals the extent to which the EB

*Table 13.1* ICFTU Executive board seats and affiliated membership (000) by region

| | 1972 | | 1983 | | 1992 | |
|---|---|---|---|---|---|---|
| | Seats (%) | Mbp (%) | Seats (%) | Mbp (%) | Seats (%) | Mbp (%) |
| Africa | 3 (12) | 868 (2) | 4 (11) | 546 (1) | 5 (11) | 1997 (2) |
| Asia | 5 (20) | 4295 (11) | 6 (17) | 11047 (14) | 8 (18) | 19628 (20) |
| West Asia | 1 (3) | 1800 (2) | 1 (2) | 800 (1) | | |
| Middle East | 2 (8) | 844 (2) | 2 (6) | 865 (1) | 2 (4) | 882 (1) |
| Latin America | 3 (12) | 1552 (4) | 4 (11) | 12608 (16) | 5 (11) | 10812 (11) |
| Caribbean | 1 (4) | 122 (–) | 1 (3) | 311 (–) | 1 (2) | 149 (–) |
| *Third World* | *14 (56)* | *7681 (20)* | *18 (51)* | *27177 (34)* | *22 (50)* | *34268 (35)* |
| GB | 2 (8) | 10002 (26) | 2 (6) | 11006 (14) | | |
| Europe | 6 (24) | 17803 (46) | 8 (23) | 24896 (31) | 14 (32) | 46872 (48) |
| North America* | [2] (8) | 1300 (3) | 6 (17) | 14902 (19) | 6 (14) | 14990 (15) |
| Australia/NZ | 1 (4) | 1625 (4) | | | | |
| Oceania | 1 (3) | 2448 (3) | 2 (4) | 2063 (2) | | |
| *Industrialised* | *11 (44)* | *30730 (80)* | *17 (49)* | *53252 (66)* | *22 (50)* | *63925 (65)* |
| Total** | 25 | 38411 | 35 | 80429 | 44 | 98193 |

* 1972: 4 additional seats held open following AFL–CIO withdrawal.

** Not including; President, General Secretary, ITF and women's representatives.

*Source*: ICFTU Congress Reports.

follows the recommendations of the smaller bodies. Such important issues as the choice of a new general secretary in 1972 and 1982 were discussed first, and at great length, in the FGPC, or even by small informal meetings of individual leaders of affiliates, mostly those from North America and Europe. Over the same period, the participants in a series of committees and sub-groups set up to discuss the reform of the ICFTU structure and finances also came from northern Europe and North America , although Japanese affiliates played an important role, especially on financial issues, and the Indians on political and social issues.

The dominance of the European and North American affiliates has been offset to a degree by the important role played by figures like C. V. Devan Nair, of the National Trades Union Congress of Singapore and a leader of the Asian Regional Organisation, who stood for general secretary in 1972, P. P. Narayanan, of the Malaysian TUC, who succeeded Bruno Storti of Italy as the first ICFTU president from a developing country in 1975, and LeRoy Trotman, of the Barbados Workers Union, who followed him in 1992. To take but one example, Narayanan was a leading advocate of the advancement of women within the Confederation, and played a major role in social and economic policy when he chaired the Economic and Social Committee. However, in both the FGPC and the EB, most other representatives from the developing countries most of the time have tended to restrict their remarks to matters directly connected to their own regions. On some occasions their role has been crucial in blocking policy proposals, such as their 1972 refusal to endorse the appointment of Otto Kersten as general secretary until Devan Nair's candidacy could be given serious consideration; rarely however have they been the initiators of policy for the Confederation as a whole. One important exception was the advocacy of cooperatives and other socio-economic projects throughout the 1960s and 1970s, another the more recent role of the Inter-American regional organisation ORIT in advocating policies for the informal sector. Otherwise the dominance of a small number of affiliates from the industrialised countries stands out in the reports of the Executive Board, the FGPC and the Steering Committee. This can be explained through tradition, the background and approach of individuals, but most importantly through the size, political influence and financial resources of these affiliates.

## The role of resources in decision-making

While it has always opposed colonialism and the unequal distribution of the world's resources, the ICFTU could hardly fail to be influenced by the inequality of the society around it. Throughout the history of the international labour movement, the affiliates with most resources, those from the leading industrialised countries, have tended to supply most of the funds for international activities. For the ICFTU, ostensibly the most important source of finance has been the regular payment of affiliation fees by national affiliates. This has always proved difficult for the poorer affiliates. Affiliation fees were initially calculated on the basis of the average wage of a manufacturing worker, so that most developing countries, which were largely agricultural, were at a disadvantage. Over the years, unpredictable changes in exchange rates have often aggravated the problem. In addition, many third world national centres remain weak and under-resourced, with the real money and power in the hands of the affiliated industrial unions.[7] This has affected the national centres' ability to contribute to their regional organisations as well as to the ICFTU itself.[8] In practice, over the years, many affiliates in developing countries (and in many industrialised countries as well) have registered only a fraction of their real membership, in order to reduce their financial obligations. All these factors have accentuated the influence of those affiliates with greater financial resources, as Table 13.2 indicates.

Beyond affiliation fees, those affiliates with enough resources and willing to use them for international work have also made substantial donations to the ICFTU's International Solidarity Fund (ISF), and in later years have contributed most of the resources for project work. Throughout the 1970s and 1980s, a significant part of the financing of the regional organisations came out of the ISF, contrary to its original purpose of funding short-term and emergency activities only. This eventually led to a review of the ISF in 1986, which recommended that the funds be used for strictly humanitarian and educational purposes, not for regular administration.[9] The overburdening of the ISF was a particularly sensitive issue at a time where there were too few regular contributors to the fund. In the monetary crises of the late 1970s and 80s, even affiliates in some richer countries had difficulty in meeting their minimum financial obligations to the confederation.[10] At the same time, many affiliates initiated their own bilateral projects and decreased their contributions to the ISF accordingly.[11]

The financial question with the most direct impact on the unions of the developing countries has been the funding of development aid projects. From its foundation, the ICFTU supported projects organised or at least

*Table 13.2*   ICFTU affiliation fees by region (%)

| Region | 1960 | 1975 | 1998 |
| --- | --- | --- | --- |
| Africa | 1.4 | 1.6 | 1.4 |
| Asia and Pacific (incl. Middle East) | 4.3 | 11.8 | 15.6 |
| Europe | 57.1 | 81.3 | 58.6 |
| Latin America and Caribbean | 0.4 | 1.0 | 0.3 |
| North America | 36.8 | 4.3 | 24.0 |

*Source*: Gumbrell-McCormick, 2000b: 536.

coordinated by the Confederation itself, under its own umbrella, and was opposed to funding from outside sources.[12] Yet despite this official policy, some affiliates (in the beginning, particularly the AFL) pursued their own bilateral projects, and in the 1970s the issue became a major focus of controversy. The Asian Regional Organisation (ARO) voiced its concern in a resolution passed by its EB in 1971, warning that the increase of such projects in the absence of any real coordination from the secretariat or the affiliates would lead to a 'Balkanisation' of the free trade unions.[13] Similar concerns were expressed by many representatives of European affiliates, such as Jack Jones, who asked for an assurance that 'the ICFTU's basic role would not be impinged by this source of financing', to which the general secretary, Otto Kersten, responded that such funds were always received through the affiliates, and 'carried no national flag'.[14]

In fact, it was hard to avoid the association of particular development projects with the resources from particular unions or countries, despite the best intentions of all concerned. This problem was exacerbated by the increasing use of funds derived from governmental or other sources outside the unions themselves, particularly from northern Europe and North America, and later Japan. The resourcing of projects sponsored by the ICFTU had to go through the national affiliates first, but this did not necessarily resolve the potential problems of the use of governmental funds for union work. The matter was taken up by a sub-committee of the FGPC convened in the early 1980s to consider the ICFTU's entire financial situation, which held meetings in the different regions with donor and recipient affiliates, ITSs and the regional organisations.[15] There were also important political problems associated with development projects, with the creation of a culture of dependency among the recipient affiliates and the imposition of particular styles of trade unionism.

## The planning and resourcing of development projects

The coordination of development projects was a major theme at the Oslo congress of 1983. According to the recently-elected general secretary, John Vanderveken, the ICFTU had three functions in this respect: to act as a clearing house for information on the needs of affiliates in the developing countries and the means at the disposal of affiliates in the richer countries;[16] to provide a platform enabling all unions to maximise cooperation; and to put its own knowledge and experience at the disposal of both donor and recipient organisations. The fundamental political challenge was to provide assistance that would increase the self-reliance of the recipients and respond to the real needs of workers in the individual country or region. As one ITS representative put it: 'the objective of all development aid must be to help workers and workers' organisations become aware and understand their own situations'.[17]

A Project Committee was established in 1987, with representatives from the major donor organisations and Stefan Nedzynski, general secretary of the Post, Telegraph and Telephone Workers' International (PTTI) representing the ITSs.[18] It drew up a series of priorities and criteria for project selection, stressing the need for all projects to provide 'help for self-help', to increase the recipient organisation's self-reliance by strengthening trade union organisation and planning activities that would make them 'more effective representatives of their members and more capable of influencing and accelerating the process of development'.[19] It was recognised that the earlier model of trade union education, focusing on narrow industrial concerns with an emphasis on Anglo-Saxon models of collective bargaining, had to give way to programmes designed to enhance the trade unions' role in development. Activities involving women and rural workers were particularly important in this connection.[20] In practice many problems remained in the selection, coordination and implementation of projects, and one participant reluctantly recognised that 'the ICFTU's efforts to assure multilateralism (have) failed',[21] while Vanderveken concluded that it was a 'voluntary act of affiliates to go through the ICFTU' and that the best that could be hoped for would be for the secretariat to act as an 'honest broker'. The effect of this breakdown of multilateralism was to reinforce the leading role of a few wealthy first world affiliates, without the mediating role of the international organisation through which the voice of third world affiliates could be heard. While the views of 'recipient' affiliates were solicited in the process, in practice it was the availability of resources from the industrialised country affiliates – and their governments – that determined the selection, content and implementation of development programmes.

## Political divisions and trade union solidarity

Dependence on outside funding for development projects has been just one aspect of the impact of political factors on trade union concerns. From the beginning of international trade unionism, the confederations of national centres have been concerned with political issues, leaving the ITSs to concentrate on more narrowly industrial concerns (Van Goethem, 2000). In the course of the development of the labour movement, unions in many countries established close relationships with social democratic parties, and at the international level they confronted many political issues, from the power struggles that led to the first world war, to the rise of fascism afterwards. In the second world war, trade unionists played a considerable role in the Allied war effort, building links with governments and secret services that continued in the tense post-war situation (Carew, 1987). These links contributed to the split in the international movement in 1949, as unions felt obliged to choose sides in the cold war.

The early years of the ICFTU were thus marked by the East-West conflict, with the developing and decolonising countries viewed as a new field of competition between opposing ideologies. This may be one of the reasons that the affairs of the developing countries were of such importance to the ICFTU and its rivals, WFTU and the WCL. In Africa, Asia and Latin America, the organisation and support of 'free' trade unions was seen as an essential goal in the establishment of democracy and the defeat of communism (Carew, 1996). Education programmes and other projects were aimed at creating leaders committed to the 'free' trade union ideology, in a setting where trade unions played a major role in decolonisation and democratisation, and where union leaders often became the political leaders of newly independent states. The dangers of this approach came to a head in the 1970s, when the regional organisation for the Americas, ORIT, became the object of a major scandal with revelations of its close interpenetration by U.S. government agencies.[22] Its education programmes were often formulated and staffed in cooperation with the American Institute for Free Labour Development (AIFLD), largely funded by the U.S. government and big business, placing a strong emphasis on the 'East-West conflict', and leading ORIT to oppose unions in Latin America, however large or influential, that were seen as 'left wing'.[23]

The concentration on a particular model of 'free collective bargaining', based on the Anglo-Saxon countries, linked to a vision of trade unions as totally independent of political parties and performing a purely industrial role, was later seen as inadequate and inappropriate to the situation of many developing countries.[24] From the 1980s onwards, many individual projects with a new 'socio-economic' focus have been notably successful, in particular many of those aimed specifically at women workers in the Third World.[25] These projects have provided training for workers in Asia, Africa and Latin America, adapted to each individual case.[26] Although the content of projects has noticeably improved, the structure and funding of development projects have remained basically the same, leaving room for indirect political influence in the choice of location, content and execution of the projects. Moreover, U.S. government-backed institutes like the AIFLD, along with the Friedrich Ebert Stiftung in Germany, the Japan International Labor Foundation and similar bodies in a few other countries, have continued their involvement , despite protests from many leaders of the confederation (Gumbrell-McCormick, 2000b: 458–61).

## Solidarity or dependence?

One of the major *raisons d'être* of the ICFTU, and the other trade union internationals, has from the beginning been assistance to trade unions in the developing countries, based on a concept of solidarity between the richer and poorer workers. This was no doubt the sincere intention of the founders of the confederations, and remains so among workers and union leaders alike today. The international organisation was the main channel of information and contacts between trade unions in the developed and the developing countries. Yet increasingly, knowledge and expertise have been appropriated by individual affiliates involved in funding development projects; bilateralism has greatly reduced the ICFTU's role as an 'honest broker' and its ability to influence the relations between unions in the first and third worlds by setting a global policy based on the wishes and interests of all affiliates. The fear expressed by Asian affiliates in the 1970s of a 'Balkanisation' of the developing countries through the control of projects by a few affiliates from the industrialised world has to a large extent come true. As long as the affiliates in the developing countries are seen as 'recipients' of assistance, and those in the industrialised countries as 'donors', the inequality of their relationship remains, whatever the content of projects. Furthermore, as has been seen, while the EB has a majority of members from the developing countries, the same cannot be said of the crucial smaller committees and working groups, especially those concerned with finance.

It is a difficult task for the trade union movement, whatever its espoused policies, to escape the heavy weight of inequality between the rich and poor countries. The ICFTU has supported major initiatives in favour of debt relief and other measures to equalise trading relationships, and has opposed colonialism and exploitation; but as the influence of the trade union movement has waned in the industrialised countries over the past 20 years of neo-liberalism, so has its ability to affect the crucial decisions involving world trade and global inequality. In recent years, a more critical appreciation of the dynamics of trade liberalisation, and the growth of a more robust trade union movement both in the developing and the industrialised countries, have encouraged new ways of thinking within the international movement. There have been recent examples of international trade union solidarity, where unions from the south have given their assistance to unions in the north. Furthermore, the emerging leaders of the international movement in such countries as Brazil and South Africa are establishing close links among themselves, and may be leading the way to a more egalitarian international structure and greater autonomy and initiative from the trade unions of the developing world.

### References

Carew, A. (1987) *Labour under the Marshall Plan*. Manchester: Manchester UP.

Carew, A. (1996) 'Conflict within the ICFTU: Anti-Communism and Anti-Colonialism in the 1950s'. *International Review of Social History*, 41: 147–81.

Carew, A. (2000) 'Towards a Free Trade Union Centre'. In van der Linden, M. (ed.), *The International Confederation of Free Trade Unions*. Bern: Peter Lang, 187–339.

Fimmen, E. (1924) *Labour's Alternative: The United States of Europe or Europe Limited*. London: Labour Publishing Company.

Gumbrell-McCormick, R. (2000a) 'Globalisme et régionalisme'. In Fouquet, A., Rehfeldt, U. and Le Roux, S. (eds), *Le syndicalisme dans la mondialisation*. Paris, Editions de l'Atelier, 43–53.

Gumbrell-McCormick, R. (2000b) 'Facing New Challenges'. In van der Linden, M. (ed.), *The International Confederation of Free Trade Unions*. Bern: Peter Lang: 343–517.

Gumbrell-McCormick, R. (2000c) 'Quel internationalisme syndical? Passé, présent, avenir'. *Les Temps Modernes*, janvier-février: 178–206.

Régin, T. and Wolikow, S. (eds) (2002) *Les syndicats en Europe: A l'épreuve de l'international*. Paris: Syllepse.

Reinalda, B. (1997) 'The ITF and the non-European world'. In Reinalda, B. (ed.), *The International Transportworkers Federation 1914–1945*. Amsterdam: Stichting beheer IISG, 117–25.

Van Goethem, G. (2000) 'Conflicting Interests'. In van der Linden, M. (ed.), *The International Confederation of Free Trade Unions*. Bern: Peter Lang, 73–163.

# 14
# Partnership and the Politics of Trade Union Policy Formation in the UK: The Case of the Manufacturing, Science and Finance Union

*Miguel Martínez Lucio and Mark Stuart*

## Introduction

The central objective of the chapter is to challenge what we consider to be the *binaristic* nature of recent debates around social partnership in the UK, particularly the argument that trade unions have clear strategic choices facing them in terms of 'moderation' or 'militancy' (see Ackers, 2002; Kelly, 1996, 1998). As Roche and Geary (2002) note, this debate can be broken down into two camps: advocates and critics. The former, such as Ackers and Payne (1998), argue that partnership offers trade unions an historical opportunity to come 'out of the cold', play a leading role in corporate decision-making processes and gain 'broader social legitimacy'. At a tactical level, this presupposes that trade unions have no choice but to engage with the partnership agenda because 'both management and government, and indirectly customers, are highly intolerant of union behaviour that does not "add value" to the organisation' (see Ackers et al., 2004). This line of analysis is disputed by a wide range of critics (Kelly, 1996, 2001, 2004; Martinez Lucio and Stuart, 2004; Richardson et al., 2004; Stuart and Martinez Lucio, 2002; Wray, 2004).[1] They question the degree of independence afforded trade unions within the (essentially managerial) partnership agenda, the absence of institutional preconditions for effective delivery of partnership and ultimately the extent of mutual gains derived from engagement with partnership. To date, however, most analysis has considered the effects of partnership as a form of strategic engagement, rather than systematically examining the way in which partnership is developed and understood within specific trade unions and politically responded to.

Against this backdrop, we will explore the complex way in which union choices are made and politically constructed through a discussion of the British Manufacturing, Science and Finance (MSF) union's decision to embark on a strategy of partnership. The chapter will map the way MSF engaged with partnership in the late 1990s and how it was developed, understood and acted upon within its membership structures, in particular its workplace representatives. We argue that such strategic ventures should be evaluated and understood in relation to the politics of employment relations *and* the realities of strategic calculations within trade unions. The chapter argues that the constitution of partnership by trade unions in the UK emerges from the way in which trade unionists perceive the actions, intentions, and trajectories of management and employers. This is noticeable in the way even 'supportive' views amongst trade unionists of partnership are paralleled by very strong sets of concerns in terms of the risk of institutional engagement and the nature of management commitment. This lack of faith in the nature and attitude of British management makes the evolution of partnership policies problematic, even if the concerns vary across the different levels and arenas of union action.

The chapter advances a three-level framework of analysis for the study of the politics of partnership within trade unions. Our first level documents the genealogy of partnership within the MSF union, carefully revealing the way in which its meaning is contested (we call this the *intra-union interface*). The second level presents some survey findings on the basic attitudes and experiences of MSF workplace representatives vis-à-vis partnership, noting how the concept is understood and evaluated within the reality of contemporary workplace relations and management behaviour (we call this the *management-union interface*). The third level focuses on the workplace, briefly reporting the findings of a case study of 'partnership building' and pays particular attention to the dynamics of workplace representation and relations between trade unions (we call this the *inter-union interface*). This three-fold framework allows us to show how concerns with trust – which are vital to the 'game' of partnership – manifest themselves at different levels and in different ways, thus allowing an appreciation of the complex landscape of worker interests. It also allows us to appreciate that relations of trust have to be understood not solely in terms of management-union relations but in terms of the three dimensions outlined above. In conclusion, we consider the way in which trade union concerns and their politics are influenced by broader regulatory and managerial legacies of employment relations (Kochan and Osterman, 1994).

## Partnership and union decision making

At the time of the research the Manufacturing, Science and Finance Union[2] was one of the UK's largest trade unions, with over 425,000 members. It represented mainly skilled and professional workers (typically technical and scientific) across a variety of industries and services in the public and private sectors, and had a reputation for developing innovative trade union strategies (for example, around lifelong learning and organising). A number of high-profile partnership agreements had been signed by the union (for example, at Legal and General), but, despite this, its leadership 'displayed a generally cautious and pragmatic approach to the question of partnership' (Upchurch and Danford, 2001: 102). This cautious and pragmatic approach can be understood in terms of the different levels of union engagement and politics.

## Strategic choices and union politics: the intra-union interface

During the 1990s the MSF began to evaluate the furtherance of partnership as a possible model of industrial relations practice, although like the organising debate this was not a clear and coherent development that merely contrasted with more activist approaches. Pre-empting the election of a Labour government, key circles within the union leadership saw in the new language of partnership a model for re-establishing a dynamic role within collective bargaining and reinvigorating relations with management generally. Partnership was visualised as a way of expanding union influence within the firm along a range of new issues, such as learning, health and safety and equal opportunities. It was also seen as a way of marketing the union to employers in a context where union recognition and membership expansion would come to the fore due to proposed regulatory changes.

Whilst the union had already signed a number of high profile partnership agreements, this had not been underpinned by any systematic outline of the meaning and objectives of partnership by the union leadership. Partnership was seen as an extension of the over-arching project to 'modernise' the union and create a new form of relationship with employers and government based on an acceptance of the exigencies of the new economy and a widening of trade union influence within the firm into both social and business related matters. However, in 1999, the MSF leadership confronted a motion from key branches within its annual Conference. The Conference held a debate on partnership that resulted in a majority of delegates voting for a counter motion that emphasised the importance of 'mutual respect' with employers and guarantees of union independence. The concern was that without such guarantees partnership would be 'unequal and compromising for unions'. This motion would also allow, it was argued, for independent and radical campaigning to be prioritised. Carter and Poynter (1999) point to this emerging tension in terms of the contradiction between the organising and partnership dimensions of the MSF's activities.

The leadership responded by outlining a strategy that was, in theory, sensitive to these concerns. The argument forwarded was that partnership would be developed 'within a framework of independent, campaigning trade unionism' (MSF, 1999: 7). However, whilst effective collective bargaining would be a central feature of partnership its character would vary from company to company depending on the industrial relations tradition (MSF, 1999). The issue here was that partnership would still constitute an extension of union remits and roles but this would be contingent on the nature of union involvement. What is more, partnership continued to be a part of both the MSF's modernising discourse and its attempt to create a more 'moderate' – in this case New Labour oriented – union.

At the annual conference in 2000 the issue of guarantees and activist concerns re-emerged (despite the publication of a series of national MSF guidelines and documents in the interim). The issue of union independence and alternative strategies, along with the perception that 'good' partnership agreements were few and far between, resurrected a range of motions and amendments that carried favour amongst the conference delegates and which, whilst not undermining the strategic shift towards partnership, did argue for its rethinking as a central plank of policy making and union action. It was asserted, for example, 'that such policies confuse and disarm trade unionists and help them to maintain the existing system which gives resolute power to employers, whose sole purpose is to satisfy shareholders' interests...' (MSF, 2000: 5). Although this debate did not significantly shift the leadership's position, it did force key players to try and formulate a critical tone to the approach to partnership. The debate continued in the union's 2003 conference when a form of synthesis emerged. The constituency of delegates presenting critical motions decided to table a new motion that continued to question the viability of partnership but which sustained that partnership could only be supported if it was underpinned by a series of conditions and principles. These principles were extracted from the British Trade Union Congress's (TUC) approach to partnership which emphasises, for example, recognition of differences between management and unions, investment in quality of working life issues and training and greater trade union participation within the firm (see Martinez Lucio and Stuart, 2002; TUC, 1999; Terry, this volume). The conference and leadership supported the motion.

Such developments, whilst located at the institutional and policy level of the union, illustrate the instability of the meaning of partnership and its varied forms. A large constituency saw the partnership concept as an extension of earlier discussions on the union's role vis-à-vis new management practices. The concern was that the union risked having its independence undermined by a close relation with management in the implementation of such projects. In other words, partnership was seen to be an issue that had consequences for union purpose and identity. The instability in the term was also related to the way it was used as part of a broader political project and shift in union identity. Hence, the policy debates focused on defining *guarantees* and establishing common understandings of '*good*' *industrial relations practice*.

## Management-union interface: the attitudes and experiences of workplace representatives

Moving from the level of policy making, we now turn to an evaluation of the meanings and understandings of partnership at the level of the workplace. Having detected an ambiguity in the term, we need to locate this in the way partnership was viewed by those at the forefront of the implementation process. It is always difficult to evaluate the effect of formal, organisational discussions within a union on a specific topic within its broad membership, particularly when materials handled by workplace representatives regarding the subject are rarely linked to union conference processes. Nonetheless, with this caveat in mind, we draw here selectively from a large-scale survey of MSF senior workplace representatives' perceptions and experiences of partnership, conducted during April and May 2000. In total, 2,084 questionnaires were distributed, generating 317 usable responses (a response rate of 15 per cent).[3] The survey sought to assess trade unionists' experiences of contemporary employment relations and the management of change, including their attitudes towards the principles and practices of partnership. Our aim was to map the changing nature and forms of employment relations across MSF's key sectors, and to assess the extent to which partnership-type arrangements were taking root. The distribution of questionnaires was not, therefore, restricted to those organisations with partnership agreements.

Just under a third of the MSF representatives surveyed indicated that they had a clear understanding of the union's policy towards partnership. This level of understanding was found to be much higher in those 17 per cent of cases where a partnership agreement had been signed. Nonetheless, given the relatively low levels of awareness amongst workplace representatives of official MSF policy towards partnership, it is worthwhile examining the extent to which respondents held positive or negative attitudes towards the principles of partnership, as this provides an indicator of the degree of receptivity to the furtherance and implementation of partnership strategies at the workplace level.

Table 14.1 presents data on attitudes towards the principles of partnership. Respondents were generally positive about the principle that 'effective industrial relations are based on a shared understanding of the business goals of the organisation'. Eighty four per cent agreed with this statement. Similarly, nearly six out of ten respondents agreed that employee commitment is dependent upon non-adversarial industrial relations (57%). These findings are consistent with an outlook amongst trade unionists that is broadly supportive of the business agenda of partnership. Nonetheless, if trade unionists are to engage in partnership with management, it is important that it is furthered on a mutual recognition by management of the potentially conflicting roles of trade unions. Again, our findings here are supportive. A majority of respondents (57%) agreed that management at

*Table 14.1* MSF representatives' attitudes to the principles of partnership (valid percentage)

| | Strongly agree | Agree | Neutral | Disagree | Strongly disagree | Mean score |
|---|---|---|---|---|---|---|
| Effective industrial relations are based on a shared understanding of the business goals of the organisation | 39 | 45 | 9 | 4 | 3 | 1.86 |
| The business goals of this organisation are clearly explained to the union and its members | 12 | 34 | 26 | 18 | 11 | 2.82 |
| Management has become more willing to share, and develop jointly, the future business goals of this organisation | 5 | 29 | 25 | 23 | 18 | 3.21 |
| Management recognises that at certain times there might be legitimate differences in the interests of the employer and employee | 9 | 48 | 20 | 17 | 7 | 2.64 |
| There is a high degree of mutual trust between management and unions at this organisation | 5 | 14 | 25 | 30 | 26 | 3.57 |
| Employment security should be dependent upon the development of greater flexibility | 6 | 34 | 37 | 15 | 9 | 2.88 |
| Management has become more committed to employment security | 5 | 18 | 35 | 26 | 16 | 3.30 |
| Measures to improve the employability of staff have become an increasing priority | 2 | 23 | 34 | 26 | 15 | 3.30 |
| There has been an increased investment by the organisation in the quality of members' working lives | 1 | 10 | 29 | 39 | 22 | 3.69 |

*Table 14.1* MSF representatives' attitudes to the principles of partnership (valid percentage) – *continued*

| | Strongly agree | Agree | Neutral | Disagree | Strongly disagree | Mean score |
|---|---|---|---|---|---|---|
| Training and development are regarded as non-conflictual issues between unions and management at this organisation | 6 | 40 | 28 | 20 | 7 | 2.82 |
| Opportunities for non-vocational training exist at this workplace | 4 | 24 | 20 | 30 | 23 | 3.43 |
| Management shares information, and discusses openly, the future plans of the business | 4 | 29 | 21 | 24 | 23 | 3.33 |
| Unions have the opportunity to express their members' views on key business issues | 10 | 45 | 16 | 16 | 14 | 2.80 |
| Unions may have to accept conditions of confidentiality on certain issues and manage their membership communications in new ways | 18 | 48 | 21 | 8 | 5 | 2.33 |
| Employee commitment is dependent upon non-adversarial industrial relations | 16 | 41 | 24 | 15 | 4 | 2.50 |
| The future role of the union at this organisation should be dependent upon its success in contributing to performance improvements. | 6 | 23 | 27 | 29 | 16 | 3.26 |

Due to rounding the totals per item may not always add to 100.

their workplace 'recognises that at certain times there might be legitimate difference in the interests of employer and employee', with just under a quarter disagreeing (24%).

At the heart of partnership working is the idea that both management and trade unions trade reciprocal commitments for the good of the organisation. To this end, 40 per cent of MSF representatives agreed that employment security should be dependent upon the development of greater flexibility, with just under a quarter of respondents disagreeing. MSF representatives also appeared to be relatively committed to the furtherance of training and development opportunities, with just 27 per cent questioning whether training and development were non-conflictual issues between management and unions at their place of work. Positive levels of involvement were also visible in relation to the development of business issues. Respondents were more likely to agree (46%) than disagree (29%) that the business goals of the organisation are clearly explained to the union and its members. Likewise, a majority (55%) reported that they had opportunities to voice their members' views on key business issues. Such information disclosure, particularly around future business plans, may, however, carry an expectation of confidentiality, a principle that our respondents appear to accept. Thus, 66 per cent agreed with the statement that 'unions may have to accept conditions of confidentiality on certain issues and manage their membership communications in new ways'.

Nonetheless, the degree of involvement and information sharing may, in practice, be rather limited and 'one directional'. MSF representatives were more likely to disagree (41%) than agree (34%) that the future business goals of the organisation were something that the union could develop jointly with management. Indeed, only a minority (33%) reported that management were willing to 'share information, and discuss openly, the future plans of the organisation'.

The findings on perceived improvement in the quality of working life and investments in human capital were no more impressive. Less than a quarter of respondents reported that management at their organisation had become more committed to employment security, compared to 42 per cent who reported that this was not the case. Likewise, 'measures to improve the employability of staff' had become an increasing priority in just a quarter of cases, and 'opportunities for non-vocational training' were available in less than three out of every ten cases (28%). Given these results, it is unsurprising that just 11 per cent of MSF representatives reported 'an increased investment by the organisation in the quality of members' working lives'.

The limited nature of involvement with regard to business decisions and the lack of investment in human capital can clearly influence 'mutual-trust' at the workplace and stall the development of genuine partnership relations. Less than a fifth of MSF representatives reported a high degree of mutual trust between management and unions at their organisation, compared to 56 per cent of respondents who reported that this was not the case. Perhaps as a consequence, MSF representatives were more likely to disagree (45%) than agree (29%) that 'the future role of the union at this organisation should be dependent upon its success in contributing to performance improvements'.

In summary, the findings suggest that MSF representatives were sensitive to the changing context and needs of contemporary organisations. They were open to the challenge of workplace change and were realistic about management constraints. Yet as far as involvement, information sharing and the working environment were concerned MSF representatives were much more ambivalent about the extent of workplace change. This is vital for understanding the development of partnership and the prospects for change at the British workplace. According to the survey findings that addressed investment around what we called the three pillars of partnership – involvement, quality of the working environment, and training – the extent of investment in change was minimal (Martinez Lucio and Stuart, 2001).

What we find then is that at one level whilst the respondents were open to the aspirations of partnership, they recognised that the process of 'building' partnership was contradictory, uneven and not central to managerial and employer agendas. Thus, support for the critical positions that emerged within union conferences appeared underpinned by a general unease with the *context* and *deliverables* of partnership – if not necessarily the *process*. This is suggestive of critical understandings and positions within ostensibly 'moderate' views of relations with management. In other words, there was not just a problem of partnership in terms of its content and definition there was a problem in terms of the perceived <u>context</u> within which it was to develop. In this respect, partnership was being read by trade union representatives in relation to other contextual factors: the institutional environment, the character and legacies of management, and the changing experiences of work. The more supportive view of partnership as a new agenda of employment relations served as a basis of the leadership's position, yet the reality of relations with management tended to undermine any attempt to create a clear consensus on the issue. Within the union's branches, the basis for strategic ventures such as partnership was undermined by the legacy of uncertainty and the lack of trust generated within the workplace.

### Workplace politics and the issues of representation and trust: inter-union interface

Having discussed partnership as an object of political engagement, both within the union and in the *perceived* relations between union representatives and management, we now focus on how partnership is defined and utilised within the political relations that exist at the level of the workplace. We draw here from a qualitative case study designed to track the evolution of partnership. The case draws from interviews and the observation of joint management-union meetings related to partnership in a medium-sized food ingredients manufacturer (employing approximately 300 people), which we refer to as FoodCo. A concerted effort had been made over a number of years to move towards a partnership-based approach to employment relations. This was driven by the desire of a new HR manager to move away from an employment relations tradition typically characterised by the set-piece negotiations of the annual pay round, which tended to be prolonged and adversarial. The basis for partnership was laid over a two-year period via a 'working together' management-union forum, and advice and guidance from the Arbitration, Conciliation and Advisory Service (ACAS). Despite a strong initial interest and commitment from management and union constituencies, the transition to partnership did not materialise. It was eventually derailed by the poor financial performance of its parent company and its eventual takeover by an (anti-union) American multinational, although as we document below the process of partnership building had reached an impasse well before this. The case reveals three related themes that explain some of instability in the politics and practice of partnership relations: the fragility and unevenness of voice mechanisms; the potential impact of inter-union relations; and the problems of low trust that can emerge due to the exploitation by management of inter-union rivalries.

At FoodCo, clear problems around the development of *voice mechanisms* emerged. The joint management-union forum developed for discussing the issue of partnership became hamstrung with debates around the meaning of partnership. The lack of clarity in management intentions in terms of partnership was seen to exacerbate this problem. Certain union representatives – in particular those of the MSF – were concerned that partnership appeared to be an extension of the management's ongoing concern to develop new forms of work organisation based on direct involvement and individualised employee relations (i.e. developments that could bypass collective forms of representation). The more critical trade unionists, when not distrustful of management intentions, accepted partnership when presented to them as a deepening of traditional consultative roles and forms of joint regulation, which was not necessarily obvious as far as the management rhetoric was concerned. In this respect, partnership was viewed as a possible extension of the contemporary trade union agenda of enhancing the democratic role and thematic influence of labour. This contrasted, however, with a management approach that viewed partnership as central to 'cultural transformation'. From management's point of view, changes at such a level, through the development of new line management structures and individual forms of employee communication and involvement, would, it was believed, be facilitated by union support through partnership structures. This perspective further exacerbated the concerns of key trade unionists that partnership represented a by-passing of collective forms of communication.

In this respect, the problem was one of emphasis in terms of the way the meanings of partnership were tied to distinct organisational readings of participation and involvement, which were further compounded by the lack of national regulatory supports for 'voice' mechanisms at the workplace (especially in the private sector) (Towers, 1997). The two unions at the plant (USDAW[4] and MSF) were also concerned with the potential threat of de-recognition. There was a view that the risk to unions of engaging in new forms of partnership could undermine their long term prospects due to the way individual voice mechanisms would be legitimated and due to the way cultural changes could be used to privilege one union over another. This issue of risk is central to the development of partnership structures. This lack of trust, and the associated risk of engagement, was also influenced then by the nature of *inter-union relations*. In the case of FoodCo it was felt that USDAW – a union renowned for its political commitment to partnership – was less likely to be de-recognised, according to the MSF branch at the plant. Whether issues of de-recognition were ever on the management agenda was another matter, but concerns for this issue were apparent in the strategic calculations and behaviour of both unions. Matters came to head in a management-union workshop designed to ratify the defined approach of partnership in the organisation. In the case of USDAW, full time officials were observed to force a partnership agreement onto the shop stewards during workshop 'breakouts'. This differed from the way the MSF branch was allowed to develop a more critical line around its lead representative, with the support of his members and officials. These inter-union tensions had a profound effect on the strategy, and political will, of management to further the partnership agenda. In essence, the line advanced by the MSF on partnership served to expose the previously ill defined intentions of management, based around a more business and culturally driven understanding of partnership. Hence, the process of building partnership was, in effect, derailed and management chose to pursue its re-evaluation of employment relations more closely with USDAW, to the gradual isolation of MSF.

These inter-union dynamics were also exacerbated by the way in which trust relationships were strained by further developments related to organisational change. The de-merger of the company that owned FoodCo did not involve any consultations or discussions (formal or informal) with the trade union branches. The changing personnel within senior management and the failure to involve local representatives in key developments regarding ownership intensified the fragility of the partnership process. This led to a greater reliance on informal information and hearsay and undermined consistent relations between unions.

Of relevance to this chapter is the fact that the development and definition of partnership was conditional and dependent on negative perceptions of the regulatory environment and the context of management intentions, the impact of unstable systems of union representation and the poor legacies of *involvement*. These factors were creating a politics of partnership that were not emerging from any *a priori* political or ideological discourses related to moderation and militancy – although there is no doubting that in some cases such conscious discourses and educational processes did play a role. The question appears to be the way concerns about union *voice* and union *roles* had been defined within the workplace historically and were then woven into the current institutional dynamic of employment relations.

## Conclusion: Union strategy and context

This chapter has forwarded an analysis that is sensitive to the politics of partnership at three levels of employment relations: the intra-union, the management-union, and the inter-union interfaces. Choices in terms of partnership are made in the context of political processes that influence the way such concepts evolve, not just as strategic 'ventures' but as sites of struggle in their own right.

Firstly, within the macro politics of the union an intriguing set of engagements emerged as the union's leadership and various constituencies of activists tried to forge meanings of partnership around questions of union identity. In this case, the issue was the nature of the relationship with employers and management in terms of the union's independence and role. The concern within the annual conference related less to the process of partnership than with the 'cost' it would have on the purpose and scope of union action. These concerns led to a series of accommodations and reconfigurations in the meaning of partnership within the politics of the union. However, these accommodations could not stifle the concerns that constantly re-emerged within the annual conference and at the level of the workplace.

Secondly, at the level of workplace representatives, the issue of union independence remained important but was underpinned by a broader set of concerns about management. Our study reveals that support for partnership as a form of involvement and information sharing was seriously undermined. The issue at this level was the perception that partnership was not just an ideological problem but also a practical one due to the nature of employment relations and poor management predispositions. Support for the critical positions that had emerged at Conference appeared underpinned within the workplace by a general unease with the *context* and *deliverables* of partnership, but not necessarily the *process*.

Finally, the chapter noted that these concerns with the purpose and practicalities of partnership were exacerbated by the complex relations between unions within the workplace and the concern with their managerial manipulation during the development of partnership agreements and structures. The failure to crystallise and develop systematic voice mechanisms within industrial relations is a salient feature of partnership in Britain (Stuart and Martinez Lucio, 2002). Hence, it is difficult for observers to evaluate partnership and its meaning when the relations of trust and the clarity of roles it is contingent upon are unclear. In this respect, the analysis of political processes remains central to the evolution of partnership and new forms of employment relations.

## References

Ackers, P. (2002) 'Reframing employment relations: the case for neo-pluralism', *Industrial Relations Journal*, 33(1): 2–19.

Ackers, P. and Payne, J. (1998) 'British trade unions and social partnership: rhetoric, reality and strategy' *International Journal of Human Resource Management* 9(3): 529–50.

Ackers, P., Marchington, M., Wilkinson, A. and Dundon, D. (2004) 'Partnership and voice, with or without trade unions: changing British management approaches to participation', in Stuart, M. and Martinez Lucio, M. (eds), *Partnership and Modernisation in Employment Relations*. London: Routledge.

Carter, B. (1991) 'The making of MSF: politics and process in the making of the Manufacturing, Science and Finance Union (MSF)' *Capital and Class*, 45: 35–72.

Carter, B. (1997) 'Adversity and Opportunity: Towards union renewal in Manufacturing, Science and Finance' *Capital and Class*, 61: 8–18.

Carter, B. and Poynter, G. (1999) 'Unions in a Changing Climate: MSF and Unison in the new public sector' *Industrial Relations Journal* 30(5): 499–513.

Kelly, J. (1996) 'Union militancy and social partnership' in Ackers, P. Smith, C. and Smith, P. (eds), *The New Workplace and Trade Unionism*. London: Routledge, 77–109.

Kelly, J. (1998) *Rethinking Industrial Relations: Mobilization, Collectivism and Long Waves*. London: Routledge.

Kelly, J. (2001) Social Partnership Agreements in Britain: union revitalisation or employer-counter-mobilization? Presented at Conference *Assessing Partnership: The Prospects for and Challenges of 'Modernisation'*, Leeds University Business School, Leeds, 24–25th May.

Kelly, J. (2004) 'Social partnership agreements in Britain', in Stuart, M. and Martinez Lucio, M. (eds), *Partnership and Modernisation in Employment Relations*. London: Routledge.

Kochan, T. A. and Osterman (1994) *The Mutual Gains Enterprise: Forging a Winning Partnership among Labour, Management and Government*. Boston, MA: Harvard University Press.

Martinez Lucio, M. and Stuart, M. (2001) *Partnership and Modernisation in Employment Relations*, London: Manufacturing, Science and Finance Union.

Martinez Lucio, M. and Stuart, M. (2002) 'Assessing the principles of partnership: workplace trade union representatives' attitudes and experiences', *Employee Relations*, 24(3): 305–320.

Martinez Lucio, M. and Stuart, M. (2004) 'Swimming against the tide: social partnership, mutual gains and the revival of 'tired' HRM'. *International Journal of Human Resource Management*, 15(2): 404–418.

MSF (1999) *Annual Conference documentation*, London: MSF.

MSF (2000) *Partnership*, London: MSF.

Richardson, M., Stewart, P., Danford, A., Tailby, S. and Upchurch, M. (2004) 'Employees' experiences of workplace partnership in the private and public sector', in Stuart, M. and Martinez Lucio, M. (eds), *Partnership and Modernisation in Employment Relations*. London: Routledge.

Roche, B. and Geary, J. (2002) 'Advocates, Critics and Union Involvement in Workplace Partnerships: Irish airports', *British Journal of Industrial Relations*, 40(4): 659–688.

Stuart, M. and Martinez Lucio, M. (2002) 'Social Partnership and the Mutual Gains Organisation: Remaking Involvement and Trust at the British Workplace', *Economic and Industrial Democracy* 23(2): 177–200.

Towers, B. (1997) *The Representation Gap: Change and Reform in the British and American Workplace*. Oxford: Oxford University Press.

Trades Union Congress (TUC) (1999) *Partners for Progress*. London: TUC.

Upchurch, M. and Danford, A. (2001) 'Industrial restructuring, "globalisation" and the trade union response: a study of MSF in the South-west of England', *New Technology, Work and Employment*, 16(2): 100–17.

Wray, D. (2004) 'Management and union motives in the negotiation of partnership: A case study of process and outcome at an engineering company', in Stuart, M. and Martinez Lucio, M. (eds), *Partnership and Modernisation in Employment Relations*. London: Routledge.

# 15

# 'Partnership': A Serious Strategy for UK Trade Unions?

*Michael Terry*

The statistics of union decline in the United Kingdom since 1979 are familiar, depressingly so to those who hold a strong trade union movement to be a central guarantor of a degree of economic and industrial democracy. Union membership fell from 12.6 million in 1979 to 7.1 million in 1998, a fall in the membership density of the employed workforce from 56 per cent to 30 per cent (Waddington and Kerr, 2000: 231). By 2000 membership had fallen to below 7 million. In the last few years there has been a flattening-out, even a slight upturn, but not enough to mask the trauma of decline, most marked in the private sector. In 1980 well over half of all private sector employees were union members; by 1998 this had fallen to a quarter, and by late 1999 estimates put it as low as 19 per cent.

Many explanations for the decline have been put forward. The core of my preferred account is that the decline in membership reflects, and in turn exacerbates, growing union weakness and ineffectiveness. Behind these lie two linked changes: a dramatically-changed structure of international private capitalism that weakens the collective bargaining power of unionism in general, and decentralised, workplace-based unionism in particular; and a managerial strategy designed to weaken and eventually eliminate union influence not over pay and working conditions directly but over the organisation, pace and nature of work. While not confined to the UK, these factors were particularly marked there during the 1980s and 90s, and were aided by the politics of governments hostile to collectivism.

Union ineffectiveness is clearly visible in the findings of the latest (1998) UK Workplace Employee (previously Industrial) Relations Survey (WERS). Setting these data alongside earlier surveys, case studies and other research of the 1960s and 1970s leads to the inescapable conclusion that workplace trade unions no longer *negotiate* to any significant extent on behalf of their members (see Brown et al., 2000). The concept of 'joint regulation' as the normative cornerstone of British industrial relations, clear evidence of unions' capacity to shape, through collective bargaining, the policies and practices of employers, has to be set aside.

## Voluntarism, decentralisation and oppositional trade unionism

British trade unions have traditionally operated within a unique context of law that furnished no clear framework for their operation; in virtually no other European country has post-war unionism developed in the absence of any positive legal supports, direct or indirect. An obvious consequence of such a 'voluntaristic' framework has been that trade unionism reflected the collective bargaining power of groups of workers. Unionism developed where circumstances facilitated a degree of bargaining strength sufficient to extract recognition from employers or where, for pragmatic or political reasons (the state sector) unionism was encouraged. Generally, and in particular in the private sector, unionism and the protection of collective bargaining were available more to the skilled than the unskilled, to the worker in the large rather than the small workplace, to the permanent rather than the temporary and part-time, to men rather than women, and to white rather than black.

From the 1960s onwards the rapid decentralisation of collective bargaining focused union bargaining attention on matters of immediate workplace concern; pay, employment protection, and the linked and increasingly important issue of the control of work organisation, pace and content. One of the favourite metaphors for workplace industrial relations of the time – the 'frontier of control' – conjured up images of a continuous entrenched struggle between organised workers and employers over jobs and work, and this image was convincingly reinforced by case studies. Such *oppositional* trade unionism could be powerful and effective but limited both in the range of its demands (economistic and sectional) and in its horizons (short-term and opportunistic). The inability of such unionism to construct both a more strategic, proactive agenda and the intra- and inter-organisational structures to transcend the limitations of sectionalism, has been much discussed and debated. But workplace-based democratic unionism, in the absence of legal or broader institutional supports, is rationally and understandably directed towards the immediate, day-to-day concerns of members, a point reinforced by the argument that German unions, by contrast, can take a longer-term, more strategic, view precisely because the day-to-day concerns of members carry relatively little internal weight (Jacobi et al., 1998). On the one hand we see participative democracy and limited ambitions; on the other more centralised, bureaucratic unionism but a more developed agenda. As argued below, this is one of the dilemmas raised by the 'Partnership' debate.

Despite the limitations of UK workplace unionism outlined above it is a central contention of this chapter that any eventual renaissance of trade unionism in the private sectors of British industry must be based on *workplace*-level activity, if for no other reason than that there is no other organisational base on which to build. There is no interest on the part of employers in reconstructing any form of sectoral engagement with trade unions, even on relatively 'safe' issues such as training. And, whatever may have been the hopes associated with the electoral success of the Labour Party in 1997, after seven years in government there are few signs of a return to any form of state involvement that might significantly enhance the unions' national standing.

Recently Richard Hyman identified five alternative strategies available to trade unions in Europe of which one, acting as the forger of 'productivity coalitions' with management is of particular relevance to this discussion (Hyman, 1996a: 70–1). Hyman makes clear that this strategy, collaborating with management 'in policies to enhance competitive performance' is a reflection of the altered balance of power between unions and employers (to the latter's advantage), which he implies is unlikely to change. The main beneficiaries of this approach are employers, and unions insofar as they may enjoy enhanced organisational status, at least in the eyes of their coalition partners. But the members – the employees – can take little comfort from this, since

> in severe economic circumstances...productivity coalitions may imply a competitive underbidding of either job protection or conditions of employment...with unionism organisationally reinforcing the fault lines of intra- and international divisions of employee interests (1996a: 71).

On this account the prospect of a resurgence of 'oppositional' trade unionism at workplace level appears out of the question, at least in the traditional context of voluntarism. The remainder of this paper will examine whether this pessimism appears warranted, and in particular will do so on the basis of recent ideas and data dealing with the concept of 'partnership'.

## Partnership: union capitulation or renaissance?

The use of the term 'partnership' as a means of characterising a reformed, co-operative set of relationships between unions and employers in contrast to traditional antagonism has been used in UK parlance for a decade (see Kelly, 1996: 78). Vigorous debate between academic advocates and detractors has been flourishing. Ackers and Payne, presenting the most optimistic set of arguments, conclude that 'by including unions in [to managerial decision making], partnership marks out a favourable industrial relations terrain, in which unions can regain the initiative and work to rebuild their institutional presence in British society' (1998: 544–5). In particular, they argue, trade unions may be able to take advantage of the language and rhetoric of partnership, now widely accepted, they claim, by government and employers. John Kelly, by contrast, will have none of it, nor indeed, of any approach that has the intended or unconscious effect of deflecting shopfloor union activists from a strategy of militancy (Kelly, 1996; see also Taylor and Ramsay, 1998). For Kelly, militancy, as opposed to any form of co-operation or collaboration with employers, is not only the appropriate language and practice for shopfloor unions, it is also their best chance of institutional survival and membership support and growth (1996: 92–6).

Hyman's analysis of productivity coalitions steers a middle way, by noting that a union orientation of collaboration in policies to enhance competitive performance 'is not new; trade unions have rarely welcomed the bankruptcy of their members' employers' (1996a: 71). As he argues elsewhere

> Uncompromising militancy is a recipe for defeat and exclusion; unqualified collaboration invites grass-roots alienation and perhaps revolt. Any effective system of representation is a contradictory combination of conflict and accommodation (1996b: 67).

It is difficult to see any one disagreeing with that as formulated. The question then becomes whether these contradictory elements persist within the emerging forms of workplace trade union representation; whether the language and practice of 'partnership' themselves enter the equation, moving both significantly towards the accommodation dimension.

Although the partnership concept predated the 1997 General Election, the approach was given a significant boost by the incoming Labour government and by Tony Blair's personal endorsement of partnership as their preferred approach to industrial governance. In May 1999 both he and the Secretary of State for Trade and Industry endorsed the concept at a conference organised by the Trades Union Congress and announced the creation of a Partnership at Work Fund, with up to £2.5m to spend on projects to improve partnership at work. A report published in 2000 claimed that the year had witnessed a 'frenzy' of partnership approaches to employers by unions – more than 700 (IRS, 2000: 3). The TUC launched its own 'Partnership Institute' providing consultancy and advisory services to unions and employers looking to establish partnership arrangements.

So what is this new big idea? Like many other phrases in fluid systems such as the UK it has no clear definition. But its essential elements – at least in any version sufficiently robust to mark it as a novel approach – can be identified. One such is provided by the TUC whose document *Partners for Progress: New Unionism at the Workplace* (1999) identified six features.

> First, there should be a shared commitment to the business goals of the organisation. Second, there should be a clear recognition that there might be quite legitimate differences of interest and priorities between the parties, differences that need to be listened to, respected and represented. Third, measures to ensure flexibility of employment must not

be at the expense of employees' security, which should be protected by taking such steps as ensuring the transferability of skills and qualifications. Fourth, partnership arrangements must improve opportunities for the personal development of employees. Fifth, they must be based upon open and well informed consultation, involving genuine dialogue. Sixth, and finally, effective partnerships should seek to 'add value' by raising the level of employee motivation. (Brown, 2000: 305)

Most supporters of partnership, including the government and many supportive employers, would endorse this list. The central point of difference between them and the TUC is that the latter see trade unions as central to the process, while employers and the government, have stressed that they see the approach as equally applicable to non-unionised workplaces.

Whatever else this list may be it is dramatically different from the language deployed by unions 20 years ago; then it would have been seen as representing unacceptable class collaboration, and not only by left-wing activists. The language and approach are, as Brown notes, a reflection of union weakness; an acknowledgement, at least as indicated by the speeches of John Monks, until recently TUC General Secretary, and other union leaders, of the failure of traditional 'confrontational' approaches. They are a statement of a view that in the private sector at least, unions can only survive if they can persuade employers that it is in their material interests to continue to deal with them. Equally clearly, this is no longer an agenda of traditional negotiation; it is an approach based on *consultation*, a process that, in UK usage, explicitly recognises the ultimate right of unilateral management action, for which reason it has consistently been rejected by unions in the past as very much a second-best.

But partnership agreements are, after all, only words on paper. In the context of the UK they have only voluntary effect, having no standing in law. So why do some practitioners and analysts see them as marking a significant development? In trying to answer this I will take in turn the features identified as central to partnership.

i. Shared commitment to business success
In many partnership agreements, this is the starting point. The agreement at Blue Circle Cement starts

The purpose of this Agreement is to establish the framework within which constructive employment relations can be maintained and developed. It is designed to support the objectives of the business in its journey towards excellence.

More succinctly, the agreement signed at the Legal and General insurance and finance company has as its first objective 'to work together to further the success of the business by enabling a flexible approach in a time of rapid and continuous change'. And so on.

On one reading, as noted above by Hyman, this may represent nothing novel. Employees (union members) would rather work for successful than struggling employers; their jobs are more secure, their wages probably higher. But there is a second implication, namely the involvement of unions in decisions affecting corporate performance, and thus opportunities to engage with broader, more strategic issues than the conventional fare of terms and conditions of employment. Against that must be set the (implied) loss of union autonomy in setting out demands. The managerial expectation is that, to take the most obvious example, wage claims will be set more by reference to managerial analyses of what is financially viable than to members' demands. To present any claim that might jeopardise commercial success would be seen as contradicting the unions' own undertaking, and threatening the partnership. The union role would thus be reduced to that of helping to assign priorities within an agreed 'budget'. At its most extreme – and there is no question that this is the view of at least some managers, particularly those concerned with production and operations rather than IR – the partnership commitment should mean that the unions should not contest any change seen by management as commercially necessary. For many union activists in workplaces this is giving local management *carte blanche*.

ii.   The trade-off between flexibility and employment security

An explicit relationship is established in many agreements between these two, and may be seen as seeking to mimic continental European, especially German experience of works councils, whose champions argue that they promote and encourage work flexibility in a context of employment security. The contrast with the UK experience, where job loss has been an almost invariable corollary of organisational restructuring, is clear. In assigning this priority to employment security trade unions are clearly reflecting their members' preferences which have shifted steadily from reward to security in the turbulent labour market environment of the 1980s and 1990s. The agreement at Blue Circle Cement, one of the most influential early partnerships, seeks to promote 'an environment in which employees can develop, acquire additional skills, practise those skills and demonstrate maximum flexibility, whilst the company is committed to providing maximum employment security' (cited in IDS, 1998: 5) Similarly in the case of Welsh Water 'essential to the agreement was union acceptance of the linkage between continued cooperation in the organisational and technological changes designed to promote efficiency and the No Compulsory Redundancy Policy' (IPA, n.d.(a): 2). Most agreements stress that all that is being offered is a degree of employment security (with the same company, if necessary with appropriate re-training and perhaps redeployment), not job security, and even this is usually set aside in the event of serious economic difficulty. In the UK, and this is of critical importance in the contrast with mainland Northern Europe, employment security guarantees embedded in collective agreements have no legal force; they are statements, and often relatively weak statements, of intent.

For management the crucial side of this equation is 'flexibility', the holy grail of the 1980s and 1990s. There is little doubt that one managerial intention is to eliminate union influence over the day-to-day performance of work; finally to expunge union-based 'job controls' or, as employers would term them, 'restrictive practices' which, in Conservative government and employer views, contributed to economic failures of the 1970s. More than that, the twin commitments to flexibility and business success are seen by employers as entitling them to union support in managing change, against employee resistance if necessary, as 'partners in successful change management'.

Does this approach constitute a radical change in the micro-patterns of workplace industrial relations? On the face of it certainly it seems to exclude unions from a significant area of activity in protection of their members' interests. But it is not quite as simple as that. Unions have always had an ambivalent relationship to the exercise of job controls and have on many occasions in the past refused to defend those they saw as unacceptable (see Terry and Edwards, 1988, passim). More recent attention has focused on the way in which job controls have operated in an *exclusivist* fashion, often operating to the relative advantage of the more skilled and secure, maintaining work patterns structured to exclude women and ethnic minorities, resisting new working patterns (part-time, flexible employment) that might provide better integration between employment and domestic activity. Defence of job controls and resistance to organisational change *per se* has rarely appealed to union activists. Few would articulate them as union objectives in the 21st century. Rather, at the bottom of current union concerns about flexibility proposals in the partnership approach lies the view that they pave the way for the (re-) appearance of managerial arbitrariness in the daily management of work. Unions and members are concerned that they may have signed away any right to challenge such behaviour.

iii.   The representation of differences of interest (or, whatever happened to collective bargaining?)

Most agreements contain some formulation that acknowledges differences of interest even in partnership. The Legal and General agreement contains the statement 'each side recognises and respects the other's different and shared interests'. The preamble to the agreement at the Co-operative Bank recognises 'the distinctive role and accountabilities of each partner', while a 'Basic Principle of Partnership' at Scottish Power is the provision 'of machinery for the effective and independent representation of the interests of the people who work in the organisation'. In different ways they all indicate a continued recognition of a pluralist environment with legitimately-differing interests and their representation.

But that is about all they do say, and the language is otherwise overwhelmingly unitarist in flavour. One mystery about many partnership agreements is the fate of the pre-existing machinery of grievance resolution, disciplinary and dismissal procedures and, above all, the procedures previously associated with the negotiation of pay and conditions of employment. Rarely are they formally abolished; rather, they are quietly ignored. Approaches to the *determination* of pay are, by contrast, frequently mentioned and again the language deployed is novel, with little of the flavour of negotiation to it. The Co-operative Bank agreement sets out a three-year pay formula which

> provides the framework for future salary reviews based on: the union's pay claim, bank performance and affordability; and external employment market conditions. The economic aspects of this agreement are made on the basis that the business will continue to prosper, in line with its Corporate Plan. In the unlikely event that this is not the case the bank will revert to the union to review these elements of the agreement.

Welsh Water introduced a pay formula which 'linked movements in pay to inflation, conditions in the Welsh labour market and profitability (via profit-related pay) [and] replaced the traditional annual pay negotiation' (Marginson, n.d.: 4). Cardiff Business School were asked to carry out an annual pay survey and share this with employees and trade unions, although this was not a formal part of the review mechanism. For Scottish Power 'bargaining is seen as part of a broader consultative and participative agenda around partnership' (IPA, n.d(b).: 7) with a specific procedure for negotiating terms and conditions designed to 'achieve agreed changes in terms and conditions....within the spirit of partnership and without employee relations difficulties'. This will be done through a procedure in which 'joint working groups cover the ground work beforehand to give the negotiations 'shape' in advance' after which 'negotiations focus on the level of settlement or change to terms without ranging over the territory covered by the working group'. Quite what these procedures amount to in practice (although again they clearly place new demands on the expertise of union representatives) has not yet been the subject of independent research. In all cases the language is clearly designed to present pay settlement as a consensual, commercially-informed process rather than a distributive negotiation.

The underlying question is the extent to which the expression and mobilisation of collective action, long accepted (in theory) as the legitimate underpinnings of effective collective bargaining relationships, are compatible with the approach and structures of partnership. Partnerships do not mention conflict or strikes. A characteristic approach is that found at Scottish Power when any disagreements, collective or individual, eventually find their way to the 'Partnership Council', a body committed to 'promoting and developing [the company's] business values and the partnership agreement'(IDS, 1998: 20).

While the language is non-conflictual, its practical effect is impossible to establish, primarily because there is virtually no strike or other collective action in the UK private sector at present, so no basis for arguing whether partnership has had an impact. Kelly recently noted 'the first [successful] strike threat by workers operating under a social partnership agreement' (at Scottish Power; Kelly, 2000: 6). Of itself, a single dispute proves nothing; the advocates of partnership arguing that it underlines the pluralistic, stable nature of the arrangements, and opponents that it indicates the failure of a strategy directed at membership demobilisation.

## A union revival?

The arguments outlined above are based on specific cases – virtually all of them within sectors or companies with a strong union presence pre-dating the partnership innovation – that serve to highlight the central features and dilemmas of the partnership approach. But after seven years of a Labour government committed to the approach, and a longer background of general interest in the approach, is there evidence to assess its impact on union futures and the arresting of the decline summarised at the start of this chapter?

A recent study (Smith and Terry, 2003) examined the hundred or so partnership initiatives supported by the government's Partnership at Work Fund since its inception. While this confirmed a widespread interest in the approach, one immediately striking finding was that the initiatives were overwhelmingly concentrated in companies and sectors with an existing union presence. The public sector and privatised utilities (energy, transport) were strongly represented. Very little evidence could be found that the approach was attracting enterprises in those areas – large swathes of the private service sector, small firms – where unions have to gain a toehold if decline is to be reversed. One exception was the voluntary charitable sector, where pressures both for the professionalisation of industrial relations and the recognition of trade unions have been increasing. The language and approach of partnership appeared here to provide a route to trade union recognition that accorded with the ideological orientations of charitable organisations, historically often opposed to 'antagonistic' trade unions despite wishing to act as a 'good employer'. So far, therefore, there are few grounds for anticipating that partnership will quickly foster union growth in non-traditional areas.

The second strand of the partnership argument suggested that it might contribute to an improvement in union fortunes through re-establishing what Ackers and Payne called their 'institutional centrality', in particular their greater inclusion into processes of managerial decision-making. Here the evidence is generally more positive. In a number of cases partnership agreements appeared both to reinforce the position of unions as representative agents and to widen the agenda of joint consultation, both to general business issues and to specific areas of employment relations; issues of current topicality such as safeguards against bullying and harassment and the discussions around work-life balance both appeared frequently. This development was often identified – by employers in particular – as a means of reforming existing systems, in particular to move the 'industrial relations culture' from one of perceived antagonism to joint co-operative working. This employer enthusiasm for seeking to redefine the workplace ideology of collective relations must be taken alongside evidence of widespread support for the approaches among many of the union officials involved. Indeed in a significant proportion of cases the union rather than the employer was the instigator of the partnership initiative.

### Partnership: union reinforcement and membership demobilisation?

Partnership reflects, primarily, a managerial view of trade unionism – as business-focused, consensual, responsible organisations that perceive their members' interests as best served by the pursuit of corporate success. Equally, of course, it reflects a managerial decision to continue to operate on the basis of union recognition. It is undeniable that partnership reflects union weakness, that at least early on many union representatives were deeply suspicious of the partnership approach, and that in many cases partnership agreements owe their existence and much of their content to strong managerial pressure, in some cases amounting to a formal threat of union derecognition. This is trade unionism on management's terms – but it is still trade unionism.

For Kelly, the most mordant critic of UK partnership, it represents a familiar tactic taken to new lengths. Partnership is

> a process of union co-optation by the employer. Once union officials and senior stewards have come to define the employers' interests as their own, the union organisation can be used as a mechanism for disseminating partnership ideology through the workforce, at the same time demobilising any resistance that may occur (1999: 9).

Partnership for Kelly is co-optation taken to such lengths that it must be resisted. Failure to do so will compromise the last vestiges of independent trade unionism. Courageously, Kelly has sought to examine outcomes at 'partnership' companies and compare them with their 'non-partnership' equivalents (Kelly, 1999, 2000). He argues that there is no evidence that workers in partnership companies are any better-paid or more secure and perhaps that they are worse off. His critique met with a spirited response from a shop steward at Blue Circle Cement, who argued that Kelly had underestimated the long-term benefits of the pay and security arrangements and the extended influence of the unions across a broad agenda (Warren, 2000). This debate is set to run for some time.

But a different argument can be made, namely that the key to the current union enthusiasm for partnership reflects not the advance or defence of members' interests as such, but the opportunity partnership agreements present to restate the legitimacy of trade union presence and to reinforce the organisational underpinnings of union presence in UK workplaces. In many agreements this is a central feature, and one to which union activists attach great weight. Two examples may illustrate this. At Tesco supermarket a new 3-tier (local/regional/national) consultation structure was established, with formal union representation guaranteed at each level. The Union of Shop, Distributive and Allied Workers claims that the enhanced role of the union in these structures, and its high-profile activity in establishing the partnership, have led to its gaining about 9,000 new members (an increase of around six per cent). A similar radical overhaul of joint structures took place at Scottish Power, with 'Partnership Councils', built around strong trade union representation, at corporate and local levels, with strong constitutions, wide-ranging remits, and an apparently central role in the development and implementation of policy. It is this organisational re-engagement of trade unions that lies behind union enthusiasm and that of some academic commentators. After 20 years in which the dominant drift in industrial relations has been the marginalisation and exclusion of trade unions and the reassertion of managerial unilateralism, any process that appears to re-establish unions as central actors in company affairs comes as an immense relief.

At its simplest, therefore, we may see partnership as a form of corporate level 'political exchange' in which unions formally forgo, at least in principle, significant opportunities for challenging managerial decision through the traditional assumptions of antagonistic collective bargaining, in exchange for a reinforcement of their procedural/institutional standing. Unions are thus calculating – gambling – that the advantages gained from enhanced 'institutional centrality' outweigh the losses from decreased 'substantive autonomy'. At the very least, they would argue, to do otherwise invites the continuation of the catastrophic decline summarised at the start of this paper.

It is, of course, a highly contingent calculus and exchange in which three central factors appear to be involved: managerial interest; union capacity; and the legal; and institutional setting of UK labour relations. UK management has often been characterised as unmitigatedly pragmatic; dealing with unions when it seems unavoidable or advantageous, ignoring them at other times. While some have characterised the last decades as an era of hostility to unions, calculated indifference might be an equally accurate (and often to unions equally destructive) label. The ideological hostility sometimes claimed to be widespread in North America is not a widespread UK phenomenon. But if partnership is to offer a new opportunity, as suggested above, something has to change compared with the last two decades. Ackers and Payne come up with a number of arguments that it has of which I will select two: that many employers' HR strategies have failed because of lack of union involvement (collective legitimacy); and that 'perhaps most crucial, British business has to adjust to the changing political and ideological mood, as it did to Thatcherism in the 1980s' (1998: 531). For the first claim a significant amount of largely anecdotal support may be found. It is, for example, interesting that a significant proportion of sophisticated partnership agreements have been signed in the banking and retail sectors, not areas of traditional union strength, but certainly sectors characterised by intense competition and an insistence on the rhetoric (and practice) of customer service as the key to success. Insofar as that in turn may require the implementation of sophist- icated strategies to enhance employee performance it may be seen as provid- ing some support for the argument. Otherwise, to put it baldly, why should management bother? But the implication is that partnership will be severely limited in its application, of no interest to companies pursuing 'low road' paths to commercial success. If it remains confined to such situations partner- ship will remain limited and exclusive in its coverage, offering little prospect of effective union development in sectors of low pay and low skill develop- ment. The second claim, more diffuse and intriguing, is in effect that partner- ship is cutting with a broader grain of social and political pressure for the 're-regulation' of industrial society . The evidence is, perhaps of necessity, harder to find and the statements adduced by Ackers and Payne from business leaders and politicians fail, thus far, to convince.

Important though the managerial contingencies may be, those deriving from the presumed union role in partnership are hugely more dramatic, and reflect the perception among many union activists that they are running out of alternatives. In effect partnership, if it is ever to approach the claims its advocates make, requires workplace-based unionism funda- mentally to redefine its relationships as an intermediary organisation with two groups – management, and its members. Its utility to management is primarily as a legitimator of decision change (with the corollary threat of refusal in the event of inappropriate managerial behaviour), and secondly as a source of expert, authoritative input. Both require a 'distancing' from the membership, through union engagement with managerial decisions and their implementation and through their developing professionalism. Shopfloor unionism will in that sense become increasingly less driven by the day-to-day priorities of their members. One intention of the partner-ship emphasis on employment security and pay settlement stability is to mitigate just such pressures. Strategic engagement through partnership may lead to a diminution in the organic nature of union/member relation-ships, the traditional bedrock of their participative democracy. But at the least those who have often been excluded from full access to this relation-ship (women, ethnic minority employees, part-time and low paid employ-ees) may not see this as a great loss. Equally, of course, if unions come to be seen as merely an emanation of the HRM department they lose not only membership credibility but, at the same time, their central utility to employers. If partnership – or its managerial interpretation – fails to provide appropriate scope for independent union action (oppositional), partnership as a model for the reformulation of UK private sector trade unionism collapses.

And the only significant reason for believing that it might not lies in the third contingency, the institutional, and in particular the legal framework, deriving, at least as far as the workplace level is concerned, from Britain's membership of the European Union and, in particular, the Blair govern-ment's decision to end its predecessor's 'opt-out' from the Social Chapter of the Maastricht Treaty. The gradual introduction of a weak 'works council' framework for UK workplaces, combined with the provision for a legal route to union recognition in the 1999 Employment Relations Act, may provide the UK's trade unions with the necessary minimum guarantees necessary to avoid total dependence on management on the one hand, and to speak and act with an independent, membership-based voice on the other. Equally, British employers will not, for the foreseeable future, be able to operate in a context entirely devoid of collective rights to information and consultation available to their employees. Hyman has argued that, on the balance of evidence, such a legal framework offers the only hope for private sector trade unionism since, in effect, free collective bargaining offers none (1996b: 81–2). Kelly also sees the legal changes as part of the partnership debate, except that for him they reinforce other demobilising tendencies (Kelly, 1996).

Partnership has been seized upon as offering the only hope for British unionism (and employees, by implication) after 20 lean years. But it may be at the cost, if that is what it is, of the long-accepted contours of British unions' autonomy and action in exchange for a model closer to that of the Northern continental European countries, albeit with only a pale imitation of their full legal rights and institutional integration. John Monks, then TUC General Secretary, recently argued that 'the fundamental choice is now about what kind of capitalism we want. Is it the deregulated wild-west devil take the hindmost style of the U.S.? Or is it the European approach? This combines productive economies with good welfare states, rights for people at work and environmental protection' (Monks, 2000). The adjustments that will be necessary if workplace trade unionism is not only to survive but to be part of such an approach – through partnership – are huge in their implications.

## Acknowledgement

The author is grateful to The British Academy and the University of Warwick for financial support for the work that contributed to this chapter.

## References

Ackers, P. and Payne, J. (1998) 'British trade unions and social partnership: rhetoric, reality and strategy', *The International Journal of Human Resource Management*, 9: 529–50.

Brown, W. (2000) 'Annual Review Article: Putting Partnership into Practice', *British Journal of Industrial Relations*, 38: 299–316.

Brown, W., Deakin, S., Nash, D. and Oxenbridge, S. (2000) 'The Employment Contract: From Collective procedures to Individual Rights', *British Journal of Industrial Relations*, 38: 611–30.

Hyman, R. (1996a) 'Changing Union Identities in Europe', In Leisink, P. et al. (eds), *The Challenges to Trade Unions in Europe: innovation or adaptation*, Cheltenham: Edward Elgar, 53–73.

Hyman, R. (1996b) 'Is there a case for statutory works councils in Britain?' In McColgan, A. (ed.) *The Future of Labour Law*, London: Cassell, 64–84.

IDS (1998) 'Partnership Agreements' *IDS Study* 656 (October), London: Incomes Data Services Ltd.

IPA (n.d. (a)) 'Welsh Water' *Towards Industrial Partnership*, no. 3, London: Involvement and Participation Association.

IPA (n.d. (b)) 'Scottish Power' *Towards Industrial Partnership*, no. 4, London: Involvement and Participation Association.

IRS (2000) 'Strikes decline amid union 'frenzy' over partnership and new recognition deals', *IRS Employment Trends*, 713 (October).

Jacobi, O., Keller, B. and Müller-Jentsch, W. (1998) 'Germany: Facing New Challenges'. In Ferner, A. and Hyman, R. (eds), *Changing Industrial Relations in the New Europe*, Oxford: Blackwell, 190–238.

Kelly, J. (2000) 'The Limits and Contradictions of Social Partnership' *Communist Review* (Autumn): 3–7.

Kelly, J. (1999) 'Social Partnership in Britain: good for profits, bad for jobs and unions', *Communist Review*, (Autumn): 3–10.

Kelly, J. (1996) 'Union Militancy and Social Partnership'. In Ackers, P., Smith, C. and Smith, P. (eds), *The New Workplace and Trade Unionism*, London: Routledge, 77–109.

Marginson, P. (n.d.) 'Case study 3: Hyder Utilities/Welsh Water', *Collective Bargaining on Employment and Competitiveness: Report on the UK*, Warwick: IRRU.

Millward, N., Bryson, A. and Forth, J. (2000) *All Change at Work?*, London: Routledge.

Monks, J. (2000) Speech to Liberal Democrat Assembly, http://www.tuc.org.uk/the_tuc/tuc-649-f0.cfm (26 March 2001).

Taylor, P. and Ramsay, H. (1998) 'Unions, partnership and HRM: sleeping with the enemy?' *International Journal of Employment Studies*, 6: 115–43.

Terry, M. (1989) 'Recontextualising shopfloor industrial relations: some case study evidence'. In Tailby, S. and Whitston, C. (eds), *Manufacturing Change: industrial relations and restructuring*, Oxford: Blackwell.

Terry, M. and Edwards, P. (eds) (1988) *Shopfloor politics and job controls: The postwar engineering industry*, Oxford: Blackwell.

Terry, M. and Smith, J. (2003) 'Evaluation of the Partnership at Work Fund', *Employment Relations Research Series*, No. 17, London: Department of Trade and Industry.

Waddington, J. and Kerr, A. (2000) 'Towards an organising model in UNISON: A trade union membership strategy in transition'. In Terry, M. (ed.) *Redefining Public Sector Unionism: UNISON and the future of trade unions*, London: Routledge, 231–62.

Warren, D. (2000) http://www.partnership-at-work.com/cgi-bin/webdata_ipapaw.pl (14 March 2001)

# 16

## Negating or Affirming the Organising Model? The Case of the Congress of South African Trade Unions

Geoffrey Wood

From the mid-1970s to the 1990s, union membership decreased significantly in most of the advanced societies. This resulted in a major rethink in union strategies, with renewed attention being placed on outreach, and on drawing in previously neglected categories of labour. Particularly influential was the 'organising model', which sought to shift the role of unions from simply servicing existing members in day-to-day disputes, to one where contestations are broadened into community struggles over questions of social justice (Roberts, 1999: 38). Hence, traditional forms of activity were broadened to encompass a wide range of social issues, with a far stronger emphasis being placed on recruitment and outreach (Frege, 1999: 279). Although originating in the United States, the organising model proved influential throughout the Anglo-Saxon world (Wood and Brewster, 2002; c.f. Gall, 2003).

More recently, the assumptions underlying the organising model have come under increasing criticism (Hurd, 2003; Desai, 2002; von Holdt, 2002). Critics can be divided into two camps. Firstly, there are those who argue that organising unionism, has, quiet simply failed to deliver in the U.S. context, and, hence, represents an unsuitable model for emulation elsewhere (Hurd, 2003). Secondly, there are those who question the core assumption that organising unionism's strength lies in the rediscovery of a social movement tradition. Rather, they suggest that genuine social movement unionism remains an elusive project, given geographically specific identities and contested conceptions of representivity (Von Holdt, 2002; c.f. Desai, 2002).

Indeed, it can be argued that, given inevitable tendencies towards elitism within the labour movement, a social movement role cannot be recaptured through a centrally defined organisational model; genuine social movement representation can only arise from the grassroots, through the independent actions of workplace and community activists (Desai, 2002). These arguments are of particular relevance in the South African context. On the one hand, the South African labour movement has retained a considerable following and political clout in the post-apartheid era, and is a source of inspiration to labour activists worldwide (see Moody, 1997). Seemingly, many of its strengths arise from strategies and campaigns that closely mirror the organising model (Wood, 2002). On the other hand, it can be argued that the social movement role of the South African labour movement has been gradually eroded, with tendencies towards elitism and domination at both central and branch levels (Rachleff, 2001; Von Holdt, 2002; Desai, 2002). Based on the findings of a nation wide survey of members of the Congress of South African Trade Unions (COSATU), South Africa's largest and most vibrant union federation, this article explores the extent to which key features of the organising model have persisted in the South African context, and the extent to which this can be a source of abiding strength.

The South African labour movement dates back to the 19th century. Early unions were on craft lines, but, by the early 20th century, race rather than real skill assumed ever-greater importance. Neglected in these early unionisation initiatives were African workers. Attempts to organise African workers in the 1920s and 1930s, foundered as a result of an overreliance on a few key leadership figures and sustained employer resistance. Again, the South African Congress of Trade Unions failed to make serious headway outside of a small number of workplaces in the 1950s. Again, overdependent on a small leadership coterie, it neglected shopfloor organisation, and was forced into exile by the apartheid government in the early 1960s. Informed by the lessons of the past, the independent African unions that emerged in the early 1970s[1] placed a strong emphasis on shopfloor organisation and internal democracy. By the mid-1980s, these unions had coalesced into two federations, the Congress of South African Trade Unions (COSATU), and the very much smaller National Council of Trade Unions (NACTU). The apartheid government's declaration of two successive States of Emergency and it resort to unprecedented levels of repression in the face of growing popular resistance forced COSATU into an increasingly outspoken political role. Indeed, by the close of the 1980s, COSATU had become the apartheid government's principal internal opponent. The ending of apartheid resulted in COSATU entering into the Tripartite Alliance with the formerly exiled African National Congress (ANC), and its junior partner, the South African Communist Party (SACP).

## Key features and assumptions of the organising model

Organising unionism encompasses an ability to develop a socially diverse membership encompassing neglected categories of labour, the forging of close linkages with community organisations, a strong emphasis on outreach drawing on the skills of local activists, and the 'empowerment' of members, in order that their interests may be genuinely voiced (Heery et al., 2000: 1–5). Union activity should be framed within a moral discourse, centering on the promotion of 'justice, dignity and respect at work'(ibid.: 1–5) and wider social upliftment.

Organising unionism represents an attempt to recapture the role played by many early unions as that of a social movement (Hyman, 1997). Social movement unionism can, quite simply, be defined as combining institutionalised collective bargaining practices, with modes of collective action normally associated with social movements (Hirschsohn, 1998: 633). Organising unionism aims to shift the role of unions from simply servicing members in day-to-day disputes, to one where contestations are broadened into community struggles over questions of social justice (Roberts, 1999: 38). Hence, it seeks to inject a moral tone into union activities.

Organising unionism represents a response to the failings of the servicing model that, in many of the advanced societies, had led to unions concentrating on the needs of existing members at the expense of recruitment and flexibility; it seeks to rediscover a tradition of activism and outreach (c.f. Waddington and Whitston, 1997: 515–546). In contrast to the experience of much of the Western labour movement, the South African independent unions never fully implemented the servicing model. The latter were forced to adopt an increasingly outspoken political and community role by the mid 1980s, reflecting the groundswell of mass resistance to the then apartheid regime, the persistence of racial-fordist forms of work organisation, and in reaction to the banning of a range of popular political and grassroots organisation. Furthermore, the example of the older – and visibly sclerotic – white dominated unions highlighted the danger of a narrow emphasis on servicing the needs of an existing constituency (Wood, 2003). Hence, in South Africa, the question is not so much as to whether unions can recapture a lost organising tradition, but rather whether they can reconstitute it in the 'post-struggle era'.

## Contesting organising unionism: a failure to deliver

Hurd (2003) argues that there is very much more to union renewal than effective recruitment and an emphasis on mobilisation. Above all, unions need to devote more attention to the complexities organisational change, expanding member education, overcoming conservatism amongst staff members and leadership, balancing representation and organising, and real strategic planning (ibid.; Fletcher and Hurd, 2001). Without radical institutional change, attempts at mobilisation will do little more 'than stir excitement', whilst an adverse external environment can easily 'overwhelm individual campaign victories' (Hurd, 2003). Nor will the 'empowerment' of the rank and file necessarily reenergise unions: 'there is no evidence that union members are any more willing than leaders to promote radical transformation' (Hurd, 2003).

The established union tradition has failed to inspire the new workforce, and no amount of outreach can overcome this deficiency (Hurd, 2003; c.f. Waddington and Whitston, 1997). Unions have to find new ways of reaching out to a changing workforce, that encompasses on the one hand, expanding numbers of technical and professional workers, and on the other hand, even larger numbers of poorly-paid temporary and part time workers (Hurd, 2003). Unions have to experiment with diverse new forms of representation, taking account of the needs of differing constituencies (ibid.). In summary, Hurd's critique of organising unionism revolves around two distinct issues. Firstly, that in the absence of a strategic vision centering on viable demands and clearly articulated policy alternatives, an emphasis on recruitment and internal democracy is unlikely to result in a revitalisation of the labour movement (Hurd, 2003). Secondly, unions need to take account of the needs of an increasingly diverse workforce; this may entail the development of new ways of representation both within the union and at the workplace, and the exploration of new strategies for collective action and engagement (ibid.).[2]

## Contesting organising unionism: an elusive social movement role

There is a growing body of literature that suggests that social movement unionism is a fragile and contested domain (Desai, 2002; Dibben, 2003; Von Holdt, 2002). Organising unionism's emphasis on outreach and activism will not necessarily provide the basis for a return to, or a reconstitution of a meaningful social movement role (ibid.). Rather, maintaining such a role will be difficult in view of long term changes in labour markets – with increasing numbers of peripheral workers and socially excluded 'poors' – and the persistence of deeply embedded gender, regional and ethnic divisions. The latter can neither be bridged by centralised interventions nor by an internal democracy that favours the interests who have been longest within the fold (c.f. Desai, 2002).

A number of applied studies have pointed to the inevitable tensions and contradictions between centrally derived strategies for union renewal and the diverse needs of the grassroots (see Desai, 2002; von Holdt, 2002; Dibben, 2003). The type of social movement unionism that emerges in industrialising countries represents a response to authoritarian governments and repressive workplaces (von Holdt, 2002). Mirroring the concerns of the organising model, social movement unionism seeks to build alliances with communities, to empower members and seeks to promote both justice and dignity at work and a fairer society (c.f. Roberts, 1999). In addition, South African accounts have emphasised the importance of alliance with progressive political and community organisations (Lambert and Webster, 1988; c.f. von Holdt, 2002: 285). However, von Holdt argues

that the literature tends to overemphasise the importance of external relations rather than internal debates and contestations. Can internal solidarity
and democracy ever be unproblematic? Or, is a contested arena, molded
not just by traditional working class concerns, but by non-class based identities? (von Holdt, 2002). Much of the literature on social movement
unionism – and the organising model – neglects the effects of workplace
practices, and of enduring solidarities and cleavages between differing categories of member that cannot be ascribed to class. Based on a case study of
the National Union of Metalworkers of South Africa (NUMSA), von Holdt
(2002: 286) argues that:

> ...internal conflict, often violent in nature – and contestation over prac-
> tices, strategies and meaning is central to an understanding of militant
> black unionism in South Africa.

Whilst the South African context is clearly distinct to North America, von
Holdt echoes Hurd's (2003) concerns as to the ability of unions to adequately take account of workforce diversity and the need for workplace representation to adequately articulate the needs of *all* workers, and an ability
to renew the discourse in such a manner as to promote radical transformation in changing times. On the one hand, in the South Africa of the 1980s,
an organisational culture developed that stressed non-collaboration, a
rejection of social injustice at both workplace and polity, and a desire to
make all aspects of the status quo ungovernable (von Holdt, 2002: 288). On
the other hand, deep divisions emerged with unions between township
and (migrant) hostel dwellers (ibid.). The latter constituted tightly knit
closed communities, where solidarity was often enforced by violence;
hostel dwellers tended to be concentrated in the poorest paying and tough-
est jobs. In contrast, township residents enjoyed greater representation in
'softer' and more skilled occupations, and had more pressing financial pressures (such as rent, bond and hire purchase payments) which would discourage precipitate collective action. Inevitably, these led to tensions
within the unions. Hostel dwellers had little time for increasingly complex
collective bargaining and agreements and perceived shop stewards as too
close to management. On the other hand, union activists from the town-
ships resented the ruthless manner in which hostel dwellers enforced solidarity, their unwillingness to engage debate or entertain alternative
viewpoints, and above all, the regular use of violence as a means of discipline. Whilst political liberation removed a power stimulus for mobilisation, it failed to bridge over enduring cleavages between town and country,
skill and gender (ibid.). New and technically complex forms of engagement
with management further heightened divisions within the union had the
effect of 'fragmenting and eroding' the remaining shared values and practices central to NUMSA and other COSATU unions.

Desai (2002) argues that internal contestations within COSATU have increasingly led to the ascendancy of more conservative elements. Invariably, this has led to workplace militancy being sacrificed in the interests of reaching accommodations with management, and promoting productivity. Given that established unions are neither capable of formulating new strategies for dealing with the worst consequences of neo-liberalism nor of representing the most marginalised, the future of workplace representation must lie outside the mainstream labour movement (Desai, 2002). Rather, the mantle should be assumed by grassroots groupings of workers, acting in concert with similar collectives in the community (ibid.). What these accounts have in common is a concern that centrally determined strategies for union renewal fail to take account of the needs of highly marginalised categories of labour. Again, they underscore the need for unions to develop alternative strategies that address both the immediate concerns of the grassroots, and changes in the composition of the economy and the social organisation of work.

## Reconstitution or diminishment of a social movement tradition?

Critiques of the organising model and of attempts to reconstitute a social movement tradition thus center on three distinct issues. Firstly, is meaningful social solidarity possible given increasingly diverse workforces? Secondly, in the absence of regular institutional reform, is it inevitable that leadership, and the strategic decisions they make, become far removed from the real concerns and wishes of rank-and-file? Thirdly, is it possible to generate and retain a clear vision for social upliftment given the need for inevitable compromises with state and management?

### Measuring social solidarity

As Murray and Levasque (2000: 11) note, 'internal solidarity is, of course, at the very heart of union action...to achieve its agenda, a local union must rely on the collective identity or cohesion of its members'. This, in turn, is underpinned by internal democracy – of critical importance given the 'more fragmented social identities on the labour market' (ibid.: 11). The international literature on trade union renewal repeatedly emphasises the importance of membership participation (ibid.: 11). Moreover, internal structure and democratic practices are also 'key determinants in the capacity of local unions to be involved in change at the workplace' (ibid.: 12).

More specifically, organising unionism is characterised by an ability to effectively voice the concerns not only the relatively privileged, but also more 'vulnerable' categories of labour: women, the unskilled and those with low levels of formal education (Moburg, 1999: 26; Fletcher and Hurd, 1999: 194; Moody, 1997: 178). In other words, it is necessary to 'tap the energies of a broader cross section of members...responding to internal pressures for effective representation' (Fletcher and Hurd, 1999: 213–4). This hinges on responsibility being 'pushed down to the lowest levels'; a broad cross-section of members should be actively involved in union affairs, and be imbued by strong notions of democratic accountability (Fletcher and Hurd, 1999: 210–211). I explore the extent to which this is the case within COSATU by comparing propensity to take part in union affairs (measured by frequency of union meeting meetings) and views on accountability of workplace representatives with gender, and educational and skill levels. Many writers have highlighted the differences in experiences workers may bring to the workplace, and the vital need to overcome gender, skill and age divisions (see, for example, Moody, 1997; Hyman, 1992; Rogers, 1995; Weinbaum, 1999; Wood and Psoulis, 2001). Different categories of employee may be less or more prone to attend union meetings, participate in internal elections and engage in collective action (ibid.).

### Strategic alliances: a rupture between leadership and rank and file?

As noted earlier, organising unionism is characterised by the ability to pursue a 'moral discourse' for broader social transformation, community linkages, and a broad social footprint (Heery et al., 2000: 1–5). However, whilst a crucial element of the former is the ability to wield political influence at national level, this is often constrained by alliances with political parties that provide little in the way of accountability or effective payback (Moburg, 1999: 30). Yet, such alliances may be necessary to make political gains, or at least to temper the worst effects of a changing global economy (ibid.: 30–1). An alliance is only effective if it is contingent on material delivery, with parties and candidates with links to organised labour being subject to close scrutiny, and with clear notions of accountability (ibid.: 30–2). Much of the contemporary literature on COSATU focuses on the tripartite alliance, and the extent to which participation therein sacrifices the interests of the rank-and-file on the altar of political expediency (Habib and Taylor, 1999; Southall and Wood, 1999; Saul, 1999; Barchiesi, 1999). It has been argued that the compromises entailed by the Alliance have necessarily been detrimental to the rank-and-file, which will result in increasing disillusionment at shopfloor level (Habib and Taylor, 1999).

### Retaining a vision for social transformation?

In addition to the 'political', a crucial area of union activity is the 'social', encompassing a strong interest in community and social concerns at issues at grassroots level (Moody, 1997: 301–7). The phasing out of racial fordism and the ending of legalised discrimination removed a powerful set of grievances. This may have diluted the extent to which union members have retained a clear commitment to social upliftment, and are willing to back up their demands with mass action.

## Method

This chapter is based on a nation-wide survey of COSATU members. The final sample size of 646 was computed after a pilot study had been conducted, which also facilitated in refining the questionnaire. Area sampling was employed, after four geographic areas had been identified. These were the Western Cape, Eastern Cape, KwaZulu-Natal and Gauteng, the four of South Africa's nine provinces where the bulk of the country's population lives, and where the overwhelming majority of industry is located. Within each of these four areas, individual unionised workplaces were selected randomly. The support of COSATU regional offices was obtained, and, thereafter, individual employers contacted to arrange access. Further details on the sampling process are as follows:

- Final sampling was done systematically at individual workplaces, the number of workers being selected was in proportion to the overall number of employees at the workplace. In other words, the sample was compiled during the interviewing process (Bailey, 1982).
- Whilst considerable effort was expended to select workers from the entire workforce, the researchers relied heavily on the goodwill of both management and shop stewards. It is therefore possible that workers that were hostile to both management and the relevant union could have been excluded from the selection process.
- Again, as name lists were not employed, an individual worker – who had switched jobs – could have been interviewed twice. To reduce the possibility of this taking place, the interviews were conducted over as short a time period as possible.
- Interviewers were selected who were fully familiar with the relevant vernacular language and were subject to an extensive training programme. Following the interviewers, an extensive process of cross checking took place to confirm the circumstances under which the interviews took place.
- The Chi-squared test was employed as a test of statistical significance between key variables. It is recognised that this test has serious limitations in a range of areas, and that a more detailed analysis of sub-components of the database would necessitate the use of a range of more sophisticated tools, such as Turkey's HSD.
- It should be emphasised that there was a high degree of uniformity in responses to key questions, cutting across gender, age and skill; in short, respondents represented a relatively homogenous grouping.
- Inaccuracies in membership records, unequal access to telephones and uneven standards of postal deliveries in working class areas in South Africa – most notably in informal settlements – made a telephonic or postal survey unfeasible.

- The survey enjoyed the support of COSATU leadership, following extensive consultation, and would also have not been possible without the co-operation of most of the employers contacted.
- 'The sampling procedure may be difficult to justify on purely technical grounds; it was overly multi-layered. However, given the need to secure the support of a wide range of parties, and the lack of accurate trade union membership lists, it represented the only feasible option under the circumstances. Whilst it would have been easier to have interviewed workers attending union meetings, this would have course, eliminated those who were less active in union affairs'. (Wood and Psoulis, 2001: 293–314)

The sectoral variation of the sample was as follows: 39.9 per cent in the manufacturing sector, 35.6 per cent in the non-manufacturing/service sector, and 17.6 per cent in the public service and parastatals. 34.7 per cent of respondents were from the Gauteng province, 19 per cent from KwaZulu-Natal, 26.6 per cent from the Eastern Cape province and 19.7 per cent from the Western Cape province. It is acknowledged that the survey could have resulted in an over-sampling of union activists.

However, the survey revealed that recent entrants to the workforce (and to the labour movement) had similar views on a wide range of issues to those of their longer serving peers, and were just as likely to be actively involved in union affairs (Wood, 2001). All the figures in the following cross-tabulations are percentages, calculated row-wise. It should be noted that to ensure the validity of the Chi-squared test, response categories in some instances have been collapsed, and/or some categories (where there were insufficient responses to reach any meaningful conclusions) filtered out. This, of course, will result in slight discrepancies between tables, owing to fluctuations in the number of valid responses.

## Findings

### Social solidarity[3]

The relationship between education and attendance at union meetings was not a statistically significant one (Chi-squared = 4,016, d.f. = 2, s = 0675, n = 639). The relationship between skill level and attendance at union meetings was equally not statistically significant (Chi-squared = 12.136, d.f. = 15, s = 0669, n = 639). Again, those with different skill and educational attainments were equally likely to strike. However, the survey revealed important gender divisions. Firstly, men were rather more prone to engage in collective action than women, as can be seen by Table 16.1.

This discrepancy may be partially explained by the fact that a large proportion of COSATU's female members is concentrated in the South African

Clothing and Textile Workers Unions (SACTWU).[4] The latter's low strike
profile represents a combination of a long tradition of quiescent unionism,[5]
ethnic and cultural divisions,[6] coupled with large scale downscaling in that
industry (and hence, fear of job losses) following on the dropping of protective tariffs (c.f. Baskin, 1991; Friedman, 1987). However, a lower procliv-
ity to strike could also reflect the tendency of women to be less active in
union affairs. (Wood, 2003).

Secondly, there was a statistically significant relationship between gender
and attendance at union meetings (Table 16.2):

Indeed, some 19 per cent of women never attended union meetings at all.
Conversely, only five per cent of male trade union members never went to
meetings. It is evident that many women do not participate in union affairs
nearly to the same extent as men do. Given that a disproportionately large
proportion of men regularly attend union meetings, it is likely that such
affairs will be male dominated, which, in turn, would discourage future
female involvement. Such cycles are likely to become self-perpetuating.

Hardly surprisingly in view of the above, there was a statistically
significant relationship between the gender of respondents and the likelihood of being a shop steward. Just fewer than 30 per cent of male respondents were shop stewards, compared to only 11 per cent of women.

*Table 16.1*  Gender by experience of strike action (%)

| Gender | Experience of strike action | | |
| | Yes | No | Unsure |
| --- | --- | --- | --- |
| Male | 70.2 | 26.2 | 3.6 |
| Female | 56.1 | 34.4 | 9.5 |
| Total | 66 | 28.6 | 5.3 |

Chi-squared = 15.948, d.f. = 2, s = 0.00, n = 636.

*Table 16.2*  Gender by frequency of attendance at union meetings (%)

| Gender | Frequency of attendance | | | |
| | Once every month or more | Less than once a month by more than twice a year | Twice a year or less | Never |
| --- | --- | --- | --- | --- |
| Male | 46.0 | 35.5 | 7.1 | 11.4 |
| Female | 33.5 | 33.5 | 6.8 | 26.2 |
| Total | 42.3 | 34.9 | 7.0 | 15.8 |

Chi-squared = 23.646, d.f. = 3, significance = 0.00, n = 639.

There is little doubt that such gross imbalances can only be corrected through positive intervention on the behalf of the union, and active initiatives to get women to stand as shop stewards. Again, there was a statistically significant relationship between gender, and perceptions as to how shop stewards were elected (Table 16.3). Some 13 per cent of women were not sure how they were elected, compared to only four per cent of men. Whilst roughly the same number of respondents of each gender said that shop steward elections were conducted by means of a show of hands, 54 per cent of men said that elections took place by secret ballot, compared to only 44 per cent of women. In other words, a significant number of women are so excluded from the democratic process as to have no idea as to how shop steward elections were held.

Nonetheless, despite gender inequalities in terms of participation in union democratic structures, there was not a statistically significant relationship between the gender of respondents and views on democratic accountability. Roughly the same number (and, indeed, the mode) of respondents of either gender held that shop stewards should consult workers every time they acted on their behalf. In other words, whilst women may have been less likely to participate in union affairs, they had roughly similar views as their male counterparts on the desirability of regular consultation. However, women were very much less likely to have actually had experience of removing a shop steward from office (Table 16.4). Again, this would reinforce the impression that women seem to play a rather passive role in the affairs of unions.

Meetings remain male dominated affairs, and whilst a patriarchal organisational culture persists within many COSATU affiliates.[7] In addition, the 'many incidents of sexual harassment of women comrades by male comrades...sexual exploitation taking place right within our own union structures' would also deter women from attending union meetings (TGWU quoted in Baskin, 1991: 356). As a Chemical Workers Industrial Union official remarked: 'These things are killing the struggle and women's involvement in the union' (Baskin, 1991: 356). Moreover, a major barrier

*Table 16.3*   Gender by method of electing shopstewards

| Gender | How were your shop stewards elected (if elected)? | | | |
| | Show of hands | Secret ballot | Don't know/ Cannot remember | Total |
| --- | --- | --- | --- | --- |
| Male | 42.3 | 53.6 | 4.1 | 100 |
| Female | 43.2 | 43.7 | 13.2 | 100 |
| Total | 42.6 | 50.6 | 6.8 | 100 |

Chi-squared = 18.867, d.f. = 2, s = 0.00, n = 634.

to female attendance at union meetings is housework. As Elizabeth Thabethe, a Chemical Workers Industrial Union official remarked:

> To increase women's participation in unions means changing the relationship between men and women. It needs men to share in domestic duties with women, and we have a long way to go before this happens. (Baskin, 1991: 374).

Nonetheless, a sizable number of female respondents continued to regularly attend union meetings.

Again, women were somewhat less likely to have recently participated in elections for shop stewards, although as can be seen from Table 16.5, the frequency of participation by both genders remains high.

### Views on the alliance[8]

As can be seen from Table 16.6, 74.8 per cent of respondents supported the ANC Alliance as it presently stood, and would vote for it in future national parliamentary elections. In contrast, only 10.7 per cent said that they intended to abstain from voting – a far smaller percentage than would be the case in most Western democracies. Meanwhile, the ruling party in the Apartheid era, the National Party, gained a mere 3.9 per cent. The remainder of respondents was split between the plethora of small parties operating

*Table 16.4*  Gender variations by experiences of having removed a shop steward

| | In your workplace, has a shop steward ever been removed? | | | |
| Gender | Yes | No | Do not know | Total |
| --- | --- | --- | --- | --- |
| Male | 41.1 | 54.2 | 4.7 | 100 |
| Female | 23.4 | 70.2 | 6.4 | 100 |
| Total | 35.9 | 58.9 | 5.2 | 100 |

Chi-squared = 18.055, d.f. = 2, s = 0.000, n = 634.

*Table 16.5*  Gender by when last participated in shopsteward elections

| | When last participated | | | | | | |
| Gender | <1 month ago | 1–6 month | 7–12 month | 1–2 years | >2 years | Never | D.K. |
| --- | --- | --- | --- | --- | --- | --- | --- |
| Male | 4.9 | 20.2 | 24.4 | 26.9 | 14.6 | 5.6 | 3.4 |
| Female | 2.6 | 20.0 | 18.9 | 29.5 | 8.4 | 12.6 | 7.9 |
| Total | 4.2 | 20.0 | 22.8 | 27.7 | 12.7 | 7.7 | 4.7 |

Chi-squared = 22.043, d.f. = 6, s = 0.001, n = 636.

in South Africa, most notably the Democratic Party, the Pan Africanist Congress, the Azanian Peoples' Organisation, Inkhatha, and the United Democratic Movement. None of these parties gained the support of more than four per cent of COSATU members.

Interestingly, there was not a statistically significant relationship between age, gender and support for the ANC. However, slightly more women than men favoured the National Party. This would reflect the fact that a large proportion of COSATU's female members are employed in the textile industry in the Western Cape, where the National Party continues to enjoy the support of a large proportion of members of ethnic minority groups (most employees in the Western Cape textile industry are of mixed racial origin).

As can be seen from Table 16.7, 70.1 per cent of respondents believed that the Alliance represented the best way to safeguard worker interests in parliament. Few respondents favoured the alternative options of 'an alliance with the SACP alone' or for COSATU to be politically unaligned. Almost two-thirds of respondents believed that the Alliance should

*Table 16.6*   Party allegiance

| Party | Per cent support |
| --- | --- |
| ANC Alliance | 74.8 |
| National Party | 3.9 |
| United Democratic Movement | 3.0 |
| Other parties | 2.1 |
| Undecided | 4.6 |
| Will not vote | 10.7 |
| n = 634 | |

*Table 16.7*   'What do you think of the Alliance?'

| | Percentage respondents |
| --- | --- |
| It is the best way to safeguard worker interests in parliament | 70.1 |
| Workers would be best represented by an alliance with the South African Communist Party (SACP) alone | 3.5 |
| COSATU should not be aligned to any political party | 13.4 |
| Workers should form their own party | 0.9 |
| COSATU should be aligned to another political party | 3.5 |
| Don't know | 8.6 |
| n = 636 | |

continue, and contest the 2004 elections, with only 10 per cent of respondents favouring the establishment of an independent workers' party (Table 16.8).

As part and parcel of the Alliance agreement, both COSATU and the SACP have the right to nominate a proportion of the parliamentary candidates seeking election under the ANC party list (South Africa has a modified proportional representation electoral system). As can be seen from Table 16.9, 67.4 per cent of respondents held that COSATU's decision to nominate 20 members, who were subsequently elected to parliament in 1994, was the correct one.

In other words, most respondents were convinced as to the value of parliamentary participation, even if it came at the cost of the loss of experienced leaders to the labour movement.

### Retaining a vision for social transformation

Thus, the survey revealed a strong commitment to the existing Tripartite Alliance, whatever its shortcomings. However, clear notions of accountability tempered this support. Over 77 per cent of respondents believed that if the party they supported did not carry out their wishes, they should have the right to eject it from office.

*Table 16.8* Should the alliance continue and fight the 2004 elections?

|  | Percentage respondents |
| --- | --- |
| Yes | 64.3 |
| A new alliance should be made with another party | 3.0 |
| Workers should form their own party | 9.8 |
| COSATU should be allied only to the SACP | 4.3 |
| COSATU should be allied only to the ANC | 6.5 |
| Unsure | 12.0 |
| Other | 0.2 |
| n = 633 | |

*Table 16.9* Views on parliamentary representation

|  | 'Do you think COSATU's decision to send 20 members to parliament was the right one?' | 'If a party does not do what its supporters want it to do, they have the right to remove it from office'. |
| --- | --- | --- |
| Yes | 67.4 | 77.1 |
| No | 13.2 | 17.8 |
| Uncertain | 19.4 | 5.0 |
| n | 638 | 634 |

Almost two-thirds of respondents believed that every time a party made decisions in parliament that affected its supporters, it should report back (Table 16.10). Interestingly, only 59 per cent of respondents felt that their shop stewards had to report back to them every time they acted on their behalf. In other words, respondents felt that parliamentarians should be held up to even greater scrutiny than workplace representatives. This would reflect the well-established nature of shopfloor democracy within COSATU (see Ginsburg et al., 1995) especially when compared to the relatively recent advent of democratic parliamentary representation.

Finally, the survey revealed that COSATU members closely monitored the ANC-headed government's performance (Table 16.11). On the one hand, most believed that definite improvements had taken place in the delivery of basic social services.

The above are all areas where a strong emphasis has been placed in expanding service provision, albeit that improvements have tended to be uneven, with most taking place in the core urban areas (where most COSATU members live) (c.f. Bank and Wood, 1998). Moreover, most COSATU members indicated that they would take action should the government fail to deliver improvements in their quality of life in the future. Some 77 per cent indicated that they would 'participate in ongoing mass action', and 89 per cent said that they would 'put pressure on Alliance MPs'. However, as can be seen from previous tables, there seemed to be little support for the immediate establishment independent workers' party as a means of protecting worker interests; the Alliance has resulted in material delivery to the urban working class.

*Table 16.10*   'When a party/shopstewards make(s) decisions that affects its/their supporters, they should report back...'

|  | Party making decisions in parliament (% respondents) | Shop Stewards (% respondents) |
|---|---|---|
| Every time | 65.5 | 76.1 |
| Only on important issues | 33.0 | 23.6 |
| They need not report back | 1.4 | 0.3 |
| n | 636 | 631 |

*Table 16.11*   'Has your access to ____ improved since 1994?'

| Area | % Yes |
|---|---|
| Water | 81 |
| Electricity | 81 |
| Telephones | 76 |
| Health care | 63 |

Thirty three per cent of respondents said that they were actively involved in a local community based development forum, in addition to their involvement in the labour movement, whilst exactly 67 per cent were not. There is little doubt that high levels of involvement would result in a superior capacity to forge new alliances at grassroots level, and make it easier to mobilise community support in the event of mass action. Whilst only a minority of respondents were active in community development forums, the level of participation was still far higher than would typically be the case in first world societies, reflecting the persistence of a collectivism closely binding community with workplace (c.f. Moody, 1997; Kelly, 1998: 40). In short, COSATU is, in this regard, in a rather more favourable position than its counterparts in North America and Western Europe.

## Implications

The survey revealed both high levels of internal solidarity on the lines of skill and educational status, and broad support for the strategic direction adopted by leadership. However, the latter was strictly conditional on ongoing delivery; a large proportion of respondents had personal experience of having recently engaged in collective action either in support of workplace or political objectives. This would have the effect of limiting leadership's capacity to sacrifice the interests of rank-and-file on the altar of political expediency. The survey revealed little evidence of either a rupture between rank and file, or the abandonment of a vision for social transformation.

Nonetheless, the survey revealed significant cleavages on the lines of gender, with women being rather less likely to participate in union affairs. Whilst in other respects, the degree of social solidarity was relatively high, the persistent gender divide is of some grounds for concern, particularly given that women dominate informal sector work, an increasingly important sector that remains largely ununionised.

More broadly speaking, the survey focused on what goes on within the federation. Here, two caveats are in order. Firstly, in focusing on those already within the fold, it reveals little about the attitudes of *potential* members towards the federation. In recent years, the bulk of COSATU's membership gains have been amongst relatively privileged public sector workers. Whilst these have somewhat offset the losses in the manufacturing sector as a result of restructuring and redundancies, the federation has been largely unsuccessful in drawing in the growing number of workers employed in the informal sector and other highly marginalised occupations. Moreover, organising informal sector workers is very different to their formal sector counterparts, which is only possible through new grassroots alliances with organisations representing the 'new poors' (Webster, 2003). It is evident that neither the organising models, nor similar sets of strategies, have proved capable of meeting the needs of such workers; this is a serious limitation, particularly in the case of industrialising economies.

Secondly, the use of a quantitative methodology may have resulted in certain dimensions of organisational culture and dynamics being discounted. There have been numerous recorded instances where individual COSATU unions have had to deal with wildcat action and breakaways at branch level (von Holdt, 2002; Rachleff, 2001). Nonetheless, whilst undeniably traumatic, most of these breakaways have involved relatively small numbers of workers; no breakaway grouping or union has proved capable of overturning the dominance of its COSATU parent within a specific sector.

## Conclusion

In an age of union decline, COSATU has proved capable of securing its position as a central socio-economic and political actor in post-apartheid South Africa. This has been at least partially due to a strategic vision that closely mirrors the organising model: an emphasis on meeting the needs of a socially diverse membership, close alliances with popular community and political organisations, a strong emphasis on outreach drawing on the skills of local activists, and the 'empowerment' of members through a vigorous internal democracy.

At the same time, the South African experience underscores the limitations of the organising model. A strong emphasis on recruitment and mobilisation alone is unlikely to succeed in drawing the most marginalised workers into the union fold. Informal sector work is of increasing importance in industrialising countries, yet there is little evidence that unions have developed policies that make union membership attractive to highly peripheral categories of labour. Secondly, whilst the battle lines were clearly drawn within the apartheid era, the post-apartheid era has seen a blurring of interests, with the unions entering into increasingly complex accommodations with both state and business. Recruitment and mobilisation have to do more than 'stir excitement', whilst internal democracy will not necessarily result in the emergence of new ideas and interventions inspiring to those outside the labour movement. In the end, innovative strategies can only have a limited impact in the absence of clear policy alternatives to the status quo, alternatives that are meaningful to both existing and potential members.

## References

Bank, L. and Wood, G. (1998) The Economic Implications of the Proposed East London Industrial Development Zone. East London Development Zone Initiative, East London, South Africa.

Bailey, K. (1982) *Methods of Social Research*. New York: Free Press.

Barchiesi, F. (1999) Economic Adjustment, Political Institutionalization and Social Marginalization: COSATU and the First Democratic Government (1994–99) *Transformation*, 38: 20–48.

Baskin, J. (1991) *Striking Back: A History of COSATU*. Johannesburg: Ravan.

Desai, A. (2002) *We are the Poors: Community Struggles in Post-Apartheid South Africa*. New York: Monthly Review Press.

Dibben, P. (2003) Social Movement Unionism. In Wood, G. and Harcourt, M. (eds), *Trade Unions and Democracy: Strategies and Perspectives*. Manchester (forthcoming).

Erickson, C., Fisk, C., Milkman, R., Mitchell, D. and Wong, K. (2002) Justice for Janitors in Los Angeles: Lessons from Three Rounds of Negotiations. *British Journal of Industrial Relations*, 40, 3: 543–567.

Fletcher, B. and Hurd, M. (1999) Political Will, Local Union Transformation and the Organizing Imperative. In Nissen, B. (ed.), *Which Direction Organized Labor?* Detroit: Wayne State University Press.

Fletcher, B. and Hurd, R. (2001) Overcoming Obstacles to Transformation: Challenges on the Way to a New Unionism. In Turner, L., Katz, H. C. and Hurd, R. (eds), *Rekindling the Movement: Labor's Quest for Relevance in the 21st Century*. Ithaca: Cornell University Press.

Frege, C. (1999) The Challenges to Trade Unions in Europe. *Work and Occupations*, 26, 2: 279–281.

Friedman, S. (1987) *Building Tomorrow Today*. Johannesburg: Ravan.

Gall, G. (2003) Introduction. In Gall, G. (ed.), *Union Organizing: Campaigning for Union Recognition*. London: Routledge.

Ginsburg, D., Cherry, J., Klerck, G., Maree, J., Southall, R., Webster, E. and Wood, G. (1995) *Taking Democracy Seriously*. Durban: IPSA.

Habib, A. and Taylor, R. (1999) Parliamentary Opposition and Democratic Consolidation in South Africa. *Review of African Political Economy*, 79.

Heery, E., Simms, M., Simpson, D., Delbridge, R. and Salmon, J. (2000) Organizing Unionism Comes to the U.K. *Employee Relations*, 22, 1: 1–38.

Hirschsohn, P. (1998) From Grassroots Democracy to National Mobilization: COSATU as a Model of Social Movement Unionism. *Economic and Industrial Democracy*, 19, 4: 633–666.

Holdt, K. von. (2002) Social Movement Unionism: The Case of South Africa. *Work, Employment and Society*, 16, 2: 283–304.

Hurd, R. (2003) The Rise and Fall of the Organising Model in the U.S. In Wood, G. and Harcourt, M. (eds), *Trade Unions and Democracy: Strategies and Perspectives*. Manchester (forthcoming).

Hyman, R. (1992) Trade Unions and the Disaggregation of the Working Class. In Regini, M. (ed.), *The Future of Labour Movements*. London: Sage.

Hyman, R. (1997) Trade Unions and Interest Representation in the Context of Globalization. *Transfer*, 3, 515–533.

Kelly, J. (1998) *Rethinking Industrial Relations: Mobilization, Collectivism and Long Waves*. London: Routledge.

Lambert, R. and Webster, E. (1988) The Reemergence of Political Unionism in South Africa. In Cobbett, W. and Cohen, R. (eds), *Popular Struggles in South Africa*. Trenton: Africa World Press.

Moburg, D. (1999) The U.S. Labour Movement Faces the 21st Century. In Nissen, B. (ed.), *Which Direction Organized Labor?* Detroit: Wayne State University Press.

Moody, K. (1997) *Workers in a Lean World*. London: Verso.

Murray, G. and Levasque, C. (2000) Connected, Democratic, Proactive: Challenges for 21st Century Trade Unions. Paper presented at the International Industrial Relations Association 12th World Congress, Tokyo, Japan.

Rachleff, P. (2002) The Current Crisis of the South African Labour Movement. *Labour/Le Travail*, 47: 151–169.

Roberts, M. (1999) The Future of Labour Unions: A Review. *Monthly Labor Review*, 122, 10: 38–39.

Rogers, J. (1995) How Divided Progressives may Unite. *New Left Review*, 210: 9.

Saul, John (1999) Magical Market Realism. *Transformation*, 38: 49–67.

Southall, R. and Wood, G. (1999) The Congress of South African Trade Unions, the ANC and the Election: Whither the Alliance? *Transformation*, 38: 68–83.

Waddington, J. and Whitston, C. (1997) Why do People Join Trade Unions in a Period of Membership Decline? *British Journal of Industrial Relations*, 35, 4: 515–546.

Webster, E. (2003) New Forms Of Work And The Representational Gap: A Durban Case Study. In Wood, G. and Harcourt, M. (eds), *Trade Unions and Democracy: Strategies and Perspectives*. Manchester (forthcoming).

Weinbaum, E. (1999) Organizing Labour. In Nissen, B. (ed.), *Which Direction for Organized Labor?: Essays on Organization, Outreach and Internal Transformation*. Detroit: Wayne State University Press.

Wood, G. (2001) South African Trade Unions in a Time of Adjustment. *Labour/Le Travail*, 47: 133–150.

Wood, G. (2002) Organizing Unionism and the Possibilities for Reconstituting a Social Movement Role. *Labor Studies Journal*, 26, 4: 29–50.

Wood, G. (2003) Solidarity, Representivity and Accountability: The Origins, State and Implications of Shopfloor Democracy with the Congress of South African Trade Unions. *Journal of Industrial Relations* (in print).

Wood, G. and Psoulis, C. (2001) Globalization, Democratization and Organized Labour in Transitional Economies: The Case of the Congress of South African Trade Unions. *Work and Occupations*, 28, 3: 293–314.

Wood, G. and Brewster, C. (2002) Decline and Renewal in the British Labour Movement. *Society in Transition*, 33, 2: 241–258.

# 17
# From Playstations to Workstations: Young Workers and the Experience-Good Model of Union Membership

*Rafael Gomez, Morley Gunderson and Noah M. Meltz*

## Introduction

Union membership confers certain benefits to workers. Some of these benefits, like the union wage premium, are visible to both members and non-members alike. Most others, such as the enforcement of procedural justice or the establishment of family friendly practices, are hard to identify before entering the labour market and near impossible if one has never sampled union membership (Fernie and Gray, 2002). It is only when a worker has actually been employed in a unionised environment for a long enough duration, or, when a worker has access to reliable information about the nature of unionisation, that s/he can form an accurate opinion about the value of membership (i.e., whether the benefits of joining a union outweigh any of the potential costs). If workers never experience any of these hard-to-observe benefits, they may be less inclined to become active dues paying members where unions are present, and even less likely to actively organise in workplaces lacking any union presence. This is especially the case if, as recent British and American research suggests, the largest and most visible benefit (i.e. the wage advantage conferred to unionised workers) has largely disappeared (Blanchflower and Bryson, 2003).

Organised labour, therefore, has a problem in convincing potential members that what they offer is of benefit to them. The problem is particularly acute amongst young workers; the focus of this chapter. In a separate paper the authors, together with Alex Bryson, examined youth-adult differences in the demand for, and supply of, unionisation in Canada, Britain and the United States (Bryson et al., 2004). In all three countries it was found that adult workers were roughly three times as likely to be unionised as young workers. Yet surprisingly, the extent of unsatisfied desire for unionisation among youth was greater than that for adults.[1] The question, therefore, remains: why is there such a large discrepancy between the desires of young workers for membership and their actual union status? In this chapter we argue that the answer may reside in the nature of union membership itself; which if conceived of as an *experience-good* (Gomez and Gunderson, 2004), may help explain the above paradox as well as a number of other important phenomenons associated with union membership in Anglo-Saxon economies.

The remainder of the chapter proceeds as follows. The first section describes the experience-good model of union membership and its usefulness in explaining some well (and not so well) known facts relating to unionism. It then discuses the importance of union membership's experiential qualities in the context of intergenerational transmission mechanisms, which when positive, can perpetuate union membership across the generations, but when negative, can cause membership to spiral downward. The chapter goes on to highlight the relevance for unions of focusing on young workers and ends with a discussion of the organising implications which emerge from the experience-good model.

## Union membership as an experience good

Unions can take solace in the fact that they are not the only organisations facing difficulties in attracting members. Any firm which offers a product or service with hard-to-observe attributes has to overcome the twin hurdles of 'informational' and 'experiential' asymmetries. Take the case of a fitness club that sells memberships in order to finance its operations. The club not only has to first advertise its presence, but it has to also convince potential patrons that their facilities and staff are better than the competition. Goods and services such as these – that need to be sampled before purchase in order to discern quality – are termed *experience goods* (Nelson, 1970). We argue that unionisation can also be conceived of in this way, since it too is high in experiential attributes.

Apart from the difficulty associated with discerning quality before purchase, union membership displays other important experiential properties. An experience-good tends to be accompanied by substantial switching costs after it has been purchased (Klemperer, 1995). This makes it 'durable' in the sense that an experience-good has a long shelf life, as compared to a nondurable (like a particular brand of bottled water) that has low switching costs and is purchased more frequently. The durable nature of union membership can be measured by turnover and job tenure. Union members tend to have longer job spells with one employer (higher tenure) than otherwise similar non-union workers, and unionised firms have lower quit rates (turnover) than non-union firms do.

Another characteristic of experience goods, which is also shared by union membership, is that they tend to exhibit higher than average 'brand loyalty' and 'post-purchase' levels of satisfaction. If a person has ever been unionised, he or she is more likely to remain so when switching jobs as compared to a worker who has never sampled membership. Likewise, attitudes towards unionisation are more favourable if one has ever-been a member. This is the so-called 'incumbency effect' identified by Freeman and Diamond (2001), and which remains significant even when one controls for sets of attributes which remain fixed for some time (occupational status) and which could (positively or negatively) bias attitudes towards unions.

The incumbency effect corresponds to yet another feature of union membership, which is also a hallmark of experience-goods. This feature relates to the economics of information and search – a stream of research originating 40 years ago (Stigler, 1961), but which has rarely (if ever) been applied to the study of union membership. The economics of information demonstrates that knowledge about the potential benefits of an experience good is optimally (and hence most often) disseminated via informal networks like personal recommendations, rather than through formal advertising channels. This is because 'trust' is highly correlated with 'reputation' and a personal referral is akin to someone staking his or her 'reputation' on the product endorsement in question. Thus, when quality is hard to observe, personal recommendations become the preferred channel by which potential customers are informed about hard-to-observe product attributes.[2]

The informational asymmetries generated by the experiential characteristics of a personal service are replicated in the union case if we note the strong inter-generational transmission of union status observed in longitudinal data. Machin and Blanden (2002) find that sons and daughters of union workers are 20 per cent more likely than comparable individuals to become union members. This is independent of occupation, region, and industry.

Similarly, Gomez, Gunderson and Meltz (2002) find that having a social environment consisting of friends and relatives who support unionisation makes the probability of desiring unionisation higher than those lacking in such social connections. This effect is even larger when youths and adults are separated into sub-samples and analysed (i.e., the positive effect of a social circle that is familiar and/or supportive of unionisation is twice as large for those with less labour market experience than it is for the old). Older workers – in keeping with the experiential properties of union membership – rely on their own sampling history to form opinions about unionisation, whereas young workers with less labour market experience rely more heavily on social networks and personal referrals (see Table 17.1).

Charlwood's (2002) finding that the socio-economic characteristics of the neighbourhood in which an individual lives predicts willingness to join a union, is also congruent with the experiential framework. Informal networks and social capital are likely to vary systematically with socio-economic

*Table 17.1*   Social networks and preferences for unionisation

| Independent 'Social Network' variables | Dependent variable: Desire for unionisation | | |
|---|---|---|---|
| | Youth (aged 15–24) % | Adults (aged 25–65) % | Youth–Adult difference % |
| Union family member [No union family member] | 37 | 11 | +26 |
| Positive peer attitudes towards unions [Negative peer attitudes] | 41 | 29 | +12 |

*Source*: Gomez, Gunderson and Meltz (2002: Table 4).
*Note*: Numbers represent percentage point increases in the desire for unionisation relative to the omitted reference categories in brackets. These results control for standard demographic and other variables.

environment. One only has to consider the different beliefs and values that are transmitted through membership in a working men's club compared to that of a golf club, to understand how important such social networks can be in the generation of attitudes and behaviours favourable (or unfavourable) to unions.

## Unions, work experience and sampling union membership

The results discussed above speak finally to the two channels by which people become informed about the benefits (and costs) of unionisation and with experience-goods more generally. Essentially, sampling and information gathering through personal referrals are the two most prevalent ways that potential members form favourable or unfavourable opinions about unions, or make decisions about whether to pursue membership or not.

As we have seen, union members tend to be 'brand-loyal' in the sense that those who sample union membership stick with it. The problem for the union movement in Canada, the United States and Britain in particular, is the lack of 'sampling' on the part of new labour market entrants (i.e., the young). This problem is particularly acute as 'never-membership' – as opposed to ex-membership i.e., those who have abandoned membership – accounts for the bulk of the decline in union density in Britain in the 80s and 90s.[3] This finding applies to membership decline in both recognised and non-recognised workplaces (Bryson and Gomez, 2002).

The problem of never-membership resides with the voluntary nature of due-payments in Britain (which owes its origin to EU law which prohibits agency shop arrangements). In an open-shop (i.e., right-to-work) system the default option for employees is set to 'non-union' even within recognised workplaces.[4] New workers, therefore, are less likely to pay dues unless actively compelled to do so. This is so for three reasons. First, because new workers enter a workplace as non-members, they face switching costs engendered by moving out of their non-due-paying status into a union fee-paying job. We know, from the new work in economic psychology (Rabin and O'Donoghue, 2000), that these costs need not be large (the cost of filling out a form could be enough) to induce procrastination and persistence in non-union status.

Second, as new workers, they have yet to observe the quality of union membership. Over time, workers gain greater labour market experience such that the quality of union representation becomes fully revealed. The longer a person works, for example, the more apparent becomes the need for job protection. As a worker matures, union membership loses its experiential properties and if the experience of union recognition at work is a positive one, the chances of joining a union should also increase.

Finally, the cost of switching employers increases as workers mature, thereby raising the need for voice provision. Employees are therefore more likely to be in need of union provided benefits (such as job security) as they age. All three effects (the non-union default option for new workers; the revelation of union quality; and the increasing need for voice) predict that older workers are more likely to join a union than younger workers, even within recognised workplaces.

This prediction holds true (at least in Britain). Bryson and Gomez (2003) have found that the fall in union density within the recognised sector since 1982 is due mostly to young workers who have stopped purchasing membership. In more precise terms, the proportion of those aged 30 + who are union members within recognised workplaces remained virtually unchanged throughout the 80s and 90s (0.72 in 1983 to 0.69 in 1998) but the unionisation rate amongst 18–25 year olds plunged from 0.67 to 0.41 between 1982 and 1998 respectively.

## How does the transmission of union status and preferences occur?

Although little is known from an economic perspective about the specific micro-level processes that make the intergenerational transmission of preferences and union status possible, there is a literature in social psychology that has tried to understand such behaviour and preference formation. Recently, it has been applied to the unionisation literature by Gomez, Gunderson and Meltz (2002).

The *attribution theory* of behaviour argues that instead of conceiving of individuals as utility maximisers, with a taste for unionisation that is fixed, individuals can be viewed as developing and forming conceptions of the 'self'. This self-concept is dynamic and is changing over time. The feedback loop involved can proceed in a number of ways. The elements involved are *actions, attributions* and *roles* which define a *self-concept*. In the classic (rational) case, individuals have defined roles and a clearly formed self-concept, which leads to certain actions that, in turn, lead to certain attributions that ultimately reinforce the original self-concept.

Translating this process to the case of a potential union member with some knowledge of unionisation's benefits, we can see how a person who prefers unionisation (i.e., a *self-concept* which is positive about unions) would attempt to find a job in a unionised environment. Assuming that he or she does find unionised employment, we know by way of *the incumbency effect* that they are more likely to develop positive opinions (i.e., positive *attributions* about unionisation) about that work environment. Moreover, these attributions will be independent of any original self-selection into the unionised job. The effect of this initial exposure will persist throughout the course of one's career and make it more likely that the individual will find another unionised job or remain a union member. Even if he or she does not remain unionised, their favourable opinions may influence a sibling, friend, or co-worker to join a union where one is present.

The social-psychological model above can be adapted to the case of workers with less well-defined self-concepts (i.e., workers who do not know whether unionisation is beneficial to them). People with malleable opinions about unionisation tend to be those with less labour market experience such as the young or newly arrived immigrants. So where does their feedback loop begin?

In general, the social environment is the strongest predictor of whether a worker has a positive or negative view of unionisation. In particular, and as noted earlier, parental union status imparts a 20 per cent boost on a sibling's likelihood of becoming a union member later in life. This initial exposure leads to the undertaking of certain actions – such as applying for a unionised job or helping out in an organising campaign – that, in turn, lead to the formation of attributions (i.e., 'I apply for unionisation therefore I am favourably disposed to unions'). Attributions feed into the formative stage of self-concept formation. Over time, the self-concept becomes more firmly entrenched and less susceptible to alteration. This is why social networks affect older workers much less strongly, since they are more reliant on their own individual 'sampling' history in forming opinions about unionisation (see Figure 17.1).

## Implications of intergenerational transmission for unions

Tapping into new sources of membership growth is especially important since 'initial conditions matter' in establishing behavioural attitudes. As shown above, networks and norms can be self-perpetuating over time, especially in the case of the unionisation of youths.[5] Patterns of 'state dependence' can therefore be established whereby initially starting in a particular state has an

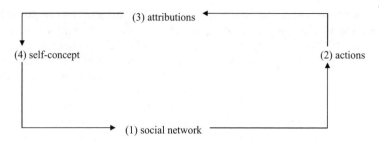

*Figure 17.1* The socialisation process of a young worker*
*The feedback loop applies to workers with less labour market experience (Montgomery 1999).

independent effect throughout one's life-course, fostering conditions that encourage remaining in that particular state. If youths are introduced to unionisation early on in their careers, they will be more likely to develop attitudes, networks and norms that foster continued unionisation. Put simply, unionism begets unionism. Conversely, if exposure to unionisation is bypassed early, then a worker may remain bypassed for their entire career. In such circumstances, unions have an added incentive for organising youths – it expands *current* membership and can sustain *future* membership. The cost of organising a young worker, which may appear unprofitable from a short-term time horizon, may be amortised over a lifetime.

Indeed, the cost may be amortised over more than one lifetime since parents who are union members or have positive attitudes towards unions are more likely to pass those attitudes and union status to their children'.[6] In such circumstances, if unions decline and parents are less likely to be union members, or to have favourable views of unions, then this can be transmitted intergenerationally, and negative attitudes towards unions on the part of their children will prevail. Unions, therefore, have an even greater incentive to organise the young given the lifetime and intergenerational effects that can result. By yielding benefits over many lifetimes, the state dependent and intergenerational effects of unionisation diminish the costs of organising the young.

Clearly, at present, unions face challenges in organising and sustaining membership in general and amongst youths in particular. Yet, meeting these challenges can yield dividends over many generations. As such, despite their low likelihood of membership, focusing on youths becomes crucially important.

## What practical use can unions make of these findings?

Clearly, unions *cannot replace* the social networks that give rise to the intergenerational transmission of union status, but they *can replicate* some of the same processes. While this may sound difficult and near impossible to achieve, in this respect once gain, the union movement's task is not unique. If unions simply translate the need to capture market share (union membership as a percentage of total workers) from a product-market setting to the labour market, they can perhaps achieve the same success that many firms have in acquiring a loyal customer base.

Unions that are unable to organise the young are nevertheless capable of influencing the formation of a self-concept that is favourable to union-isation – such as initial exposure to unions through an expansion of summer internships. Positive initial exposures are the mechanisms that make young people who come from non-union households more likely to become members later on in life.

Replicating the process by which the inter-generational transmission of a 'preferred brand' occurs is another way – drawing on what we know of experience- good promotional techniques – for unions to gain market share. Early product exposure is one way that youths become lovers of 'Pepsi' over 'Coca-Cola'. Unions could similarly try to mould the prefer-ences of youth. If the union movement were to somehow sponsor parts of the school curriculum (as do Pearson Education and Microsoft who sponsor textbook purchases and the provision of interactive media in the class-room) or offer a prominent array of university scholarships (as do many firms with formerly bad consumer reputations such as BP and Shell), then perhaps a whole new generation of youth would be sensitised to unions throughout their life-course.

Unions and trade union congresses around the world that are employing successful recruitment techniques are generally those that have (at least implicitly) understood the experiential nature of union membership. The case of the Norwegian Union of Graphical Workers (Norsk Grafisk Forbund, NGF) is illustrative of this new marketing approach. In January 2002, NGF launched a 'digital trade union' concept – a trial project aimed at attracting new groups of employees by means of ICT, among them the increasing number of young non-unionised employees within the ICT sector in Norway. It was meant to act as an alternative trade union organisation for employees in the ICT sector and to lower the sampling costs of union ser-vices for a segment of workers who had historically bypassed union mem-bership. The new union is accessible only via the Internet, which means that it has no shop stewards and does not run traditional union meetings. Nevertheless, NGF supplies its services 24 hours a day seven days a week to all its internet-based members. In the one year since its inception, member-ship among ICT workers grew by almost ten per cent, even as the ICT sector was losing jobs.

The Internet allows unions to lower membership sampling costs and to reduce the perceived risk of joining a union for new labour market entrants. The Internet also permits unions to by-pass the workplace altogether and distribute their services directly to employees (Freeman and Rogers, 2002). This is the direct or relationship marketing method that has been used by many start-up companies, such as low cost airlines EasyJet and RyanAir, with great success. Such companies offer their services via the Internet at a lower cost than if they would have distributed their services through a retailer or vendor. Even following September 11th, as major airlines like United and Swissair declared bankruptcy, internet-based airlines generated some of their largest profits ever. Freeman and Rogers have recently coined the term open-source unionism to describe similar, though more nascent, attempts by unions to target their services directly to prospective employees. The TUC recently (May 2001) held a one-day conference on the effect of the Internet on unionisation, indicating that the message of direct marketing is slowly diffusing to the union sector in Britain.

Ultimately, a full listing of optimal recruitment practices based on the lessons gained in experience good markets, requires more research. Nevertheless, making unions aware that they are 'selling a service that is high in experiential attributes' is perhaps the first step in a long process of rejuvenation that may transform unionised workplaces from hard-to-observe enclaves of beneficial employee voice, to ones that are spread over a greater part of the industrial landscape.

## Conclusion

We have argued that union membership is like an 'experience-good' in the sense that most union benefits (procedural justice, job security, the provision of family-friendly policies) are hard to observe before joining. Moreover, even if attributes are made visible (through information campaigns) union provided benefits are still of indeterminate quality before purchase (i.e., 'you don't know how good a union is until after you join') and hence still subject to the same experiential properties.

The indeterminate level of quality associated with union membership generates 'risk', which means that joining a union is a decision akin to the purchase of a product whose payoff is only fully observed after purchase. Experience-goods consequently have certain properties that make them hard to 'market' to potential customers, especially new ones, which in our case means that young workers are particularly likely to by-pass membership unless otherwise compelled to do so by agency shop arrangements. Experience goods are hard to promote since they rely on word-of-mouth and personal referrals rather than formal advertising campaigns. Unions, as a result, face the same problems as many firms that need to acquire members.

Unions need to be aware that the growing proportion of workers who have never sampled union membership (never-members) is a major factor underlying continued union density decline in Britain and perhaps in the United States and Canada as well. Unions, consequently, have to find a way of lowering sampling costs for new workers. Sampling is important because we know, by way of the incumbency effect, that early exposure to unionisation positively sensitises workers to membership throughout their life-course.

## References

Arulampalam, W. and A. L. Booth (2000) 'Union Status of Young Men in Britain: A Decade of Change', *Journal of Applied Econometrics*, 15 (3): 289–310.

Barling, J., Kelloway, E. and Bremermann, E. (1991) 'Preemployment Predictors of Union Attitudes: The Role of Family Socialization and Work Beliefs', *Journal of Applied Psychology*, 76: 725–731.

Blanchflower, D. and Bryson, A. (2003) 'Changes over time in union relative wage effects in the UK and the U.S. Revisited', In *International Handbook of Trade Unions*. John T. Addison and Claus Schnabel (eds), Edward Elgar, Cheltenham England and Northampton.

Booth, A. L. and M. Chatterji (1995) 'Union Membership and Wage Bargaining when Membership is not Compulsory', *Economic Journal*, 105, 345–360.

Bryson, A. and Gomez, R. (2002) 'Marching On Together? Reasons for the Recent Decline in Union Membership', in Bromley, C., Park, A. and Thompson, K. (eds), *British Social Attitudes: The 20th Report*. Aldershot.

Bryson, A., Gomez, R., Gunderson, M. and Meltz, N. (Forthcoming). 'Youth-Adult Differences in the Demand for Unionisation: Are American, British and Canadian Workers All That Different?' *Journal of Labor Research*.

Charlwood, A. (2002) 'Why do Non-union Employees Want to Unionize?' *British Journal of Industrial Relations*, 40 (3): 321–339.

Farber, H. and Western, B. (2001) 'Ronald Reagan and the Politics of Declining Union Organization', Working paper 460. Industrial Relations Section, Princeton University.

Fernie, S. and Metcalf, D. (1995) 'Participation, Contingent Pay, Representation and Workplace Performance', *British Journal of Industrial Relations*, 33(3): 379–416.

Fernie, S. and Gray, H. (2002) 'It's a Family Affair: the Effect of Union Recognition and Human Resource Management on the Provision of Equal Opportunities in the UK', Discussion Paper no. 525, Centre for Economic Performance, LSE.

Freeman, R. and Rogers, J. (2002) 'Open-Source Unionism: Beyond Exclusive Collective Bargaining', Paper presented in the 23rd Middlebury Economics Conference 'Changing Role of Unions', April 13–14, 2002.

Freeman, R. B. and Diamond, W. (2001) 'Liking the Workplace You Have: The Incumbency Effect in Preferences Towards Unions', Working paper no. 1115, Centre for Economic Performance, LSE.

Fullagar, C. and Barling, J. (1989) 'A longitudinal test of a model of the antecedents and consequences of union loyalty'. *Journal of Applied Psychology*, 74: 213–227.

Fullagar, C., Gallagher, D., Gordon, M. and Clark, P. (1995) 'Impact of Early Socialisation on Union Commitment and Participation: A Longitudinal Study', *Journal of Applied Psychology*, 80: 147–157.

Gomez, R. and Gunderson, M. (2004) 'The Experience-Good Model of Union Membership', In *The Changing Role of Unions*. Phanindra V. Wunnava (ed.), New York: M. E. Sharpe.

Gomez, R., Gunderson, M. and Meltz, N. (2002) 'Comparing the Demand for Unionisation Between Youths and Adults', *British Journal of Industrial Relations*, 40 (3): 421–439.

Grayson, P. (2000) 'Students who are willing to join unions'. Paper presented at the Canadian Industrial Relations Association Annual Meetings.

Heshizer, B. and Wilson, M. (1995) 'The Role of Referent Beliefs in the Socialisation of Union Attitudes', *Journal of Social Behavior and Personality*, 10: 771–790.

Kelloway, E., Barling, J. and Agar, S. (1996) 'Preemployment Predictors of Children's Union Attitudes: The Moderating Role of Identifying with Parents', *Journal of Social Psychology*, 136: 413–415.

Kelloway, E. and Watts, L. (1994) 'Pre-employment Predictors of Union Attitudes: Replication and Extension', *Journal of Applied Psychology*, 79: 631–634.

Klemperer, P. D. (1995) 'Competition when Consumers have Switching Costs: An Overview with Applications to Industrial Organization, Macroeconomics, and International Trade', *Review of Economic Studies*, 62: 515–539.

Machin, S. and Blanden, J. (2002) 'Cross-Generation Correlations of Union Status For Young People in Britain', CEP mimeo.

Montgomery, J. D. (1999) 'The Self as a Fuzzy Set of Roles: Role Theory as a Fuzzy System'. *IIM Discussion Paper no. 4*. London School of Economics.

Nelson, P. (1970) 'Information and Consumer Behaviour', *Journal of Political Economy*, 78 (2): 311–29.

Payne, J. (1989) 'Trade Union Membership and Activism Among Young People in Great Britain', *British Journal of Industrial Relations*, 27: 111–32.

Rabin, M., and Ted O'Donoghue (2000) 'The Economics of Immediate Gratification', *Journal of Behavioral Decision Making*, 13(2): 233–250.

Stigler, G. J. (1961) 'The Economics of Information', *Journal of Political Economy*, 69 (3): 213–25.

# 18
# Non-governmental Organisations and Trade Unions – The Case of India

*C. S. Venkata Ratnam and Anil Verma*

## Introduction

Both non-governmental organisations (NGOs) and trade unions form an integral part of the institutional framework in any democratic civil society. Over the years, trade unions have played a major role at both macro and micro levels. Structural and other changes in the world economy have posed critical challenges to trade unions in many countries. In traditional industries, trade union strength is declining and in new, modern, high-tech workplaces unionisation is becoming difficult. For the developing world, the vast untapped rural and informal sector, however, continues to present a major challenge and opportunity for unionisation and holds the promise for resurgence in trade union movement. In contrast, there is a growing tendency among national governments and international agencies to recognise the role of NGOs and even covert and overt attempts to coopt them into the development process. In developing countries like India while both the NGOs and the trade unions have been viewed with mixed perceptions, it appears that, over all, the attitude towards trade unions is relatively less favourable than towards NGOs.

This paper discusses the ambiguity in distinguishing trade unions from the NGOs, because in a broad sense trade unions also are NGOs. NGOs are classified into three categories: social service, developmental and activist. Based on the dominant emphasis, activist NGOs are further classified into five subgroups, viz., physical, social, intellectual, individual and moral. Case study of one major NGO, SEWA, that deals with women and informal sector workers is presented. SEWA works with a major section of the population and its activities overlap with and impinge upon the work of trade unions. In the light of such discussion, the roles of and relations amongst NGOs and others, including government, funding agencies and trade unions are analysed. Finally broad conclusions are drawn stressing the need for complementarity and synergy in their roles.

## NGOs and trade unions as distinct organisational forms

The definition of a non-governmental organisation (NGO), in its broad sense, can include trade unions as well. There are many similarities between the aims and objectives of NGOs and trade unions. They are both interested in labour and social welfare. However, there are many dissimilarities making them distinct types of organisations.

The number of trade unions registered under the Trade Unions Act, 1926 in India is over 50,000 as of the late 1990s. A Government report put the number of NGOs receiving foreign contributions in 1994 at more than 100,000, double the number of registered trade unions. The number of NGOs registered under the Societies Act, 1869, is even larger. While trade unions' sphere of activity and influence is confined to less than ten per cent of the workforce, the activities of NGOs have permeated through the vast rural and informal sector. Their presence in the urban areas and metropolis is also not insignificant.

Trade union leadership in the past was confined mainly to elitist sections of the society, but not any longer. NGO leadership is still largely elitist and becoming increasingly bureaucratic. The number of paid officials in trade union movement is still very small. The pay and working conditions in the trade union movement are largely unattractive and compare favourably with the salaries and working conditions enjoyed by their members. In contrast, in several NGOs, particularly urban based NGOs, a new culture is developing where service minded activists are being increasingly replaced by careerists. Of late, retired and serving bureaucrats are getting into leadership positions in the NGO movement and such people have been able to exercise their influence, network with a host of other institutions and mobilise resources, manage results, orchestrate publicity, and enhance and diversify the scale and range of activities.

## A typology of labour-oriented NGOs

Pandey (1991) provides a three-fold classification of NGOs based on their objectives and means of action to achieve those objectives: social service oriented NGOs, development-oriented NGOs and activist NGOs. NGOs with a labour orientation would be primarily classified as activist although some of their activities would fall under the other two categories.

Activist NGOs achieve their goals in a variety of ways. Some of them resort to physical action such as the Naxalite movement in Andhra Pradesh which has used violence and threats of violence to press for labour demands. Other NGOs engage in social action to achieve their goals. Their methods include the 3P's: Public interest litigation, Protests, and Public relations through deft handling of media. There are some NGOs like Bandhua Mukti Morcha (BMM) and Common Cause (CC) that espouse causes through public interest litigation that have a bearing on the work of trade unions.

The accomplishments of activist groups organised around one or more causes driven by a spirit of supreme personal sacrifice and outstanding moral values should serve as a reminder to trade union leadership about the immense potential and opportunities to realise their goals. Also, such illuminating examples illustrate the scope and the need for learning alternative ways of influencing people to fight social evils and provide basic amenities for good citizenship and good living. With growing ills of urbanisation and industrialisation the need for counselling deviant workers is increasing and we need, among trade unions, individuals who can exercise such moral influence both to cure and to prevent such social problems as chronic alcoholism, domestic violence, etc.

## SEWA: Self Employed Women's Association

While there are several thousand NGOs in the country, we consider here, for somewhat detailed discussion, the Self Employed Women's Association (SEWA). Women represent half the population and the unorganised labour, which National Centre for Labour (NCL) seeks to represent accounts for 90 per cent of the work force in India. One may argue, as we have discussed hereunder, whether SEWA is a trade union or an NGO. The evidence suggests that it is both given its unique blend of methods to reach the most vulnerable workers in a developing economy.

Formed in 1972, the Self Employed Women's Association (SEWA) is one of the most widely acclaimed and internationally known NGOs operating from India. SEWA considers itself as a 'sangam' or confluence of three movements: the labour movement, the co-operative movement and the women's movement. In organising the self-employed women workers SEWA has adopted a strategy of joint action with union and co-operatives. The groups targeted by SEWA are largely from the informal and rural sectors: hawkers and vendors, home-based workers, manual labourers and service providers like agricultural labourers, construction workers, contract labourers, head loaders, cart-pullers, laundry and domestic workers, among others.

Any self-employed female worker in India can become a member of SEWA by paying a membership fee of Rs.5 per year. Though initially SEWA's activities were restricted mainly to Ahmedabad in Gujarat, it spread gradually to other parts of the state and beyond. It has established global networks with other NGOs, international trade secretariats and other international organisations. About 75 per cent of its claimed membership of 218,797 in 1995 was drawn from Gujarat and the rest from the following four Indian states: Madhya Pradesh, Uttar Pradesh, Bihar and Kerala.

Roughly two-thirds of its members in Gujarat are drawn from rural areas of whom nearly 55,000 are home-based. It spearheaded a legislative bill for their protection in Gujarat and pushed for an ILO Convention on home-based workers in 1995.

Is SEWA an NGO or a trade union? SEWA evolved from within the Textile Labour Association (TLA). It began as a women's wing with a view to educate the textile worker's wives. When their husbands faced hardship due to the decline of the handloom industry, many of the textile workers wives took to informal sector activities. The scope of SEWA's activities expanded gradually as women activists pressed for greater autonomy. The TLA suggested that they form an NGO or a charitable trust. But the women wanted to function as a trade union as well. They wanted change in labour laws and labour bureaucracy which did not recognise the right of home-based/self employed workers to form a trade union. After a long battle, and with some help from the TLA leadership and local bureaucracy, SEWA was registered as the first trade union of informal workers in the country.

As TLA's popularity began to wane due to gradual decline of the textile industry in Ahmedabad, the popularity of SEWA grew. TLA leadership of the day did not take kindly to this development and attempted to hurt SEWA financially and otherwise. SEWA, nevertheless managed to withstand such pressures by cultivating political patronage of those who did not agree with TLA leadership and who happened to be political leaders at the time. SEWA also reached out to international organisations, by affiliating itself with the International Federation of Food, Beverages, Tobacco and Allied Workers (IUF) and the International Federation of Plantation, Agricultural and Allied Workers (IFPAAW).

Among other roles it plays, SEWA is the largest trade union for self employed women in India. For SEWA 'Unionising is not merely confrontation'. It also means responsible and constructive organisation for nation building. The union is not meant merely for solving workers' economic problems. It also attempts to address the totality of their lives and ensure that they obtain the recognition that is their due in our society. To achieve these goals and ideals, the means also have to be ideal. That is where the Gandhian tradition of organising provided both inspiration and direction. According to Gandhian thinking, the means to all ends are important. They should be principles based on truth, non-violence and harmony.

SEWA's principal goals are to increase employment and wages while promoting self-reliance. Increasing minimum wages for home-based workers and manual labourers has not been easy. Increasing unemployment, public apathy, an ineffective labour inspectorate and government policies that favour city beautification over the interests of hawkers and vendors, have made the job very difficult. Often greater energy is spent on reinstating women who lost their jobs/work than in recruiting new members. In urban areas, SEWA's struggles have included liaison and lobbying with regulatory authorities for better labour inspection, increasing minimum wages and issuing of vending licences for displaced vendors and hawkers.

SEWA organisers were often attacked both in the fields as well as in courts. Many village women involved in the struggle lost their low-paid jobs as the price for their union action. SEWA learned its lessons and reoriented its strategy towards increasing local employment opportunities. It focused on three areas: land-based work, live-stock based work and crafts and other home-based production of goods. Its experience in the Kheda district of Gujarat which accounts for 80 per cent of tobacco production in the country, is a good example of this strategy. About 40,000 persons are employed in the tobacco fields and the factories in the district. SEWA adopted a twin strategy of organising them into a union and simultaneously pursuing other avenues to create alternative sources of livelihood. In its role as the union, SEWA works closely with the Labour Department to ensure payment of minimum wages, providing workers with identity cards and ensuring compliance with other legal provisions for their social security support. Creation of alternative employment opportunities through savings and credit groups has improved women's bargaining power and reduced the supply of seasonal labour for the employers. In 1995 alone, the minimum wages of tobacco workers in Kheda district reportedly went up by 25 per cent.

SEWA also runs a bank that provides integrated insurance schemes in cooperation with the Life Insurance Corporation and the United India Assurance Corporation. These plans cover more than 12,000 people against death, accidental death, sickness, maternity, widowhood, loss of household goods and work tools in case of flood, fire, riot or storm. In 1995, 1,529 claims valued at nearly Rs.1.6 million were approved and disbursed.

Since SEWA and its members and member organisations have had to face a host of problems concerning the law and police, it has started providing legal aid and support to its members in court cases. SEWA's legal aid services cover problems relating to 'low wages, blatant violation of labour laws, the rapid spread of contract labour, the grip of middle men, competition arising from license requirements for certain trades pursued by self-employed women, police harassment, slow moving and delayed court and legal proceedings, open opposition from organised sector unions, exploitation of women, their labour and even their bodies'. In 1995 alone, it handled over 200 cases covering more than 10,500 members in labour courts, traffic courts, high courts and other courts. SEWA has also started new services like SEWA Design to provide marketing support for its artisan co-operatives, SEWA Academy to train its members and activists, SEWA newsletters, SEWA Video, etc., which mark its foray into mainstream print media as well as multi-media ventures that help the organisation reach out better to its members, the community and the wider world, outside the community, both within and outside India.

The success of SEWA gave birth to similar other unions in other parts of the country, notable among these is the Women Workers Forum (WWF) which is active in the southern states of India. But SEWA is more than a union in the sense that it has diversified its activities into several co-operative ventures, including a cooperative bank and is involved as an NGO in designing and implementing a host of development schemes.

## NGOs and government relations

In India, the government is a major player in the provision of social services and development activities. The role that NGOs can play is inversely proportional to the degree of coverage and efficacy of government's role in these matters. NGOs essentially fill the vacuum created by government inaction or failure. Constitutional, legal and institutional frameworks serve as gateways or barriers in defining the scope of NGO roles. NGOs need money to operate, which they often get either through their own government or from foreign sources. NGOs' own sources of finance, including membership dues, are seldom adequate to meet their needs. Till the mid-1970s Government attitude and response to NGOs was generally supportive. It set up a number of agencies like the Central Social Welfare Board (CSWB), the Council for Advancement of People's Action and Rural Technology (CAPART), the Council for Advancement of Rural Technology (CART) among others, and provided funding through various ministries to finance NGO activities.

As the NGO sector began to grow in size, popularity and finances, it generated greater political interest and in turn, led to political interference. During the Emergency (1975–77), the Foreign Contribution Regulation Act (FCRA) began to regulate funds received from foreign sources. These provisions were made more stringent in early 1980s. The amended law required prior registration or permission to receive foreign contributions and made it mandatory to maintain separate accounts and submit periodic reports to the concerned authority in the central government. During the Janata Party rule at the centre in the late 1970s, NGOs received considerable support and tax exemptions to business houses which donated funds to them. When the 1981 elections brought Congress back into power, the government found certain NGOs too critical of them and suspected links between village level Gandhian institutions and growing violence. It set up the Kudal Commission in 1981 and subsequently abolished tax exemption for business houses making grants to certain NGOs and barred some NGOs, including several religious organisations, from receiving foreign funding.

After 1985, the Congress government, under the leadership of Rajiv Gandhi, modified its attitude towards NGOs and attempted to create a national council for NGOs with a defined code of conduct. The seventh Plan added a new chapter on the voluntary sector and earmarked Rs.2000 million, a sum equivalent to foreign contributions received by them at that time, for disbursement to finance the activities of various NGOs. The government's policy towards NGOs was largely that of control through cooperation and cooption. After the defeat of the Congress government in 1989, the national council idea was dropped amidst considerable opposition from a large section of NGOs and the Kudal Commission report shelved. The new government filled several positions in the Planning Commission with known social activists who played a prominent role in the NGO movement in the country. But the government did not last long and when the Planning Commission was reconstituted by the successor government, the doyens of NGO movement were replaced largely with career bureaucrats. Subsequent developments reflect the ambivalent love-hate relationship between NGOs and government.

The Council for Advancement of People's Action and Rural Technology (CAPART) in the Ministry of Rural Employment has blacklisted 376 of some 5,500 NGOs registered with them. (Down to Earth, vol. 4, no. 4). Several other ministries have begun to insist on minimum contribution of about 10 per cent to 20 per cent in the projects manned and/or managed by them. Some of the NGOs, in turn, suggest that 20 per cent of government spending on social services and developmental projects should be routed through them (Singh, 1996: 14). In the wake of controversies regarding misuse of grants given to NGOs, the Planning Commission has put a question mark on the grant of funds to any NGO hereafter (Down to Earth, vol. 5, no. 8, Sept. 15, 1996, p. 11). Yet, the Planning Commission did not close its doors on the NGOs. Instead, it held a meeting with 83 NGOs to discuss their role in the context of the ninth Five year Plan, 1997–2002. The NGOs are concerned, however, about becoming mere agents of delivering social services and want to have a more broad-based role which includes participation in the planning process itself (Singh, 1996: 14).

## NGOs and trade unions

The most striking aspect of the relationship between NGOs and trade unions concerns the relations between formal sector workers and informal sector workers. Given the dualism in labour market where some tend to brand workers in the formal as 'labour aristocracy', the interests between the formal and informal sectors is painted by some as antithetical or conflictual. The privileged and the protected organised labour sees the underprivileged and unprotected labour as a threat to the perpetuation of their current position (Sandbrook, 1982; Harrod, 1987).

One of the most prominent leaders of SEWA, Ela Bhatt, made no secret of such antipathy in one speech where she waxed eloquently:

> How can I forget the day at an Annual Conference of one Central Labour Union where I was a delegate of SEWA, representing the unorganised

women workers and speaking about their problems of exploitation and I was hooted out. The others made me sound ridiculous! There was no one delegate to support me there at that time except my own members! We had to swallow the humiliation.... what place it (unorganised sector) has in the labour movement?... The labour of the unorganised sector remains totally unrepresented at all the significant forums of decision making. We want our representation there.... I say that the unorganised sector labour remains unpresented because of the combined bias of our Government and the Organised Trade Unions who have merely 7 per cent workforce of the country within which only 25 per cent to 30 per cent are unionised.... Let us build up our organised strength to reclaim our rightful place in the mainstream. When unorganised labour will be recognised by the main-stream (we are the mainstream, in fact), the whole structure of society – economic and social – will be changed. Private and Public Sectors of course will remain, but the People's Sector will become the most impor-tant backbone of the national economy. And we are the People's Sector. We are the majority (Bhatt, 1995).

Sanyal (1994: 53) observes that, 'the informal workers perceive their chances of joining the formal labour market as restricted by the high wages that the organised formal workers have managed to extract from their employer'. As a result, the two labour sectors are inherently antithetical, and it is virtually impossible to create institutional linkages between them. Some have taken this argument further by suggesting that even if the level of antagonism between the two groups were reduced, NGOs of informal workers should never join trade unions of formal workers because the former would be 'swallowed up' and used by the latter to pursue their own agenda.

## Roles and activities: competitive, cooperative, or complementary?

To the extent that there is an overlap in the roles of NGOs and trade unions, there will be always opportunities for both cooperation and com-petition. In this section we consider four areas in which the potential for competition exists along with possible collaboration.

### Trade union matters

*Organising the unorganised.* The attitudes of the leadership of the central trade unions in India concerning the role of NGOs in organising the unor-ganised, particularly in the non-formal or informal sector activities has been generally positive. They recognise that the task is huge and they need the support and collaboration of as many partners as possible.

Individual responses are, however, considerably varied. Some unions spurn the NGOs role particularly when the latter are seen to make tall claims and undermine the role the former. Others admit that logistically and otherwise NGOs are better suited to undertake field work at the grass-roots level. With only some exceptions, the trade union leadership in India is increasingly focused, of necessity, on trends in urbanisation, industrial-isation and bureaucratisation which moves them further away from the needs of the informal and rural workers.

*Litigation and legislation.*   The role of trade unions, particularly their national organisations, is significant in pursuing the cause of unorganised workers. Casual and contract workers who have a regular, day-to-day inter-face with the organised sector benefited from a landmark judgement by the Supreme Court in Gujarat Electricity Board vs. Hind Mazdoor Sabha in 1995. This judgement gives the labour courts authority to intervene if con-tractors are not living up to the terms of the contract. This judgement also allows labour courts to limit subcontracting.

## Gender issues: women and work

The Union Ministry of Labour has recognised four social welfare organisa-tions under the Equal Remuneration Act, 1976 for the purpose of filing complaints in courts against employers for violation of the provisions of the Act. The Women Labour Cell in the ministry has sponsored/assigned studies and training programmes to about 20 NGOs, but none to a trade union. The Ministry of Labour also provides grant-in-aid to NGOs to encourage employers to establish creche facilities for women industrial workers. This plan enables employers/establishments who are not statut-orily required to provide crèches.

Despite these efforts and the participation of women in the labour force, very few women can be found among the trade union leadership. The 9th Plan Working Group Report on Labour Policy, 1997–2002 does not refer to the role of trade unions, but makes repeated references to the role of SEWA in the upliftment of women workers in the informal sector. Thus, as far as women are concerned, there appears to be a divide between trade unions and NGOs that have done far more for women workers.

## Child labour

Trade union interest in child labour followed, not preceded, the International Programme on the Elimination of Child Labour (IPEC) (Varma and Jain, 1995). Kulshrestra, (1982: 186) argued that, 'except for the media and the voluntary organisations, virtually none, including the inspectors, who have been made responsible for the enforcement of various legislations regarding child labour, the trade unions, who will be one of the beneficiaries in case of total eradication of child labour, and the political parties, who claim to hold up and high the flag-mast of social justice, is concerned in the least in securing social justice for [child workers]'.

Since the late 1980s, however, trade unions have become somewhat active in this regard. In 1988 the ICFTU's Executive Board has adopted a resolution for systematic action for the elimination of child labour. In 1993 Indian National Trade Union Congress (INTUC, 1993: 53–55) outlined the following agenda for trade union action with the ultimate goal of elimination of child labour:

(a) Fixing of the wage for the children on par with adult workers.
(b) Demand for improvement in their working conditions.
(c) Determine and regulate the hours of work and fix the suitable work load.
(d) Combine work with education and training without disruption.
(e) Make education and health care obligatory on the part of the employers.
(f) Insist on compulsory schooling for children.

INTUC also envisaged that trade unions can become the focal point.

a. in creating awareness and a congenial climate for a mass movement against child labour;
b. strengthening public opinion and launching a rigorous campaign for the nation-wide boycott of the products involving child labour; and,
c. evolving and submitting a master plan with a demand for resource allocation for investment for the overall improvement in the standard of living of the poor.

At the NLI-IPEC conference (Varma and Jain, 1995: 40–62), both the Bharatiya Mazdoor Sangh (BMS) and the All India Trade Union Congress have admitted that the trade unions have not been working on the eradication of child labour and have been somewhat indifferent to the issue due partly to the very nature of the problem and due largely to the lack of resources and experience. Perhaps for this reason the dean of NLI, A. P. Varma observed (Varma and Jain, 1995: 9) that one of the objectives of the Workshop was to equip the trade union members with the required skills to prepare their respective area-based, project-based proposals on the subject.

Trade Unions Act, 1926, prohibits membership of persons under the age of 15. But The Child Labour (Prohibition and Regulation) Act, 1986 also restricts employment of children under the age of 15. Trade unions in India can deem it their duty and obligation to see that a child is not employed because this undesirable practice would depress the wages of their own members. But often even trade unions seem to share the ambivalent attitude that most people in India seem have about child labour: both concern and indifference. Trade unions in India have, in the past, entered into collective agreements that provided lower wages for children compared to the wage paid to adult labour. In the 1990s, in tea plantations in Kerala, for instance, this was corrected and clauses providing for a separate wage for child labour were removed through collective bargaining. This is a major positive step which removed the incentive to employ child labour.

By and large, as is the case for women workers, for child labour, several of the Government schemes were initiated and implemented through NGOs rather than trade unions. Usually the Government provides grants-in-aid for such projects with 75 per cent financial assistance. Trade unions may be lacking either the expertise in preparing projects and/or lacking the ability/willingness to finance 25 per cent of the project costs. In nine cases NGOs have been entrusted with projects in various areas of child labour concentration. It is only after the IPEC project was started through the ILO that some trade unions have started undertaking projects aimed at regulation and prohibition/elimination of child labour.

Besides the service, development and activist roles, trade unions can also play a major role in preventing engagement of child labour in prohibited areas of employment and in forcing employers, through collective agreements, to remove wage inequality based on age.

## Conclusions

Based on our discussion, some conclusions for future policymaking and research can be drawn. The methods of mobilisation of trade unions need to be compared and contrasted with that of NGOs. It is easy to see what unions do, but difficult to prescribe what they should do. The latter is something that unions themselves should decide based on the assessment of the needs and circumstances. Many unions consider their job as 'asking for more and more and more' to improve the lot of their members. In contrast, NGOs build one or more of the different social work programmes into their means of action, which Kanth and Varma (1994) recount as the following six: preventive, ameliorative, promotive, curative, rehabilitative and reformative. It is possible some trade unions may be undertaking some of these social work programmes as well. Those trade unions who see their job as merely presenting charters of demands and fighting for realising their demands would do well to consider what else they can and must do. In this, the means of action of NGOs and the strategies and tactics that they adopt provide valuable insights and lessons. It is time, therefore, for trade unions to take up social service and developmental activities alongside interest articulation. Some trade unions may already have been engaged in social service, developmental and other non-bargaining activities. But since the scale and the history of such activities is limited and recent, there is a need to step up attention and action in this direction.

One of the major strengths of NGOs is that they are usually grass-roots organisations and therefore close to their roots. Trade unions also begin their existence by being close to the roots. They need to take care to see that subsequently the grass-roots contacts and field orientation do not suffer. NGOs which seem to have confined their attention to the micro level in dealing with specific issues in a limited geographical area seem to have had substantial impact. Trade union organisation structures need to take lessons from the organisation structures of grass-root level NGOs.

It is naive to consider that all is well with NGOs, but not with the trade unions. Both seem to suffer from the same set of weaknesses in as much as societal weaknesses are reproduced in their own organisations as well. As such one occasionally sees abuse of power, lack of democratic orientation, absence of transparency and refusal to be open to scrutiny. The growth pangs bring with them bureaucratic orientation even among the NGOs and the trade unions which need to be arrested to the extent they cause alienation and result in anomie. Both are not free from the fear or threat of cooption by the State. Additionally, if NGOs suffer from possible cooption by the funding agencies, trade unions may suffer from cooption by employers. While some NGOs are accused of being 'lords of poverty', some trade unions are accused of 'being managers of discontent'. If one looks at some NGOs and trade unions these appear wild exaggerations, but when one looks at some others, they appear as gross understatements. With due introspection and sensitivity, both NGOs and trade unions can develop conscious and cautious mechanisms to get over such limitations.

There is nothing wrong if NGOs and trade unions compete between themselves. Some competition is productive, though if stretched to its extreme limits, it can certainly be counterproductive. The stress should be on supplementing rather than supplanting or complementing the efforts of each other rather than mere duplication. Both NGOs and trade unions should learn to both compete and cooperate. The prescription is 'co-optation', a combination of competition and cooperation. The problems of the groups that both seek to serve are so gigantic, complex and are growing at such fast pace, that they both need to strive individually and collectively to address themselves to unfolding challenges. The phenomenal magnitude of the task that await them is such that they need to make peace, not war. They both could win by serving the cause of the depressed, oppressed and disadvantaged sections of the workforce. They should never strive to win at each other's expense.

Lastly, trade unions and NGOs will need to develop mutual trust, understanding and co-ordination amongst themselves if they are to develop any synergy between their activities.

## References

Ambekar Institute for Labour Studies and Maniben Kara Institute (1988) *Cooperation between trade unions and voluntary agencies.* New Delhi: Friedrich Ebert Stiftung.

Bhat, Ela (1995) Inaugural Speech at the Formation of National Centre of Labour, Bangalore, 25 May.

Edwards, M. and Hulme, D. (eds) (1994) *Making a Difference*. London: Earthscan Publications Ltd.

Edwards, M. and Hulme, D. (eds) (1995) *Non-Governmental Organisations – Performance and Accountability*. London: Earthscan Publications Ltd.

Kanth, A. and Varma, R. M. (1994) *Neglected child: changing perspectives*. New Delhi: Prayas.

Kulshrestha, J. C. (1982) *Indian child labour*. New Delhi: Uppal Publishing House.

NIPCED (National Institute of Public Cooperation and Child Development) (1993) *Orientation course for functionaries of voluntary organizations engaged in programmes for street and working children*. New Delhi.

Pandey, S. R. (1991) *Community action for social justice: Grassroots organisations in India*. New Delhi: Sage.

Sanyal, B. (1991) 'Organising the self-employed: The politics of the urban informal sector'. *International Labour Review*, 130 (1): 39–56.

Sanyal, B. (1994) *Cooperative Autonomy: The dialectic of state–NGO Relationship in Developing Countries*. Geneva: International Institute for Labour Studies. Research Series, 100.

Sen, R. (1996) 'The future of trade unionism and trade unions in the future'. *IIRA Newsletter*, March. II (3): 15–20.

Singh, K. (1996) 'NGOs want to take part in planning process'. *Times of India*, 21 November 14.

Susman, S. D. (1995) 'Transformation of standing in public interest litigation'. *Legal News and Views*, 9(11) March: 4–20.

Varma, A. P. and Jain, M. (eds) (1995) *Trade unions, child labour and IPEC: Workshop Report*, Noida: National Labour Institute.

# Notes

## 1 Unions in the 21st Century: Prospects for Renewal

1. This introduction builds on and extends the brief discussion in Verma, Kochan and Wood (2002).
2. For another articulation of likely scenarios for the future, see Verma, Kochan and Wood (2002).

## 3 Extended Networks: A Vision for the Next Generation Unions

1. This paper is drawn from Chapter 4 of Paul Osterman, Thomas Kochan, Richard Locke, and Michael Piore, *Working in America: A Blueprint for Change*, Cambridge, MA: MIT Press, 2001.
2. Daniel Yankilovich, (national survey data from 1997 on file with the authors).
3. See the report of the Collective Bargaining Forum, 'Principles for New Employment Relationship', *Perspectives on Work*, vol. 3, no. 1 (1999): 22–29.
4. Thanks are due to Amy Dean for first coining this term.
5. Others have also proposed viewing unions as networks. See for example, Charles Heckscher, *The New Unionism* (New York: Basic Books, 1987); and Saul Rubinstein and Charles Heckscher, 'Labor Management Partnership: Two Views', in Thomas A. Kochan and David B. Lipsky, Negotiations: From the Workplace to Society, 2000.
6. For a discussion of alternative forms unions have taken in prior time periods, see, Dorothy Sue Cobble, 'Organizing the Postindustrial Work Force: Lessons from the History of Waitress Unionism', *ILRR*, vol. 44, April 1991.
7. Graham L. Staines and Robert P. Quinn, 'American Workers Evaluate the Quality of Their Jobs', *Monthly Labor Review* (Washington, January 1979).
8. See, Thomas A. Kochan, Harry C. Katz, and Nancy R. Mower, 'Worker Participation and American Unions', in Thomas A. Kochan, ed., *Challenges and Choices Facing American Labor* (Cambridge, MA: MIT Press, 1985): 271–306.
9. Seymour Lipset and Noah Meltz, 'Canadian and American Attitudes Toward Work and Institutions', *Perspectives on Work*, vol. 1, no. 3 (1998); Richard Freeman and Joel Rogers, *What Workers Want* (Ithaca, NY: ILR Press, 1999); AFL-CIO. *High Hopes, Little Trust: A Study of Young Workers and their Ups and Downs in the New Economy*, (1999). (http://www.aflcio.org/articles/high_hopes/index.htm).
10. Richard Freeman and Joel Rogers, *What Workers Want*.
11. National survey conducted for the AFL-CIO by Peter D. Hart Research Associates, March 1999.
12. Morton Bahr, *From the Telegraph to the Internet* (Washington: National Press Books, Inc., 1998).
13. Harry C. Katz and Owen Darbashire, *Converging Divergences* (Ithaca, NY: Cornell University/ILR Press, 1999).
14. Business Roundtable, 'Training Problems in Open Shop Construction', (The Construction Industry Cost Effectiveness Project, 1990). www.brtable.org.
15. Janice Fine, 'Community Unionism: The Key to the New Labor Movement', *Perspectives on Work*, vol. 1, no. 2, (1997): 32–35.

16. Maureen Scully and Amy Segal, 'Passion with an Umbrella: Grassroots Activism in the Workplace', MIT Sloan School of Management Task Force Working Paper #WP13, 1999.
17. Raymond A. Friedman and Donna J. Carter, 'African American Network Groups: Their Impact and Effectiveness' (Executive Leadership Council: Washington, D.C., 1993).

## 10 Unions and Procedural Justice: An Alternative to the 'Common Rule'

1. I am grateful to other members of the 'Future of the Unions' project and those attending the University of Toronto Conference in honour of Noah Meltz in April 2000, for their comments on a preliminary presentation of the ideas in this paper. This paper draws on evidence from the CEP's work on performance pay in the British public services. The work has been funded variously by the ESRC, the Leverhulme Foundation, and the Anglo-German Foundation.
2. 'Blunkett humiliated in pay row: Judge rules that formula to decide teachers' wages is illegal', The Guardian Newspaper, 15.7.02).

## 11 Changing Patterns of Unionisation: The North American Experience, 1984–1998

1. As discussed below, the decline in U.S. unionization was very similar to that in Canada in terms of percentage points of union density, but proportionally much larger because of the substantially lower initial level in the United States.
2. The probit results are available on request.
3. The LFS questions on educational attainment changed in January 1990, with the post-1990 questions providing more detailed educational categories. We group the 1984 SUM and 1998 LFS educational categories so that they are very similar.
4. The Survey of Work History (SWH), carried out as a supplement to the LFS in 1981, was an earlier Canadian household survey that included a question on union membership. However, the SWH did not include questions on coverage. Furthermore, several other features of the SWH – including industry and occupation coding – make it non-comparable to the 1998 LFS.
5. About ten per cent of covered workers in Canada are not union members (Riddell, 1993; Akeampong, 2000). The comparable figure for the United States is very similar (Riddell, 1993), albeit higher in right-to-work states (Budd and Na, 2000).
6. Due to differences in the way occupations are categorised between the LFS and CPS and empty cells, we use 11 occupational groups for the CPS data. Using the two digit coding, this gives occupations that are fairly comparable between the two countries.
7. Estimates using the complete set of industry and occupation controls are available on request.
8. These inter-country differences could be partly due to the lack of a job tenure variable in the U.S. data.
9. If community services is used as the reference group, the constant term absorbs this amount.

## 13 The ICFTU and Trade Unions in the Developing Countries: Solidarity or Dependence?

1. An earlier version of this chapter was published (in French) in Régin and Wolikow, 2002.
2. For convenience, I have used the terms 'developing countries' and 'Third World', but neither is really satisfactory. In the main, I am referring to the countries in the ICFTU regions outside Europe, North America and Oceania. Unfortunately, the ICFTU's broadly constituted regions lead to anomalies such as the grouping of wealthy countries like Japan with impoverished countries in the same region, or the inclusion in Oceania of not only Australia and New Zealand but also Fiji.
3. See also Gumbrell-McCormick (2000a and 2000b).
4. Interview notes, John Vanderveken, former ICFTU general secretary, Edi Horii, former ICFTU official, Georges Debunne, former president of the Belgian affiliate ABVV-FGTB and ICFTU vice president.
5. Four of the seats for North America were left vacant as a result of the disaffiliation of the AFL-CIO from the confederation in 1969; the U.S. national centre re-affiliated in 1981.
6. ICFTU, *Report of the Tenth World Congress*, 1972, p. 20; *Report of the Thirteenth World Congress*, 1983, p. 45; *Report of the Fifteenth World Congress*, 1992, p. 37. In each case, the total numbers include the general secretary, but not the president, who sat *ex officio*. The general secretaries over this period, Otto Kersten and John Vanderveken, were both Europeans.
7. Interview notes, Vanderveken. Luis Anderson, now general secretary of ORIT, adds that in the 1970s, having the 'correct' ideology was seen as much more important than the payment of dues.
8. This is particularly the case in Latin America (interview notes, L. Anderson).
9. ICFTU, *Report of the 15th World Congress*, 1992, pp. 275–280; interview notes, Vanderveken.
10. For example, in 1977 the devaluation of the British pound meant that the TUC's affiliation fees amounted to £452,000, or 23 per cent of its total income (TUC, *Report to the General Council*, 1977, pp. 602–3). Other affiliates, such as those in Italy and Israel, were similarly affected (69EB/ 2,18(a), 1977).
11. Interview notes, Vanderveken and Tom Etty (International Secretary, FNV).
12. Interview notes, Vanderveken, see also Carew (2000): 252–4, 270–3.
13. ICFTU, 55EB/ 8, 1972.
14. ICFTU 69EB/ 2,18(b), 1977, interview notes, Jack Jones (TUC).
15. 85EB/ 13(a), 1984; 89EB/15, 1986.
16. This had already been proposed by the Dutch affiliate NVV as early as March 1975, in a letter to the EB (63EB/5(d), 1975). Throughout the 1970s and 80s, the NVV and its successor, the FNV, played an important role in pushing for more stringent financial control and accounting of projects, and greater coordination by the ICFTU (85EB/13(a), 1984; 96EB/12(a), 1989; interview notes, Etty).
17. Nedzynski, in 86EB/14(a), 1984.
18. 91EB/16(a), 1987; interview notes, Nedzynski.
19. 92EB/15, 1987.
20. Interview notes, Elsa Ramos (ICFTU Women's Bureau); 86EB/13, 1984, and 92EB/15, 1987.
21. Interview notes, Etty.
22. 64EB/2, 1975.

23. Interview notes, Anderson.
24. Interview notes, Anderson and Stephen Pursey (former head of ICFTU Economic and Social Policy Department).
25. 97EB/7, 1990; interview notes, Ramos and Mamounata Cissé (ICFTU Women's Bureau).
26. 68EB/2,11(b), 1977; 89EB/9, 1986.

## 14 Partnership and the Politics of Trade Union Policy Formation in the UK: The Case of the Manufacturing, Science and Finance Union

1. This is not to suggest that there is necessarily a common position amongst the critical camp, rather we see a variety of critical hues.
2. MSF was formed through a merger of TASS (Technical and Supervisory Staff) and the ASTMS (Association of Scientific Technical and Management Staffs) in the 1980s (see Carter, 1991, 1997). MSF itself merged with the Engineering and Electrical Union (AEEU) to form AMICUS in 2002.
3. For a more detailed account of the survey methodology see Martinez Lucio and Stuart (2001).
4. The Union of Shop workers, Distributive and Allied Workers.

## 16 Negating or Affirming the Organising Model? The Case of the Congress of South African Trade Unions

1. As a result of the efforts of the worker service and advice organisations that had been founded by liberal students and intellectuals and former union activists.
2. Based on a case study of the 'Justice for Janitor's Campaign', Erickson et al. (2002: 565) reach a rather more optimistic conclusion. Coalition building and collective action that seeks to win public support can play a vital role in garnering support for unions. However, they concede that it is in jobs that cannot easily be relocated or 'globalized' that such organisational tools are likely to be most successful.
3. This section represents a modified version of an argument more fully developed in Wood (2003).
4. Significant numbers can also be found in the National Education, Health and Allied Workers Union (NEHAWU), the South African Municipal Workers Union (SAMWU) and the South African Democratic Teachers Union (SADTU). However, the survey concentrated on COSATU's members in the private sector.
5. Former affiliates of the conservative (and now defunct) Trade Union Council of South Africa) formed the core of SACTWU.
6. SACTWU has a strong following amongst ethnic coloured and Indian workers; these groupings had more rights under apartheid than African workers, making it difficult to build an effective non-racial union, a task made even harder by differences in home languages (Baskin, 1991: 394).
7. COSATU's internal journal, the *Shopsteward*, regularly airs concerns of sexist behaviour within some COSATU unions.
8. The following two sections represent a modified version of an argument more fully developed in Wood (2002).

## 17   From Playstations to Workstations: Young Workers and the Experience-Good Model of Union Membership

1. Adults who desired a union job were 3.26 times more likely to be unionised in Canada than comparable youth, the U.S. and British figures being 2.73 and 2.38 respectively.
2. A mechanic, for example, does not generally advertise on television. Indeed, we tend to be suspicious of any mechanic who does. Instead, the mechanic generates his customer base through personal referrals, or, more generally by 'word of mouth'.
3. Britain is the only country for which we have consistent data extending this far back.
4. Note that this is also true of Right to Work laws in the United States. Such practices, however, do not exist in Canada.
5. The importance of initial exposures to unionisation for youths is emphasised in Freeman and Diamond, 2001; Fullagar and Barling, 1989; Fullagar, Gallagher, Gordon and Clarke, 1995; and Payne, 1989.
6. Evidence on the impact of family is given in Barling, Kelloway and Bremermann (1991), Kelloway, Barling and Agar (1996), Grayson (2000), Heshizer and Wilson (1995) and Kelloway and Watts (1994), with most finding that parent's attitudes towards unions mattered more than their union status.

# Index